T0139149

Cybersecurity Issues in Emerging Technologies

Cybersecurity Issues in Emerging Technologies

Edited by
Leandros Maglaras and Ioanna Kantzavelou

CRC Press
Taylor & Francis Group
Boca Raton London New York

CRC Press is an imprint of the
Taylor & Francis Group, an **informa** business

First edition published 2022
by CRC Press
6000 Broken Sound Parkway NW, Suite 300, Boca Raton, FL 33487-2742

and by CRC Press
2 Park Square, Milton Park, Abingdon, Oxon, OX14 4RN

ISBN: 9780367626174 (hbk)
ISBN: 9781032110363 (pbk)
ISBN: 9781003109952 (ebk)

DOI: 10.1201/9781003109952

Typeset in Sabon
by Deanta Global Publishing Services, Chennai, India

Contents

7 RF Jamming Attacks and Countermeasures in Wireless
   Vehicular Networks   115

DIMITRIOS KOSMANOS AND ANTONIOS ARGYRIOU

8 Smart Cars and Over-the-Air Updates   137

PANAGIOTIS EFSTATHIADIS, ANNA KARANIKA, NESTORAS CHOULIARAS,
LEANDROS MAGLARAS, AND IOANNA KANTZAVELOU

Foreword

The explosive recent advances in a variety of information and communication technologies and the plethora of research efforts in future applications call for a holistic view on the security of the infrastructure, the applications, and the way services are offered.

The edited book *Cybersecurity Issues in Emerging Technologies* offers a thorough and holistic approach to the cybersecurity issues that a variety of technologies face, which will be predominant in our lives in the near future – with some of them quickly becoming part of our everyday transactions.

The various chapters of the book not only address specific security and privacy issues that these emerging technologies will need to cope with but also provide general approaches to the security problem from human factor issues to ways attacks are orchestrated.

The reader of the book will find the major issues that new technologies, such as 5G, blockchain, and connected cars, will face or to be more precise have already suffered from. Moreover, applications that are more industry-specific, such as autonomous ships, and basic hardware component issues, which may have a widespread impact that has not been thoroughly evaluated and examined, are covered in the relevant book chapters. The discussion in the various chapters presents ways to mitigate the impact of likely vulnerabilities in these application areas and approaches that detect and prevent serious problems. The analysis of the ransomware phenomenon and the presentation of the skill gaps highlight the problems the industry faces and the need for a skilled workforce that can work in the interconnection of cyber and physical systems.

While each chapter can be read independently of the other chapters, the presentation of the material is, to a high degree, uniform. The book can be used not only as a reference source for persons who work in or plan to enter the cybersecurity field but also as a part of a second course on security, if combined with case studies and some experimental/simulation tools.

For all of us who are working in the cybersecurity field, this book is a welcome addition to the vast literature on the topic, since it organizes the existing knowledge in an efficient and effective manner and provides approaches that one does not find in other books. The book does not attempt, by any means, to be a comprehensive treatment of cybersecurity in emerging technologies – the field is expanding rapidly and a practitioner or a theoretician as well a policy maker will find this book as a stepping-stone to delve into the specifics that each one needs in their own work.

Professor Christos Douligeris
Department of Informatics
University of Piraeus

Preface

Digital infrastructure development is one of the main targets by all the countries. Additionally, many organizations worldwide aim to apply digital transformation successfully, especially after the COVID-19 pandemic where almost all their activities are becoming digital. Any digital transformation success depends heavily on preserving the security and privacy of both data and infrastructure, whether in the public or private sectors.

The threat landscape is evolving with tremendous speed. We are facing an extremely fast-growing attack surface with a diversity of attack vectors, a clear asymmetry between attackers and defenders, billions of connected IoT devices, mostly reactive detection and mitigation approaches, and finally big data challenges. The clear asymmetry of attacks and the enormous amount of data are additional concerns to make it necessary to rethink cybersecurity approaches in terms of reducing the attack surface and make it dynamic, to automate the detection, risk assessment, and mitigation, and to investigate the prediction and prevention of attacks with the utilization of emerging technologies such as blockchain, artificial intelligence, and machine learning.

Many aspects motivated the decision for this book. Cybersecurity has gained favor due to the increasing security-related concerns, and the expansion of technology in an astonishing rapid way. The more technologies emerge the more efficient cybersecurity frameworks are required. The book has two clear goals. The first is to bring in front important security problems that arise in the advent of new technologies and the second is to highlight a variety of possible solution approaches that might be able to address them. Specialists and experts present their significant efforts to fulfill these goals.

This book includes eleven chapters with diverse Cybersecurity Issues in Emerging Technologies. These encompass smart connected cars, unmanned ships, 5G/6G connectivity, blockchain, agile incident response, hardware-assisted security, ransomware attacks, hybrid threats, and cyber skills gap.

Chapter 1 studies the security mechanisms implemented in modern hardware architectures. Several attacks bypass security mechanisms designed to protect applications, services, and protocols; thus, hardware-based security can be more effective against some of them. The generated runtime overheads are also reduced by the security checks themselves.

Chapter 2 focuses on the maritime industry and the cybersecurity of unmanned ships. A reference model of the architecture of an unmanned ship is presented and, next, the security requirements of the three most vulnerable CPSs are defined. The identified risks drive the selection of security controls towards designing a security architecture of the unmanned ship.

Chapter 3 studies incident response processes in critical infrastructures, where cyber threats are severe, frequent, and increasing. Agile methods and practices are proposed and evaluated for integration in Industrial Control Environments in order to equip a security incident response team for significant evolving response to changes and new requirements, while remaining adaptive to confront cyberattacks effectively.

Chapter 4 focuses on the advent of 5G networks and security-related concerns. The dynamic and new network architecture implies a reconsideration of traditional security-monitoring methods and techniques to adhere to new security requirements and real-time reactions. Potential solutions are identified to overcome the threats to 5G technology, how security monitoring can be set up in 5GCN, and a method of modeling multi-stage attack scenarios using graphs applicable to 5GCN is proposed.

Chapter 5 explores the limits of 5G technology and opens new research directions in the main challenges of 6G networks. Blockchain is selected as cutting-edge technology to fulfill the in-growing demands of trust and certainty. Solutions based on blockchain are examined and open issues are highlighted.

In Chapter 6, another proposal towards the detection of attacks that take place on 5G core components is described. It consists of an Application Intrusion Detection and Prevention System and an Event Processing and Visualization Platform. A proof of concept of the architecture is designed and implemented using the 5G Network Exposure Function as an example.

In Chapter 7, readers reach the introduction of an Intrusion Detection System (IDS) based on KNN, and RaFo algorithms, with a data fusion method that combines their outcomes. It is a cross-layer IDS that aims at detecting RF jamming attacks in Wireless Vehicular Networks. More accuracy is achieved by the inclusion of an application layer metric, which is combined with some features from the physical or the media access control (MAC) layer for training and testing.

Chapter 8 explores and introduces security issues and solutions regarding the creation of a smart car. The required technologies intersect different smaller automation systems, which communicate over a network. The over-the-air (OTA) updates, necessary to support these intermodule communications, insert additional vulnerabilities and expose the entire system to more risks from external networks. Solutions that address this problem are presented and discussed.

Chapter 9 discusses the ransomware phenomenon and its correlated problems. It is the first step as an attempt to mitigate and lower ransomware infection rates, thus breaking the three-year cycle of ransomware being globally the top cybersecurity threat.

Chapter 10 presents and discusses a model to tackle hybrid threats by developing immunity rather than defensive measures. It also focuses on the elements required to present an effective and efficient response to the issue. The proposed holistic immunization model offers the ability to react proactively at an initial stage of an upcoming event.

Chapter 11 proposes a multidimensional approach in demonstrating the need for acquiring specific cyber skills required for Industry 4.0, and ways we can close the gap between users and cybersecurity professionals, by educating home users and raising their awareness.

Editors

Leandros A. Maglaras is an Associate Professor in the School of Computer Science and Informatics of De Montfort University, conducting research in the Cyber Security Centre. From September 2017 to November 2019, he was the Director of the National Cyber Security Authority of Greece. He obtained a BSc in Electrical and Computer Engineering from the Aristotle University of Thessaloniki in 1998, MSc in Industrial Production and Management from the University of Thessaly in 2004, and MSc and PhD degrees in Electrical and Computer Engineering from the University of Thessaly in 2008 and 2014, respectively. In 2018, he was awarded a PhD in Intrusion Detection in SCADA systems from the University of Huddersfield. He is featured in Stanford University's list of the world's top 2% scientists for the year 2019. He serves on the Editorial Board of several international peer-reviewed journals such as *IEEE Access*, Elsevier *Array*, is the author of more than 150 papers in scientific magazines and conferences, and is a Senior Member of the IEEE.

Ioanna Kantzavelou is an Assistant Professor at the Department of Informatics and Computer Engineering at the School of Engineering of the University of West Attica. She received a BSc in Informatics from the Department of Informatics of the Technological Educational Institute of Athens, an MSc by Research in Computer Security from the Department of Computer Science at the University College Dublin of the National University of Ireland, and a PhD in Intrusion Detection in Information Technology Security from the Department of Information and Communication Systems Engineering at the University of the Aegean. She has worked in R&D projects funded by the Greek government, the Irish government, and the EU. Her published work includes chapters in books (IOS Press), conferences, and journals, recording remarkable citations in her research work. She has joint editorship of three IOS Press collections.

She has been a repetitive reviewer in many international conferences, such as "ACM SEC", "IEEE TrustCom", "IFIP SEC", "ESORICS", "IEEE CIS", and she is currently a Reviewer for high-ranking journals of IEEE, Elsevier, Springer, and Emerald. She is a Member of the Greek Computer Society (GCS), the ACM, and the IEEE Computer Society.

Contributors

Mohamed Amine Ferrag
Guelma University
Guelma, Algeria

Antonios Argyriou
University of Thessaly
Volos, Greece

Elias Athanasopoulos
University of Cyprus
Cyprus

Nestoras Chouliaras
University of West Attica
Athens, Greece

George Christou
Foundation of Research and
    Technology Hellas
Heraklion, Greece

Allan Cook
De Montfort University
Leicester, UK

Luís Cordeiro
One Source Consultoria
    Informática Lda.
Coimbra, Portugal

Tiago Cruz
University of Coimbra, DEI, CISUC
Coimbra, Portugal

Panagiotis Efstathiadis
University of Thessaly
Lamia, Greece

Daniel Fernandes
University of Coimbra, DEI, CISUC
Coimbra, Portugal

Fenia Ferra
De Montfort University
Leicester, UK

Othmane Friha
Guelma University
Guelma, Algeria

André Gomes
One Source Consultoria
    Informática Lda.
Coimbra, Portugal

Ying He
University of Nottingham
Nottingham, UK

Sotirios Ioannidis
Technical University of Crete
Chania, Greece

Helge Janicke
Cyber Security Cooperative
    Research Centre
Perth, Australia

Ioanna Kantzavelou
University of West Attica
Athens, Greece

Anna Karanika
University of Thessaly
Lamia, Greece

Sokratis Katsikas
Norwegian University of Science
    and Technology
Gjøvik, Norway

Georgios Kavallieratos
Norwegian University of Science
    and Technology
Gjøvik, Norway

Dimitrios Kosmanos
University of Thessaly
Volos, Greece

Athanasios Kosmopoulos
Panteion University
Athens, Greece

Leandros Maglaras
De Montfort University
Leicester, UK

Sotiris Moschoyiannis
University of Surrey
Guildford, Surrey, UK

Emmanouil Panaousis
University Of Greenwich
Greenwich, London, UK

Robert Pell
University of Surrey
Guildford, Surrey

Vasco Pereira
University of Coimbra, DEI, CISUC
Coimbra, Portugal

Jorge Proença
University of Coimbra, DEI, CISUC
Coimbra, Portugal

Pedro Quitério
University of Coimbra, DEI, CISUC
Coimbra, Portugal

Marco Sequeira
One Source Consultoria
    Informática Lda.
Coimbra, Portugal

Paulo Simões
University of Coimbra, DEI, CISUC
Coimbra, Portugal

Richard Smith
De Montfort University
Leicester, UK

Aikaterini Vardalaki
Research Institute for European
    and American Studies
Leiden, Netherlands

Ismini Vasileiou
De Montfort University
Leicester, UK

Giorgos Vasiliadis
Foundation of Research and
    Technology Hellas
Heraklion, Greece

Vasileios Vlachos
University of Thessaly
Volos, Greece

Chapter 1

The Evolution of Hardware-Assisted Security

George Christou, Giorgos Vasiliadis,
Elias Athanasopoulos, and Sotirios Ioannidis

In this chapter, we study the security mechanisms implemented in modern hardware architectures. In essence, hardware-based security can be more effective against powerful attacks, while at the same time minimize the imposed runtime overheads of the security checks themselves.

The chapter is organized as follows. In Section 1.2, we present an overview of various prominent attacks in the current software ecosystem. Section 1.3 presents an overview of recently proposed mechanisms, either from academia or from the industry, which aim to thwart security-related threats. In Section 1.4, we present hardware-based memory isolation techniques that utilize a bare minimum TCB (Trusting Computing Base) and can be deployed in order to provide strong security guarantees. Finally, Section 1.5 presents vulnerabilities that originate from the complex hardware design and the various optimizations available in modern commodity processors.

1.1 INTRODUCTION

Software applications, services, or protocols are usually protected by a plethora of different security tools and architectures, the majority of which are based on solid foundations in order to be effective. However, attackers still manage to bypass them, typically by redirecting their attacks to software layers that lay below seemingly strong defensive mechanisms. Forming a chain of software components, a system is considered as secure as the weakest link, and thus a system is really secure, if and only if every layer of the software stack is secure. The application, system libraries, operating system, drivers, and hypervisors must all be hardened. However, even this may not be sufficient. The hardware itself must be secure and provide the appropriate primitives and capabilities for all the software layers built on top of it to be secure.

To remedy the problems described above, it is inevitable to push security mechanisms down the system stack, from the software layer to the hardware. Hardware security mechanisms have the benefit of being hard, if not

DOI: 10.1201/9781003109952-1

impossible, to be bypassed by attackers. The main reason behind this is the fact that hardware is not typically modifiable, as is the case with software. At the same time, hardware security mechanisms have the advantage of being more efficient in terms of performance, simplicity, and power usage. Finally, the hardware layer maintains a complete overview of the entire system state. Due to the rapid growth in chip surface area, many functionalities are being pushed to the hardware layer, without concern about depriving the software layer of the resources necessary for efficient application execution. Building solid and secure foundations is an important first step toward a complete secure system solution.

1.2 THREAT LANDSCAPE

1.2.1 Common Software Vulnerabilities

The majority of software vulnerabilities stem from the existence of software bugs in today's applications. Software bugs can cause undefined behavior in the program's execution. The adversaries aim to take control of these undefined conditions in order to form the primitives required for their attacks. These primitives can be arbitrary read or write primitives in the process address space, as well as, the alteration of the control flow of the vulnerable process.

Buffer overflows are the most common software bugs in type-unsafe languages exploited by adversaries. During a buffer overflow, a program writes data to a buffer without checking the actual size, overruns the boundaries allocated for the buffer, and overwrites adjacent memory areas. An adversary can utilize buffer overflow bugs in order to write data in arbitrary locations and even hijack the control flow of the process by overwriting control-flow values (e.g. return addresses).

Buffer over-read is similar to buffer overflow, but instead of overwriting adjacent data, the program reads beyond the bounds of a buffer. These bugs can be utilized by adversaries in order to map the process's address space.

Use-after-free is a software bug where a pointer to a memory area is not invalidated after the memory is freed. When the memory is allocated again, the stale pointer may be used in order to reference the memory area, leading to undefined program behavior.

1.2.2 Software Exploitation

Code Injection is a well-known security exploit [30]. By sending specially crafted data to the system it is possible to overwrite (due to a buffer overflow bug) code sections with malicious code, hijacking the system's functionality. Another method is to write malicious code and direct the execution to it. This can happen by overwriting a return address with the address where the buffer holding the malicious code begins. Since the return and data buffers both reside in the stack, a buffer overflow can overwrite the return address with the address the adversary desires. These attacks are not limited to only the binary level.

Return-to-libc is the natural evolution of code injection attacks, which typically are not possible anymore due to the non-executable data protection mechanisms [7]. Since data execution prevention (DEP) arrests the execution of injected malicious code, modern attacks do not depend on injecting malicious code and transferring execution to it. As a result, attackers shifted the focus to using code already present in executable address spaces for their nefarious purposes. A "return-to-libc" attack relies on overwriting a return address on the call stack, with an address of a subroutine already present in the process memory. In many programs, a vast majority of system libraries are loaded with the application, giving the attacker a plethora of functions to be used in order to compromise the system.

Code reuse attacks (CRAs) rely on executing code already present in the vulnerable application. The most common CRA found in *the wild* is Return-Oriented Programming. Return-oriented programming (ROP) is a software exploitation technique that focuses on hijacking the control flow of the target program in order to force it outside the normal instruction execution sequence. It affects many commonly used processor architectures, including x86, ARM (Advanced RISC Machine) [25], and SPARC (Scalable Processor Architecture) [13]. It's a more advanced version of stack smashing, in that it utilizes vulnerabilities that modify the stack in order to overwrite the return address stored within. The new return address is then used to change the control flow of the executable to the attacker's desired path.

Since the attacker now has control over the stack, and subsequently the return addresses, he can jump to any executable memory in the program's address space. The logical next step is to identify the code that he wants to run and set the return address to point to it. The identified pieces of code are called gadgets. Gadgets are small sequences of instructions that typically end with a return instruction. The attacker chains these gadgets together by pushing the address of each to the stack, through a stack-related vulnerability like a buffer overflow. Since gadgets end with a return instruction, at the end of its execution, a gadget will jump to the next address pushed to the stack. The attacker can identify what functionality a gadget will provide either by disassembling the program or, whether the binary is not available for analysis, by observing the effects each gadget has on the stack and the control flow in general, as demonstrated by Bittau et al. in Hacking Blind [11]. In CISC processors, gadgets are more common, and since the attacker can point execution to any byte of an instruction, thus can cause the interpretation of an instruction to shift away from its original functionality.

1.3 SECURITY MECHANISMS IN HARDWARE

In the following section we review many popular processor features that aim to increase the security of a system. We also present new extensions, which are present in newer processors but not yet made standard in current software. Thankfully, the adoption of those technologies in upcoming software is gaining popularity. The slow progress of including those features in the software is due to the need for source code recompilation, source code refactoring, and the need for the adoption of security-oriented programming styles. Furthermore, compilers have to adapt their processes to include those features in order to produce executables that are optimized in terms of performance and security and the utilization of these new technologies.

1.3.1 Protection Rings

The concept of protection rings is one of the first hardware-enabled security mechanisms. In essence, they enable isolation between the operating system and the applications that run on top of it. Typically, the operating system is allowed to take full control of the machine's resources and applications. On the other hand, applications run with lower privileges in order to restrain them from controlling the rest of the machine without supervision. Common RISC architectures, like ARM and SPARC, provide only two levels of isolation, which are controlled through the *supervisor* bit. The supervisor bit is set when the processor executes the operating system's code and unset when the processor is occupied by an application. The supervisor bit prevents the execution of several machine instructions, as well as the control of machine-specific and processor control registers. CPUs with x86 architecture include many different levels of privileges (namely *protection rings*) in order to isolate device drivers and also enable hardware-assisted virtualization. The operating system always executes at Ring 0 (Figure 1.1).

1.3.2 Supervisor Mode Execute/Access Prevention

To increase the granularity of the protection rings, recent iterations of Intel processors include certain features that provide defenses against supervisor-level vulnerabilities. SMEP (Supervisor Mode Execution Protection Enable) is one such feature that restricts the operating system from executing user-level code unless the CPU switches to a higher ring level first. SMAP (Supervisor Mode Access Prevention) is complementary to SMEP and protects user-space data from being accessed from kernel code.

1.3.3 Data Execution Prevention

Data Execution Prevention (DEP) is a hardware feature that halts an application if the control flow switches to a data memory region. This mechanism

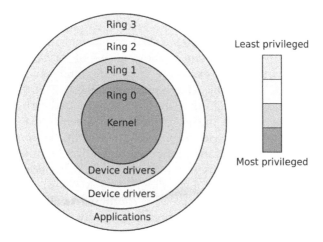

Figure 1.1 Protection rings in x86 processors by Hertzsprung at English Wikipedia, CC BY-SA 3.0, https://commons.wikimedia.org/w/index.php?curid=8950144

raises the bar against software exploitation attacks, in which malicious code is written in data memory and then redirecting the program counter (PC) to it. Attackers can only rely on existing code, within process memory, in order to achieve exploitation. Return-Oriented Programming is a sophisticated technique widely used in modern exploits to bypass this mechanism.

DEP has different acronyms depending on the processors' brand [2]. In Intel processors, it is referred to as XD bit (*eXecute Disable*). The feature is controlled through the most significant bit of a 64-bit page table entry. When this bit is set to 0, the page is assumed to hold code and can be executed. If the value is 1, the page cannot be executed since it holds data. AMD uses the same approach under the name Enhanced Virus Protection. In ARM architectures, it is part of the page table entry format as XN bit (*eXecute Never*) and is placed in the page descriptor. In SPARC V8, this mechanism is used through the Reference MMU that has permission policies of Read Only, Read/Write, and Read/Write/Execute in page table entries.

1.3.4 Intel Memory Protection Extensions

Memory protection eXtensions (MPX) is a feature introduced in Intel processors in 2015. Software deploying these extensions is fortified by associating every pointer with a lower and an upper bound. Every time a pointer is dereferenced, its associated bounds are checked. If the address stored in the pointer is out of the specified bounds, a bound violation exception is raised. Since the majority of exploits depend on out-of-bounds memory accesses (e.g. beyond the size of an array), this mechanism can effectively disclose many possible security vulnerabilities in an application.

The appealing security guarantees of this feature, however, impose a relatively high runtime overhead. If the bounds checked are not in a register, the bounds of the upcoming dereferenced pointer must be moved from a Bounds Table stored in the main memory in one of the bounds registers. This operation is relatively expensive since the pointer address must be looked up in the Bounds Table using a process similar to a TLB (Translation Look-aside Buffers) miss. Additionally, bounds associated with each pointer impose significant stress on the processor's cache system. On average, MPX deployment using ICC imposed 50% overhead in SPEC benchmarks [3].

In 2018, both GCC and Linux proposed to remove the support for Intel MPX [17, 27]. These decisions were made due to serious concerns regarding the effectiveness of MPX [29]. Even though Intel MPX is a hardware-software co-design, the overhead imposed was prohibitive. Temporal memory safety was not provided; thus multithreading was not supported. Compilers had to be redesigned in order to explicitly synchronize the memory bounds. Several programming idioms cannot be used due to the restrictions on the allowed memory layout. Thus, application developers had to substantially refactor the source code in order to deploy Intel MPX.

Prior to its introduction in Intel processors, bounds checking was a well-studied technique in the literature. Software-only implementations (e.g. [9], [14]) had several drawbacks that made them not appealing for use. Non-trivial changes were required in the source code, the violation detection was limited, and also the runtime overhead was very high. Hardware approaches like Hardbound [16] and CHERI's [40] processor pointer bound checking system are based upon the concept of Fat Pointers. Herein, each pointer's value is associated with metadata, like the base address and the length, in order to verify that when the pointer changes it remains within the bounds. These hardware approaches achieved better granularity and at the same time the overhead introduced was within an acceptable margin.

1.3.5 Intel Memory Protection Keys

Memory protection keys (MPK) [33] is a hardware mechanism that was introduced recently by Intel. It allows a user-space process to change permissions on groups of pages. Each page group is associated with a unique key and each application can have up to 16-page groups. MPK also supports per thread view, i.e., different application threads can have different access rights associated with each key (i.e. page group). The key benefit of MPK over page tables is the performance gains, since changing permissions does not require switching to kernel anymore. Moreover, different threads can be isolated within the same process. The access rights supported for the page groups are: (i) read/write, (ii) read only, and (iii) no access.

Due to the fact that MPK is a totally unprivileged mechanism that has been designed to be controlled from user-level code, it is useless when an attacker controls the PKRU register or can execute arbitrary instructions.

However, when combined with mechanisms that can prevent arbitrary code execution it can harden applications from other types of attack, such as memory disclosures.

1.3.6 ARM Memory Tagging

This mechanism is proposed for future ARM versions (8.5 and later) [8]. The key idea of this mechanism is that each 16-byte block of memory will be tagged using a 4-bit value. Each pointer will hold the tag of the valid memory blocks that can be accessed on its 4 MS bits. Thus, loads and stores can only work if the address and the target have the same tag. Memory blocks are retagged when freed. This mechanism can prevent many exploitation techniques that rely on arbitrary memory access. For example, a pointer pointing to a buffer will not be able to access contiguous memory blocks beyond the buffer bounds, thus effectively protecting adjacent memory from being overwritten if the buffer overflows. A potential problem with this mechanism is that 4-bit tags will offer reduced entropy and thus many memory blocks will have the same tag. Finally, the performance overhead of this mechanism has not been measured. If the performance overhead is substantial, memory tagging will not be a practical solution.

1.3.7 Instruction Set Randomization

Code randomization techniques [34, 32] attempt to make code reuse harder by shuffling the location of the code to be reused, but it has been demonstrated that even a simple information leak can reveal all of the process layout (especially the text section) and essentially bypass any randomization scheme [35]. Instruction set randomization (ISR) [23] and XnR [10] provide defenses against information leakage. The main principle behind hardware ISR [31] is to encrypt the instructions of executables residing in the main memory and decrypting them just before execution. This simple principle is enough to prevent the execution of arbitrary code injected into a running program by an attacker. Even if an attacker successfully injects code and

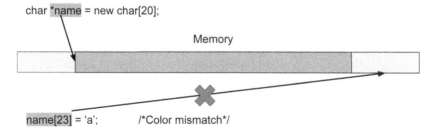

Figure 1.2 Memory Tagging Extensions overview. Pointers cannot access memory with different tags.

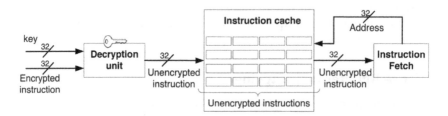

Figure 1.3 Instructions are always encrypted when in main memory, the decryption takes place during instruction cache misses.

diverts the control flow to the injected code, the result will be an execution exception, since the injected code will not translate to any meaningful machine instruction. Even though ISR was originally designed to defend against code injection attacks, it can also be effective against code reuse attacks. By encrypting the text segment with an encryption algorithm that is resistant to cryptographic attacks (anagrams, known ciphertext plaintext, etc.) an attacker will not be able to discover useful gadgets in the application's text segment since any memory leak will return encrypted contents of the text segment (the instructions are decrypted only in the instruction cache).

Originally, ISR was proposed to defend against code injection attacks since an attacker needs to know the encryption key in order to inject meaningful code. On the other hand, XnR marks every executable page as nonreadable; thus any attempt to arbitrarily disclose the text section layout will result in a memory violation. ISR can be used not only for randomizing binaries but also for interpreted languages as well (e.g., Perl).

1.3.8 Control-Flow Integrity

Instead of hiding the code, another potential avenue for stopping code exploitations is to prevent the execution of non-benign code. One promising direction is based on the observation that modern exploits introduce control flows that are not part of the program's benign Control-flow Graph (CFG) 1.4. Control-flow integrity (CFI) [5] suggests that a running program should exhibit only the control flows that are part of the program's original CFG as expressed by its source code. Essentially, CFI mandates that any indirect branch should not be possible to target the address of *any* instruction in the program but rather be constrained in an allowable set of addresses that have been a priori determined.

Although many mechanisms have been proposed and many of them are very effective in defending against software exploitation, when implemented in software they usually suffer from two issues. First, the substantial security checks required incur significant runtime overhead. Second, they can

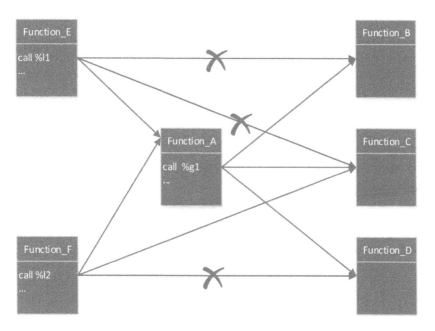

Figure 1.4 Control-Flow Integrity dictates that only Control-Flow transitions discovered with CFG analysis are allowed.

be bypassed since the trusted computing base is broad and attackers can target one of the many *trusted* components, e.g., the operating system and the firmware. For example, researchers have proposed relaxed CFI schemes in order to amortize runtime overhead [42], but it is well established today that such approaches can be bypassed [18]. On the other hand, hardware-enhanced security mechanisms have been proven to be a lot more effective in defending against exploitation and more practical in terms of performance overhead [15].

Forward-Edge CFI refers to the reinforcement of forward-edge branches, i.e., Indirect Call Instructions. Indirect calls utilize function pointers stored in memory to find their target. Unfortunately, these pointers are not safely stored in memory and are susceptible to corruption by tampering. Forward-Edge CFI validates that the indirect call reached a target that belongs to a group of authorized branch targets. This limits the call to extremely few indirect branch targets, hopefully, none that the attacker could exploit.

Backward-Edge CFI refers to the reinforcement of backward-edge branches, i.e., Return Instructions. Returns, like indirect calls, utilize a pointer stored in the stack as a branch target. This pointer is extremely vulnerable to tampering since it resides in the stack. Backward-Edge CFI keeps track of the return addresses and verifies that each return instruction did indeed reach its target.

1.3.8.1 Intel Control-flow Enforcement Technology

Control-flow enforcement technology (CET) [4] is a technology announced by Intel in June 2016. CET defines a shadow stack in order to protect backward-edge control flow transfers. When CET is enabled, call instructions are responsible for pushing the return address in the shadow stack, as well as in the original stack. Any ret instructions result to pop the shadow stack and ensure that it matches the return address acquired from the application's stack. In case of a mismatch, an exception is raised and the execution of the application stops. The shadow stack's integrity is protected by the MMU in order to prevent an adversary from overwriting the return addresses residing in it. Any memory instruction trying to access the contents of the shadow stack is blocked by the MMU and a page fault is raised. In order to protect forward-edge control flow transfers, ENDBRANCH instruction is used to mark the legitimate landing points for call and indirect jump instructions within the application's code. When a jump is issued CET enters WAIT FOR ENDBRANCH state. If an ENDBRANCH instruction is not the next instruction in the program stream, the processor raises a control protection fault.

1.3.8.2 ARM Pointer Integrity

This mechanism utilizes cryptographic primitives (hashing) in order to verify that the control flow pointers are not corrupted before using them. The pointer authentication code (PAC) of each control flow pointer is stored in the unused bits of the pointer (i.e., 24 MS bits of the pointer). PACs are calculated and authenticated using custom instructions:

- `PAC <pointer>, &<pointer>` (usually in stack): calculates a MAC using a process key
- `AUTH <pointer>, &<pointer>`: authenticates the MAC using the process key

Each process has a unique key, which is used to calculate and authenticate the control flow pointers. The encryption algorithm used is QARMA. This technology has been already deployed in recent Apple products using ARMv8.3. A recent study from Google's project zero identified several vulnerabilities in this technology [19].

1.4 TRUSTED EXECUTION ENVIRONMENTS

Almost any software security mechanism is incapable of defending the system's functionality if the operating system is vulnerable. Trusted execution environments (TEEs) define threat models with powerful adversaries.

Taken to the extreme, the trusted computing base defined by these security mechanisms is reduced to only include a trusted part of the processor 1.5.

1.4.1 Execute Only Memory

Many similar proposals exist in the research literature, which aim to reduce the trusted computing base so as to include only the processor's chip [26, 36]. XOM (Execute Only Memory) [26] supports isolation between many containers (called compartments) by tagging every cache-line with a container identifier. Moreover, it integrates both encryption and HMAC verification in the processor's memory controller, so it verifies the integrity of data residing in off-chip memory. However, XOM is vulnerable to memory replay attacks, in which a memory region is overwritten with old data that were previously residing in that memory region.

1.4.2 Aegis

Aegis [36] trusts only a small secure kernel, which is also responsible for isolating applications. It also uses memory encryption and integrity checking to protect data that reside in off-chip memory, as well as Merkle trees in order to prevent replay attacks on the off-chip memory.

1.4.3 ARM TrustZone

The *ARM TrustZone* [1] enables the separation of execution domains to the trusted and the untrusted ones. The trusted execution domain is reserved for the *trusted* system code, while third-party applications are executed in the untrusted domain. This separation extends to memory and peripherals

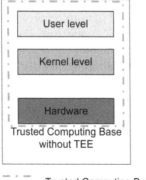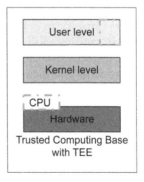

Figure 1.5 Reduced attack surface in Trusted Execution Environments. The protected application only trusts the processor chip and the code that will run in the TEE.

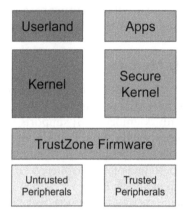

Figure 1.6 Overview of an ARM SoC with trustzone. CPU has both execution domains. Flash and SRAM define trusted and untrusted regions. Peripherals can be defined as trusted or untrusted in case of security concerns. Of course, DMA should also be constrained.

in order to achieve system-wide security, e.g., a DMA capable peripheral is forbidden access to memory areas owned by trusted execution domain software.

1.4.4 Intel Software Guard Extensions

Intel Software Guard eXtensions (SGX) was proposed in 2013 and introduced in Intel's Skylake micro-architecture in 2015. Its security guarantees provide strong isolation between parts of a user-level application, with the further enhancement of preserving the isolation even if the drivers, operating system, and BIOS are fully compromised 1.5. Effectively, the Trusted Computing Base is reduced to only the processor's hardware. Using this mechanism, developers can define code and data to be protected by encapsulating them in entities, called *enclaves*. SGX machine code instructions are used to create and initialize an enclave and move code and data in it. The underlying hardware provides confidentiality and integrity to the enclave. Enclave data residing in the main memory are always encrypted. They are decrypted only when moved inside the processor, where they also pass integrity checking tests. The component responsible for those operations is the Memory Encryption Engine [21]. Thus, even if a passive attacker snoops the bus between the processor and the main memory, the data acquired will be useless. In the case in which an active attacker overwrites SGX memory regions, the MEE will detect the forgery. Currently, the size allocated for enclaves is limited to 128 MB. The next version of SGX (2.0) will support dynamic memory allocation. Additionally, a Seal Key, unique to each processor can be used in order to store the whole enclave when the application is terminated for future use. Another selling point for SGX is secure remote computation [6]. A user who wants to use a remote computation service can verify that the software running in the remote enclave is legitimate and that the data sent to the remote host will not be accessible by the remote host owner. Thus, the user trusts only the author of the software running in the enclave and the processor's manufacturer (i.e., Intel).

1.5 HARDWARE VULNERABILITIES

The increased hardware design complexity of modern commodity processors and their various optimizations have opened the road to a new class of hardware vulnerabilities. These vulnerabilities can be abused by malicious parties to launch powerful attacks, such as disclosing sensitive data or taking full control of the base machine, even if it is protected with the strongest isolation techniques. The main cause of these vulnerabilities is that the hardware resources of the processor are aggressively shared between different processes, primarily for performance and utilization purposes.

1.5.1 Transient Instruction Execution

Spectre [24] demonstrated that instructions that are executed either speculatively or out-of-order can cause cache modifications. An attacker that can control the cache and observe the effects of the transiently executed instructions is capable of disclosing otherwise inaccessible memory. The first and most persistent variance of Spectre is the bounds check bypass. The scenario of this attack is that during a loop that accesses incremental memory addresses, the processor will speculatively access memory beyond the bounds of the array before the bounds check is calculated, due to the fact that the branch predictor will be trained to take the branch. An attacker that can run code in a sandboxed environment (e.g. JavaScript engine) could infer otherwise inaccessible data (beyond the bounds of the array). Meltdown [28] is another similar vulnerability, where transiently executed instructions could even load addresses from the kernel memory address space.

In further academic publications, it was demonstrated that a plethora of shared hardware resources could be exploited in order to leak sensitive information from a security-critical application. In Spectre-V2 [24], global branch predictors were trained in order to target an instruction sequence that can leak information and would not execute under normal execution. The speculatively executed instruction would then cause cache modifications observable by the attacker. In RIDL [39], micro-architectural state components (e.g. Line Fill Buffers and Load ports) were proven to speculatively use *stale* data without addressing restrictions during memory operations. Thus, an attacker could extract those data by executing load operations and observing side effects in the cache, since the processor would speculatively use those data until they are invalidated. These attacks can leak data even from Intel SGX [12] since the cache will be altered before the processor detects that the speculated load is incorrect.

1.5.2 Cache as a Side-Channel

It is equally important for an attacker to observe the micro-architectural state changes of the transiently executed instructions. In the different Spectre proof-of-concepts exploits, the authors utilized the FLUSH+RELOAD [41] technique. This attack is carried in three phases. Initially, the attacker flushes the cache lines of the memory area to be monitored. This can be done especially by executing clflush instructions. The attacker then waits for the victim application to execute for some time and access the monitored memory lines. In the final step, the attacker measures the time it takes to access the monitored memory area. Cache hits will mean that the victim accessed the monitored areas. This attack can affect processes that share the monitored memory areas. In cryptographic applications, an attacker can infer the key by leaking the exact control-flow path of the application. In Meltdown, this technique can be used to extract kernel memory that was accessed by transiently executed instructions. Another similar side-channel technique is Prime+Probe [37], where the attacker, instead of flushing the cache, populates a portion of the cache sets. After the victim process executes for a while and the attacker's process is scheduled, the load time of the monitored cache sets will be measured. If the victim process has accessed the monitored cache sets, it will have evicted some of the attacker's cache lines causing observable latencies that can be used to infer sensitive data. Other variances of cache side channels have been used in order to infer sensitive data from applications running inside an enclave [12].

1.5.3 Proposed Defenses

The above vulnerabilities are exceptionally hard to address, as they require disabling hardware resource sharing and aggressive speculation, an action that would substantially downgrade the CPU performance. In a similar manner, current software mitigations solve only a limited number of the different attack variations while imposing significant performance overheads. Kernel page table isolation (KPTI) is a mechanism used in Linux for preventing Meltdown exploitation. KPTI is based on KAISER [20] and effectively prevents kernel memory disclosure, by not mapping kernel pages that contain sensitive data when the processor executes in user mode. The full kernel address space is mapped when the processor switches to supervisor mode. In certain processors that do not implement process identifiers in the TLB, the kernel mappings need to be flushed when switching back to user space. In the latter case, it has been reported that the runtime overhead is non-negligible, especially in applications with heavy usage of system calls. Meltdown was effectively addressed in the next generation of Intel processors through hardware modifications.

For the first variance of Spectre, Intel proposed the use of fence instructions at the beginning of basic blocks that access sensitive memory [22]. By doing so, the processor will be forced to serialize the execution of previously fetched instructions and will not transiently execute the sensitive branch. However, this technique requires that developers will flag sensitive basic blocks in order to insert fence instructions and also may inhibit *good* speculation that significantly optimizes the performance of the application. Intel's mitigation for the Branch Target Injection variances introduces a set of mechanisms that can prevent an attacker from exploiting this set of vulnerabilities. Depending on the requirements of the application the available strategies provide: (i) the option to restrict the speculation of indirect branches, (ii) prevent branch predictors from being controlled by other threads, and (iii) Indirect Branch Predictor Barriers that can be issued in order to flush the branch predictor values when switching to an application that handles sensitive data.

To remedy the recent attacks that broke process isolation mechanisms by exploiting side channels (even in Trusted Execution Environment), researchers proposed key architectural changes that can prevent information leakage. MI6 is an out-of-order processor that can prevent information leakage from enclave execution even if the attacker can observe micro-architectural states (e.g. cache contents, internal buffers) and exploit speculation states and branch predictors. The key architectural modifications in MI6 are the strict partitioning of the hardware resources in order to prevent information leakage through delays that can be observed by an adversary. Thus, an enclave application will never share hardware resources (e.g. cache, micro-architectural state registers, etc.) with a normal application. MI6 also relies on flushing the micro-architectural state of the enclave's execution in order to erase any execution-dependent state when the processor schedules a new process. Finally, page-faults are routed directly to the enclave in order to prevent information disclosure through observing the page-faults of the enclave's execution [38].

1.6 CONCLUSION

The exploitation of modern systems is undoubtedly still possible, despite many mitigation techniques that have been enabled in production systems. To address this problem, there is a shift toward pushing security mechanisms down the system stack from software to hardware. Hardware security mechanisms have the advantage of being more efficient in terms of performance, simplicity, and power usage, while also maintaining a complete overview of the entire system state, without being modifiable, as is the case with software.

In this chapter, we presented the most popular security mechanisms that are available in modern commodity processors. These mechanisms can play an important role in hardening the security of software applications, services or protocols, and provide stronger assurances of protection against a threat landscape that is constantly evolving.

REFERENCES

1. ARM trustzone. https://www.arm.com/products/security-on-arm/ trustzone, accessed June 2021.
2. No execute bit. https://en.wikipedia.org/wiki/NX_bit, accessed June 2021.
3. Performance evaluation of MPX. https://intel-mpx.github.io/performance/, accessed June 2021.
4. Baiju V Patel, A Technical Look at Intel's Control-flow Enforcement Technology, 2016. https://software.intel.com/content/www/us/en/develop/ articles/technical-look-control-flow-enforcement-technology.html, accessed June 2021.
5. Martín Abadi, Mihai Budiu, Ulfar Erlingsson, and Jay Ligatti. Control-flow integrity. In *Proceedings of the 12th ACM Conference on Computer and Communications Security*, pages 340–353. ACM, 2005.
6. Ittai Anati, Shay Gueron, Simon Johnson, and Vincent Scarlata. Innovative technology for cpu based attestation and sealing. In *Proceedings of the 2nd International Workshop on Hardware and Architectural Support for Security and Privacy*, Vol. 13, 2013.
7. Starr Andersen and Vincent Abella. Changes to functionality in microsoft windows xp service pack 2, part 3: Memory protection technologies, data execution prevention. *Microsoft TechNet Library*, September 2004. technet .microsoft.com/en-us/library/bb457155.aspx
8. Steve Bannister, ARM. Memory tagging extension: Enhancing memory safety through architecture, 2019. https://community.arm.com/developer/ip-produc ts/processors/b/processors-ip-blog/posts/enhancing-memory-safety, accessed June 2021.
9. Todd M. Austin, Scott E. Breach, and Gurindar S. Sohi. Efficient detection of all pointer and array access errors. In *Proceedings of the ACM SIGPLAN 1994 Conference on Programming Language Design and Implementation, PLDI '94*, pages 290–301. New York, NY, ACM, 1994.
10. Michael Backes, Thorsten Holz, Benjamin Kollenda, Philipp Koppe, Stefan Nürnberger, and Jannik Pewny. You can run but you can't read: Preventing disclosure exploits in executable code. In *Proceedings of the ACM SIGSAC Conference on Computer and Communications Security*, pages 1342–1353. ACM, 2014.
11. Andrea Bittau, Adam Belay, Ali Mashtizadeh, David Mazieres, and Dan Boneh. Hacking blind. In *Security and Privacy (SP), 2014 IEEE Symposium on*, pages 227–242. IEEE, 2014.

12. Ferdinand Brasser, Urs Müller, Alexandra Dmitrienko, Kari Kostiainen, Srdjan Capkun, and Ahmad-Reza Sadeghi. Software grand exposure:{SGX} cache attacks are practical. In *11th {USENIX} Work- shop on Offensive Technologies ({WOOT} 17)*, 2017.

13. Erik Buchanan, Ryan Roemer, Hovav Shacham, and Stefan Savage. When good instructions go bad: Generalizing return-oriented programming to risc. In *Proceedings of the 15th ACM Conference on Computer and Communications Security*, pages 27–38. ACM, 2008.

14. Jeremy Condit, Matthew Harren, Zachary Anderson, David Gay, and George C. Necula. *Dependent Types for Low-Level Programming*, pages 520–535. Berlin, Heidelberg, Springer, 2007.

15. Thurston H.Y. Dang, Petros Maniatis, and David Wagner. The performance cost of shadow stacks and stack canaries. In *ACM Symposium on Information, Computer and Communications Security, ASIACCS*, Vol. 15, 2015.

16. Joe Devietti, Colin Blundell, Milo M. K. Martin, and Steve Zdancewic. Hardbound: Architectural support for spatial safety of the c program-ming language. In *Proceedings of the 13th International Conference on Architectural Support for Programming Languages and Operating Systems, ASPLOS XIII*, pages 103–114. New York, NY, ACM, 2008.

17. GCC. Remove MPX support, 2018. https://gcc.gnu.org/ml/gcc-patches/2018-04/msg01225.html, accessed June 2021.

18. Enes Göktas, Elias Athanasopoulos, Herbert Bos, and Georgios Portoka-lidis. Out of control: Overcoming control-flow integrity. In *Security and Privacy (SP), 2014 IEEE Symposium on*, pages 575–589. IEEE, 2014.

19. Google Project Zero. Examining pointer authentication on the iPhone XS, 2019. https://googleprojectzero.blogspot.com/2019/02/examining-pointer-authentication-on.html, accessed June 2021.

20. Daniel Gruss, Moritz Lipp, Michael Schwarz, Richard Fellner, Clémentine Maurice, and Stefan Mangard. Kaslr is dead: long live kaslr. In *International Symposium on Engineering Secure Software and Systems*, pages 161–176. Springer, 2017.

21. Shay Gueron. A memory encryption engine suitable for general purpose pro-cessors. *IACR Cryptology ePrint Archive*, 2016, 204, 2016.

22. Intel. Intel analysis of speculative execution side channels, 2018. https://www.intel.com/content/www/us/en/architecture-and-technology/intel-analysis-of-speculative-execution-side-channels-paper.html, accessed June 2021.

23. Gaurav S. Kc, Angelos D. Keromytis, and Vassilis Prevelakis. Countering code-injection attacks with instruction-set randomization. In *Proceedings of the 10th ACM Conference on Computer and Communications Security*, pages 272–280. ACM, 2003.

24. Paul Kocher, Jann Horn, Anders Fogh, , Daniel Genkin, Daniel Gruss, Werner Haas, Mike Hamburg, Moritz Lipp, Stefan Mangard, Thomas Prescher, Michael Schwarz, and Yuval Yarom. Spectre attacks: Exploiting speculative execution. In *40th IEEE Symposium on Security and Privacy (S&P'19)*, 2019.

25. Tim Kornau. Return oriented programming for the arm architecture. Master's thesis, Ruhr-Universitat Bochum, 2010.

26. David Lie, Chandramohan A Thekkath, and Mark Horowitz. Implementing an untrusted operating system on trusted hardware. *ACM SIGOPS Operating Systems Review*, 37(5), 178–192, 2003.

27. Linux. x86: remove Intel MPX. http://lkml.iu.edu/hypermail/linux/kernel/1812.0/04478.html

28. Moritz Lipp, Michael Schwarz, Daniel Gruss, Thomas Prescher, Werner Haas, Anders Fogh, Jann Horn, Stefan Mangard, Paul Kocher, Daniel Genkin, Yuval Yarom, and Mike Hamburg. Meltdown: Reading kernel memory from user space. In *27th USENIX Security Symposium (USENIX Security 18)*, 2018.

29. Oleksii Oleksenko, Dmitrii Kuvaiskii, Pramod Bhatotia, Pascal Felber, and Christof Fetzer. Intel mpx explained: A cross-layer analysis of the intel mpx system stack. *Proceedings of the ACM on Measurement and Analysis of Computing Systems*, 2(2), 28, 2018.

30. Aleph One. Smashing the stack for fun and profit, *Phrack Magazine*, 7(49), 365, 1996.

31. Antonis Papadogiannakis, Laertis Loutsis, Vassilis Papaefstathiou, and Sotiris Ioannidis. Asist: Architectural support for instruction set ran- domization. In *Proceedings of the ACM SIGSAC Conference on Computer & Communications Security*, pages 981–992. ACM, 2013.

32. Vasilis Pappas, Michalis Polychronakis, and Angelos D. Keromytis. Smashing the gadgets: Hindering return-oriented programming using inplace code ran- domization. In *Proceedings of the 2012 IEEE Symposium on Security and Privacy, SP '12*, pages 601–615. Washington, DC. IEEE Computer Society, 2012.

33. Soyeon Park, Sangho Lee, Wen Xu, HyunGon Moon, and Taesoo Kim. libmpk: Software abstraction for intel memory protection keys (intel MPK). In *USENIX Annual Technical Conference (USENIX ATC 19)*, pages 241– 254. Renton, WA, USENIX Association, 2019.

34. PaX Team. Address Space Layout Randomization (ASLR), 2003. http://pax.grsecurity.net/docs/aslr.txt

35. Kevin Z. Snow, Lucas Davi, Alexandra Dmitrienko, Christopher Liebchen, Fabian Monrose, and Ahmad-Reza Sadeghi. Just-in-time code reuse: On the effectiveness of fine-grained address space layout randomization. In *Proceedings of the 34th IEEE Symposium on Security and Privacy*, 2013, May.

36. G. Edward Suh, Charles W. O'Donnell, and Srinivas Devadas. Aegis: A single-chip secure processor, *Information Security Technical Report*, 10(2), 63–73, 2005.

37. Eran Tromer, Dag Arne Osvik, and Adi Shamir. Efficient cache attacks on aes, and countermeasures, *Journal of Cryptology*, 23(1), 37–71, 2010.

38. Jo Van Bulck, Nico Weichbrodt, Rüdiger Kapitza, Frank Piessens, and Raoul Strackx. Telling your secrets without page faults: Stealthy page table-based attacks on enclaved execution. In *26th {USENIX} Security Symposium ({USENIX} Security 17)*, pages 1041–1056, 2017.

39. Stephan Van Schaik, Alyssa Milburn, Sebastian österlund, Pietro Frigo, Giorgi Maisuradze, Kaveh Razavi, Herbert Bos, and Cristiano Giuffrida. Ridl: Rogue in-flight data load. In *2019 IEEE Symposium on Security and Privacy (SP)*, pages 88–105. IEEE, 2019.

40. Jonathan Woodruff, Robert NM Watson, David Chisnall, Simon W. Moore, Jonathan Anderson, Brooks Davis, Ben Laurie, Peter G. Neumann, Robert Norton, and Michael Roe. The cheri capability model: Revisiting risc in an age of risk. In *Computer Architecture (ISCA), ACM/IEEE 41st International Symposium on*, pages 457–468. IEEE, 2014.

41. Yuval Yarom and Katrina Falkner. Flush+ reload: A high resolution, low noise, l3 cache side-channel attack. In *23rd {USENIX} Security Symposium ({USENIX} Security 14)*, pages 719–732, 2014.

42. Mingwei Zhang and R. Sekar. Control flow integrity for COTS binaries. In *Usenix Security*, pages 337–352, 2013.

Chapter 2

Cybersecurity of the Unmanned Ship

Sokratis Katsikas and Georgios Kavallieratos

2.1 INTRODUCTION

There is an intense activity of the maritime industry towards making remotely controlled and autonomous ships sail in the near future; this activity constitutes the instance of the Industry 4.0 process in the maritime industry and is termed Shipping 4.0. Such vessels comprise a number of cyber physical systems (CPSs) that perform functions critical to the safe operation of the vessel; hence, it is important to address their cybersecurity challenges.

The concept of an unmanned ship is not new; visions of such ships were reported as early as the 1970s and have continued to appear regularly [5]. In 1973, Sch¨onknecht et al. [37] stated their vision of the unmanned ship as follows:

> In this age of rationalization and automation it would not be difficult to imagine a ship without a crew. [...] It is indeed quite possible that at some distant future date the captain will perform his duties in an office building on shore. In his place he will leave a computer on board ship which will undertake all the tasks of the navigator's art, [...] controlling the ship, and will in fact perform the task much more effectively.

In 1980, the Japanese Intelligent Ship project aimed at "bringing about 'intelligent ships' that can function without help from the crew" and proposed the Master-Slave ship model, according to which robot ships would form convoys. In 1994, Kai Levander proposed the "Ship without crew" for short-sea shipping:

> A ship with no crew on-board could travel aided by the GPS chain and guided from the traffic stations. Pilots could board near the harbour and take the [ship] into port. An automated mooring system secures the [ship] to the quay without help from the crew.

DOI: 10.1201/9781003109952-2

In 1996, Bertram and Kaeding suggested that a combination of artificial intelligence (AI) and teleoperation was feasible for ships. Back then, however, the concept was still not attractive to shipping companies due to high maintenance costs. The concept re-emerged in a 2007 paper on the future development of the maritime industry by Waterborne TP, a cluster of European maritime stakeholders. Although this paper suggested that more advanced automation and improved sensors might be desirable, it stopped short of advocating full automation. Five years later, inspired by this idea, European research groups launched the collaborative MUNIN (Maritime Unmanned Navigation through Intelligence in Networks) project, co-funded under the EU's FP7 research program. MUNIN concluded that an unmanned and autonomous merchant vessel was possible but only for deep-sea voyage and not in congested or restricted waters, where a crew should operate the ship [31]. In 2013, Oscar Levander of Rolls-Royce proposed the building of "unmanned containerships", by leveraging a combination of AI and teleoperation. In 2014, DNV GL proposed the concept of ReVolt, a 60-meter long, battery-powered, unmanned container feeder vessel to sail the territorial waters of Norway [9]. In 2016, Rolls-Royce initiated a joint industry project in Finland called Advanced Autonomous Waterborne Applications to create the technology for a remotely controlled or fully autonomous ship to operate in coastal waters [36]. Many companies, mostly from Scandinavian countries and Japan, are working on full-size autonomous ships with the goal of obtaining cargo vessel or even passenger vessel capabilities and relevant major research projects are underway [11]. *Yara Birkeland*, the world's first fully autonomous and electric container vessel, is expected to be ready to sail in 2022 [47]. The concept and prototype of an autonomous all-electric passenger ferry for urban water transport have been developed by the Norwegian University of Science and Technology within the ongoing Autoferry project [33].

The International Maritime Organization (IMO) uses the term MASS (Maritime Autonomous Surface Ship) for the autonomous ship [34]. According to the IMO, the levels of autonomy for a MASS are defined as follows:

- *AL0: Ship with automated processes and decision support:* Seafarers are on board to operate and control shipboard systems and functions. Some operations may be automated.
- *AL1: Remotely controlled ship (with seafarers on board):* The ship is controlled and operated from another location, but seafarers are on board.
- *AL2: Remotely controlled ship (without seafarers on board):* The ship is controlled and operated from another location. There are no seafarers on board.
- *AL3: Fully autonomous ship:* The operating system of the ship is able to make decisions and determine actions by itself.

AL0 describes the conventional ship, where the ship's operations are the same as those of traditional vessels. Although many contemporary information and communications technology (ICT) systems can be on board in order to support processes related to navigation and engine control, human operators maintain the central role. For the remotely controlled variants (AL1, AL2), most of the ship's systems are capable of performing predefined actions without human intervention. The ship's operations depend on communication with the Shore Control Center (SCC) and, at the same time, are influenced by onboard crew and CPSs. The human operator at these levels gives directions and controls the vessel's systems either locally (AL1) or remotely (AL2), while operations such as mooring, navigating, cargo loading, and unloading are performed entirely by remote control. At the last level of autonomy (AL3), most of the ship's operations rely on the onboard CPSs, although some of the operations may be supervised by an SCC. Furthermore, the ship is equipped with contemporary navigation, engine, and control systems, such as collision avoidance systems (CA). At this level, the human vector does not exist and advanced systems are responsible for the availability, maintainability, and reliability of the operations.

Therefore, the concept of the unmanned ship implies two generic alternatives:

- the remotely controlled ship (AL1, AL2); and
- the autonomous ship (AL3).

Regardless of the level of autonomy, the adoption of ICT in any industry has always been accompanied by enlargement and diversification of the risks that the industry is facing, with existing risks being increased and new risks being introduced. This is mainly due to the fact that while traditional operations were designed with no need for cybersecurity in mind, modern ICT-enabled operations are allowed to be accessed and controlled through the industry's enterprise information system, through interfaces that are rarely sufficiently secure. As the enterprise system is usually connected to the Internet, the end result is that security-unaware systems, such as control or navigation systems, are made accessible to outsiders. Therefore, it is not surprising that almost all known attacks against industrial control systems have been launched by first compromising the enterprise system and subsequently using it as a stepping-stone to attack the control system [20].

In this chapter, we give an overview of the state of play of cybersecurity of the unmanned ship. We first discuss a reference model of the architecture and the generic system architecture of an unmanned ship. We then leverage these to analyze the cyber risks of such a generic architecture. Next, we systematically elicit the security requirements of the three most vulnerable CPSs on board an unmanned ship, namely the Automatic Identification System (AIS), the Electronic Chart Display Information System (ECDIS), and the Global Maritime Distress and Safety System (GMDSS). These,

along with the analysis of risks, are used to drive the selection of baseline security controls towards designing the security architecture of the
unmanned ship.

2.2 ARCHITECTURAL VIEWS

In this section, two architectural views of the unmanned ship will be discussed. The first is the *extended Maritime Architecture Framework (eMAF)*
that has been developed to describe the relationships between technical
systems, users, and related governance aspects in the maritime domain so
as to facilitate the coordination of the development of new systems in the
domain. The second is a generic architecture of the CPSs of an unmanned
ship, including their interconnections and the dependencies among them,
that has been developed to allow the security analysis of the unmanned
ship.

2.2.1 TheExtended Maritime
Architecture Framework

A Maritime Architecture Framework (MAF) was proposed in [46] to facilitate the development and adoption of new systems and technologies in the
maritime domain. The development process of the MAF followed that of
the Smart Grid Architectural Model [8]; accordingly, the MAF has been
developed taking into consideration existing maritime architectures, including the Common Shore-Based System Architecture [1] and the International
Maritime Organization's (IMO) e-Navigation architecture [17].

The main element of the MAF is the *multidimensional cube* that combines different viewpoints to provide a graphical representation of the
underlying maritime domain and the examined system architecture.
The cube captures three dimensions, alias *axes*, namely interoperability,
hierarchical, and topological. The topological axis represents the logical
location where a technology component is located. The interoperability
axis addresses communication, data and information, usage, and context
of a maritime system. The hierarchical axis covers management and control systems of the maritime domain; it starts with the classification of
the examined system into its field of activity and continues with system-
specific operations before the system will break down into technical services and their components as well as interfaced physical components
[46]. Each axis breaks down into a number of *layers*. The layers of the
topological axis (Ships, Link, and Shore) are derived from IMO's break-
down of the maritime domain [32]. The layers of the interoperability axis
(Regulation and Governance, Function, Information, Communication,
and Component) cover organizational, informational, and technical aspects and include the different levels of interaction (Operational,

Functional, Technical, and Physical) as stated in IMO's e-Navigation vision [16]. Finally, the layers of the hierarchical axis (Fields of activity, Operations, Systems, Technical services, Sensors and actuators, and Transport objects) cover economic, technical, and physical aspects of a maritime system.

Information, technology, and people are crucial elements of the unmanned ship ecosystem [12], and the MAF is able to capture these elements. Therefore, the MAF can in principle be used for representing and analyzing the unmanned ship ecosystem. However, the MAF in its original form cannot capture specific characteristics of unmanned vessels. As argued in [26], in order to describe the relevant new concepts and technologies, the topological axis should be extended to include layers for the unmanned ship, the SCC, and the link between them. The *Unmanned ship layer* represents ship-side entities, such as the vessel's infrastructure, operational and functional goals, processes, and systems. The *SCC layer* represents entities of the shore-side infrastructure, along with processes, and systems that facilitate the interaction with other entities within or outside the maritime sector. The *Link layer* represents the telecommunication methods and protocols between the unmanned ship, the SCC, and other entities (including vessels). The resulting extended MAF (eMAF) [26] is shown in Figure 2.1.

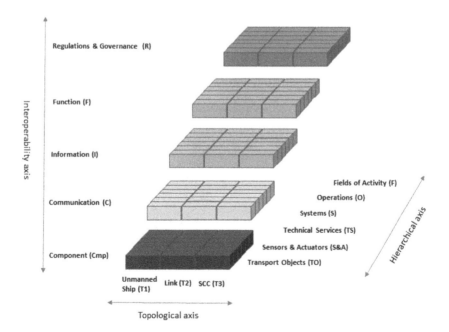

Figure 2.1 Extended MAF.

2.2.2 The CPSs of the Unmanned Ship

A generic architecture of the CPSs of the three layers of the e-MAF (Unmanned ship, SCC, and Link) based on information provided in the literature, including [31], [6], and the IEC 61162 series of standards, was proposed in [25]. The schematic of the architecture is shown in Figure 2.2. In the sequel, we focus on the unmanned ship layer.

Within the unmanned ship, the next layer comprises the *Engine Automation Systems (EAS)*, the *Bridge Automation Systems (BAS)*, and the *ICT infrastructure*.

The EAS include all the systems that generate and manage the ship's power and propulsion systems. These are:

- The *autonomous engine monitoring and control (AEMC)*, which monitors the mechanical parts of the ship and includes the *autonomous control of the engine room (AC-ER)* that monitors and controls the propulsion system, the power generation system, the fuel system, rudder systems, and the evaporation system; the *emergency handling (EmH)*, which includes the alarm systems; and the *engine data logger (EDL)*, which records all information about the operation of the ship's engines.
- The *engine efficiency system (EES)*, which monitors and controls the ship engine's efficient operation and includes preventive tools for maintenance.
- The *maintenance interaction system (MIS)*, which provides for technical, managerial, and administrative maintenance in the engine room. It also includes an instance of the EmH.

The *bridge automation system (BAS)* includes all the sub-systems on the bridge, most notably those for navigation and control of the ship. These are:

- The *automatic navigation system (ANS)*, which provides navigating for the ship, i.e. for determining aspects such as position, speed, and direction during travel. The ANS includes the *voyage data recorder*

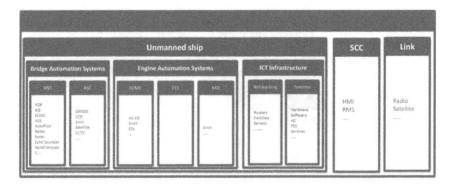

Figure 2.2 Systems architecture.

(VDR) that gathers and stores all the information about the ship's condition, its position, its movements, and recordings from engine and radio systems; the *automatic identification system (AIS)*, which is a communication system using four worldwide channels in the VHF maritime mobile band for the exchange of navigation data; the *electronic chart display and information system (ECDIS)*, which is a geographic information system used for nautical navigation that complies with International Maritime Organization (IMO) regulations as an alternative to paper nautical charts; the *advanced sensor system (ASS)*, which provides information about the ship's position and a number of navigational aids, such as the *autopilot, radar, sonar, echo sounder, gyrocompass,* and *collision avoidance system (CA)*.

- The *autonomous ship controller (ASC)* complements the SCC in assessing the data provided by the sensors to control the ship's operations. It includes the *global maritime distress and safety system (GMDSS)*, an internationally agreed upon set of safety procedures, types of equipment, and communication protocols used to increase safety and make it easier to rescue distressed ships, boats, and aircraft, which consists of several systems intended to perform the following functions: alerting (including position determination of the unit in distress), search and rescue coordination, locating (homing), maritime safety information broadcasts, general communications, and bridge-to-bridge communications, as well as providing redundant means of distress alerting and emergency sources of power; the *cargo management/cargo control room (CCR)*, responsible for the efficient control and management of the cargo; an instance of the *EmH*; *satellite communication systems*; and *surveillance systems (CCTV)*.
- The *ICT infrastructure* includes all the networking and computing equipment used in the vessel; systems such as the *Access Control system (AC)*, responsible for controlling access to the ship, be it physical or remote; and the *passenger service system (PSS)*, which serves the ship's customers/passengers with the goal of implementing efficient identity management and access control in the ship's infrastructure; and services.

The *Shore Control Center (SCC)* controls and navigates one or more ships from the shore; it includes the *human-machine interface (HMI)* and the *remote maneuvering support system (RMSS)*, an information system that allows the execution of secure autonomous procedures under the control of the SCC.

The *Link* includes all the communication systems used by the vessel to communicate with entities in its environment, including the SCC and other vessels.

To complete the architectural description of the unmanned ship, the interconnections, dependencies, and interdependencies among the CPSs need to be also identified. Two CPSs are *interconnected* when there exists information exchange between them; when two CPSs are connected and the state of one system influences the state of the other, the systems are *dependent*. Two systems are *interdependent* when there exists mutual dependency between them. The interconnections and the dependencies among the unmanned ship's systems are shown in Figures 2.3 and 2.4, respectively, where the nodes of each graph represent systems and the edges represent connections/ dependencies.

2.3 CYBER RISKS OF THE UNMANNED SHIP

A wealth of cyber risk assessment methods applicable to general-purpose IT systems exists. While these can be and have been applied to IT systems in the maritime domain, they cannot accurately assess cyber risks related to CPSs [2]. Cyber risk assessment methods for CPSs more often than not are domain-specific, as they need to take into account safety as an impact factor in addition to the "traditional" impact factors of confidentiality, integrity,

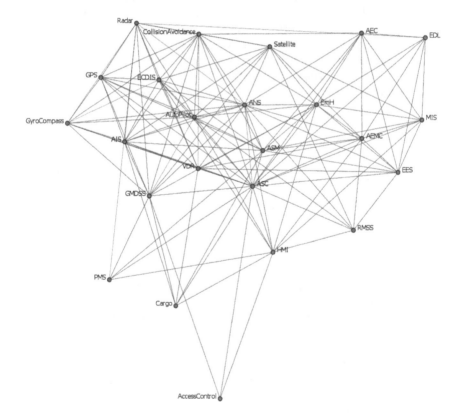

Figure 2.3 Interconnections.

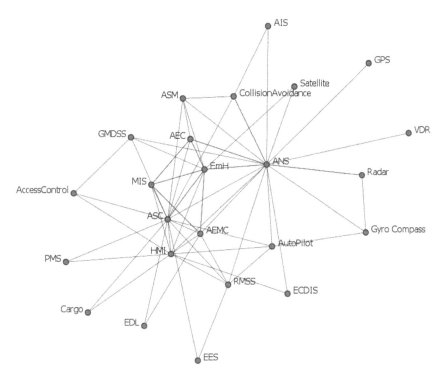

Figure 2.4 Dependencies.

and availability [6]. In the maritime domain, a review of cybersecurity risk assessment methods appeared in [48]. Rødseth et al. in [35] proposed a risk assessment method for an unmanned merchant ship. Although the method aims to identify both safety and security risks, particular focus is given on hazard identification and the accordant risks, with cybersecurity left largely unaddressed. Tam et al. in [43] proposed the MaCRA model-based framework for maritime cyber risk assessment and applied it to a number of example scenarios [44]. However, the aim of MaCRA is not to assess the risks or flaws of specific systems but rather to facilitate the understanding of cyber risks in the maritime domain. Svilicic et al. in [41] proposed a framework for assessing cyber risks in ships and applied it to the case of the electronic chart display and information system (ECDIS).

Several works in the literature have analyzed security threats and risks for specific systems used in specific types of autonomous and remotely controlled vessels. Among these, Bolbot et al. in [7] identified and analyzed safety-related cyberattacks in an autonomous inland ferry; their analysis covers safety aspects regarding the navigation and propulsion systems of the ferry. Silverajan et al. in [39] explored security issues and cyberattacks targeting systems of smart ships. Awan et al. in [3] analyzed 59 documented accidents to better understand the vulnerabilities of Integrated Bridge System (IBS) components. Svilicic et al. in [42] presented a study on the cyber resilience of a shipboard integrated navigational system (INS) installed on a RoPax ship engaged in international trade. Wang et al. in [45] proposed a secure relative integrated navigation method to counteract injected fault measurement attacks. Balduzzi et al. in [4] presented a security evaluation of the automatic identification system (AIS), by introducing threats that affect both the implementation (by online providers) and the protocol specification. Lund et al. in [28] described a proof-of-concept attack on an INS and its integrated ECDIS, and demonstrated the attack on a vessel.

Kavallieratos et al. in [25] and [24] developed and used modified versions of the STRIDE [38] and DREAD [29] methods to identify potential cyberattack scenarios and evaluated the accordant risks for a number of CPSs of the unmanned ship ecosystem. These methods can effectively analyze highly interconnected CPSs comprising heterogenous components [22] and they are most appropriate for analyzing systems under development, whose detailed operational and functional requirements have not been yet established, in contrast to other approaches that need such requirements to produce valid results.

Tables 2.1 and 2.2 depict the resulting risk value of each CPS for each STRIDE threat calculated by applying DREAD. Table 2.1 suggests that Spoofing and Denial of Service are the most critical threats both among the engine room and the SCC systems. Similarly, Table 2.2 suggests that the Spoofing, Tampering, and Denial of Service threats present the highest risk levels among the bridge systems of the unmanned ship. Tampering and Information disclosure are medium-risk threats, and Repudiation and Elevation of privileges are low-risk threats. Moreover, a single risk value for each examined system can be assigned, equal to the largest among the risk values for the same system; these values are shown in the last row of each of Tables 2.1 and 2.2.

Table 2.1 Cyber Risks in Engine and Shore Control Center (SCC) Cyber Physical Systems (CPSs)

	EAS	AEMC	EDL	ASM	EES	MIS	SCC	RMSS	HMI
S	1.33	1.75	1.5	2.25	2	1.5	2.05	1.75	2.16
T	1.67	1.5	1.25	1.28	1.75	2.25	1.67	1.5	2.16
R	1.25	1.25	1.25	1.25	1	1.25	1.42	1.25	1.25
I	1.42	1	1.25	1.66	1.25	1.5	1.42	1.75	2
D	2	1.5	1.25	2	1.75	1.75	2.05	1.75	2.16
E	1.26	1.25	1.25	1.25	1.5	1.5	1.25	1.5	1.5
DREAD	**1.67**	**1.75**	**1.5**	**2.25**	**2**	**2.25**	**2.05**	**1.75**	**2.16**

Table 2.2 Cyber Risks in Bridge CPSs

	BAS	AIS	ECDIS	GMDSS	ASC	ANS	EmH	C.A.	Radar	VDR	Cargo	CCTV	AP
S	1.83	2.33	2.42	2.25	2.17	1.92	1.25	1.91	2.25	1.5	1.5	2.16	1.5
T	1.67	2.42	2.17	2.5	2.5	1.92	1.25	2.08	2.08	1.5	1.5	1.83	1.75
R	1.25	2.33	1.25	1.5	1.75	1.5	–	1.25	1.66	1.25	1.5	1.5	1.25
I	1.83	2.33	2.33	2.25	1.75	1.75	1.25	1.41	–	1.5	1.75	1.91	1.5
D	2	2	2.5	2.5	2.58	1.92	1.5	1.91	2	1.5	1.25	1.91	1.75
E	1.25	1.92	2.33	2.17	2	2.17	–	1.25	1.5	1.5	1.5	1.75	1.5
DREAD	**2**	**2.42**	**2.5**	**2.5**	**2.58**	**2.17**	**1.5**	**2.08**	**2.25**	**1.5**	**1.75**	**2.16**	**1.75**

2.4 CYBERSECURITY REQUIREMENTS FOR THE UNMANNED SHIP

Because the unmanned ship ecosystem is characterized by high complexity and complex interconnections, dependencies and interdependencies among its constituent CPSs, a systematic approach needs to be followed when attempting to establish cybersecurity requirements, both of the ecosystem as a whole and of each individual CPS in the ecosystem. A security requirements elicitation process for the unmanned ship ecosystem that combines the eMAF reference architecture with the SecureTropos method [30] was proposed in [21]. This process is depicted in Figure 2.5.

In [21], the security requirements derived from applying this process to the overall unmanned ship ecosystem and the three most vulnerable onboard CPSs, namely the AIS, the ECDIS, and the GMDSS, are also reported. These are grouped into two groups: *system-specific* requirements and *common* requirements. The former group includes requirements pertinent to each individual system, whereas the latter includes requirements applicable to all three studied systems. These are, as follows, classified according to the classification scheme of the ISO/IEC 27001:2013 and ISO/IEC 27002:2013 standards.

- Human resource security:
    - (i) The system administrator must be well trained and aware of system functional and non-functional requirements (e.g., AIS modes and communication capabilities).
- Asset management:
    - (i) Data and signals must be identified and classified into protection levels;
    - (ii) Documentation of third-party components, versioning, and published system vulnerabilities must be maintained.
- Access control:
    - (i) A strong password policy must be enforced, which will specify the length and the lifetime of each combination of the credentials (e.g., Passwords to log in to the ECDIS should be regularly changed);

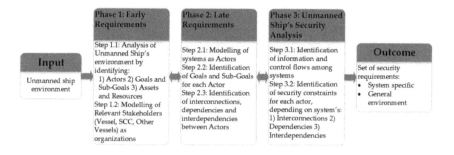

Figure 2.5 Security requirements elicitation process.

(ii)   The non-repudiation and traceability of actions performed either from the SCC or physically to the onboard system must be ensured with appropriate authentication mechanisms;

(iii) The system must be able to implement lock mechanisms when requested by the system administrator or after a configurable time of idleness;

(iv)   The number of consecutive login attempts to the system must be specified;

(v)   The system must support multi-factor authentication;

(vi)   The system must accept inputs only from authorized entities, by authorized maritime actors.

- Cryptography:

(i)   The system must support encryption algorithms that are able to promote data confidentiality and integrity, and to satisfy data transmission timing requirements during the voyage;

(ii)   Data transmitted to external and internal actors should be encrypted using appropriate – in each case – cryptographic mechanisms (e.g., Dynamic data sent from ECDIS to Radar, global positioning system (GPS), and advanced sensor module (ASM) systems must be encrypted);

(iii) Stored data should be appropriately encrypted, the strength of the encryption mechanism depending on their type and the possible pertinence of maritime legal or regulatory requirements.

- Physical and environmental security:

(i)   The physical integrity of the onboard or SCC sensors must be protected;

(ii)   The system must be installed so as to prevent physical damages, such as flooding or fire;

(iii) All physical and virtual connection points of the system must be appropriately protected or blocked (e.g., USB ports or any other human interface device).

- Operations security:

(i)   Both onboard and SCC systems must be able to operate under network stress situations such as a Denial of Service attack;

(ii)   Security mechanisms must be implemented in order to protect the system from malicious codes;

(iii) Frequent system data backup should be maintained (e.g., ECDIS voyage data should be backed up regularly to the VDR);

(iv)   The system must be able to determine whether an action taken has been performed by a system on board or by a human user remotely from the SCC;

(v)   The integrity of the static, processed, and transmitted data must be protected;

(vi)   The confidentiality of data in transit and storage must be protected;

(vii)   The freshness of data should be ensured;

(viii)   The authenticity of services, transmitted data, and software sources must be ensured (e.g., AIS updates or ECDIS charts updates should be performed by authorized sources/vendors);

(ix)   The utility of the dynamic and voyage data should be ensured; and

(x)   The measures to protect the confidentiality and integrity of data should not downgrade their utility.

- Communication security:

  (i)   The confidentiality and integrity of the data exchanged between internal (onboard systems) and external actors (SCC or other vessel) should be ensured by appropriate mechanisms depending on the actors and the type of the data in transit;

  (ii)   The segregation of the onboard components in different trust levels must be ensured;

  (iii)   The connectivity between the system and external actors and between onboard systems must be continuous;

  (iv)   Onboard systems must be mutually authenticated;

  (v)   The traffic from and to the system must be monitored;

  (vi)   The systems should be able to control the sent data considering the actor and the type of the data in transit;

  (vii)   All external actors of the unmanned ship ecosystem must be able to determine the source of data flows originating from the onboard systems;

  (viii)   The data exchange between onboard systems should be established in a way such that their authenticity can be verified;

  (ix)   The systems must use transport layer security to protect the data in transit;

  (x)   The system should support mechanisms to detect rogue data packets;

  (xi)   The services between onboard systems and external actors (SCC/other vessel) must be authenticated;

  (xii)   There should be redundancy of communication channels between onboard systems;

  (xiii)   The maximum allowable latency in system-to-system communication should conform to pertinent standards and the systems' operational requirements.

- System acquisition, development, and maintenance:

  (i)   System development and deployment must be performed following pertinent cybersecurity standards;

  (ii)   The update process must be protected against time-of-check vs time- of-use attacks;

(iii)   The source of the software must be authenticated;

(iv)   Both onboard and shore-based systems must be maintained regularly;

(v)   The system should be properly installed, taking into account network segmentation and physical access;

(vi)   System updates/upgrades must be performed only by authorized entities;

(vii)   The integrity of the maintenance process must be ensured to prevent malicious intrusions,

(viii) System maintenance must be performed only by well-trained personnel;

(ix)   The configuration and installation of the system must be performed by authorized personnel;

(x)   The vessel's infrastructure must be well designed and the corresponding systems appropriately installed according to the type of the ship; and

(xi)   The system must not allow downgrading to old system software versions.

- Supplier relationships:

  (i)   Appropriate mechanisms must be employed to validate hardware, software, and data from the suppliers; and

  (ii) A strict review of the security policies of the system's vendor must be undertaken.

- Information security incident management:

  (i)   The system must detect and produce an alert on abnormal numbers of requests, such as by a user or an external actor;

  (ii)   The system's functional and non-functional requirements should be maintained during security incidents such as GMDSS signal jamming; and

  (iii) The SCC must be notified when a system anomaly has been detected.

- Information security aspects of business continuity management:

  (i)   The continuity of system operations must be ensured;

  (ii)   The system on board or onshore must be able to operate using alternative power sources;

  (iii) The system must be able to operate 24/7; and

  (iv)   Redundant systems should be installed taking into account the operational complexity of the unmanned ship and the system operations.

- Compliance:

  (i)   Formal certification of compliance with the pertinent legislative and regulatory requirements must be obtained.

The growing convergence of information technology with operational technology and the accordant proliferation of interconnected cyber physical systems (CPSs) has given rise to the challenge of systematically identifying coherent, consistent, and non-conflicting security and safety requirements. An integrated method for safety and security requirements engineering for CPSs at the design stage of the system lifecycle, named SafeSecTropos, was proposed and applied to the most vulnerable CPSs on board the unmanned ship in [27].

2.5 TREATING THE CYBER RISK OF THE UNMANNED SHIP

An ISO/IEC 27005-compliant approach for managing the risks of the unmanned ship was proposed in [24] and is depicted in Figure 2.6, where six sub-processes are specified, along with their inputs and outputs. The Environmental Analysis sub-process for the unmanned ship was carried out in [26]; the Threat Analysis sub-process was carried out in [25]; the Security Requirements Elicitation sub-process was carried out in [21]; the Cyber Risk Assessment sub-process and the Control Selection sub-process were carried out in [24]. The security architecture design sub-process remains a subject for future work.

A number of sources (e.g. [10, 19, 18]) provide sets of security controls from which a selection can be made. All of these sources pertain to information systems rather than CPSs; hence their applicability in the case of the unmanned ship is limited. However, Appendix G of the NIST Guide to Industrial control systems (ICS) Security [40] provides the *ICS overlay*, which is partial tailoring of the controls and control baselines in [19, 18], which adds supplementary guidance specific to ICS. This source was used in [24] to select controls according to the following set of criteria, adapted from [15]:

- C1: Kind of CPS that needs to be protected; C2: Security aspects that need to be protected.
- C3: Threats that need to be eliminated.
- C4: Potential control alternatives.
- C5: The value of the CPS to protect, according to its importance. This has been assessed within the process of attack path analysis, performed in [23].
- C6: The likelihood of threat occurrence. This derives from the threat analysis performed within the risk assessment process in [24].
- C7: Risk coverage provided by alternative controls.

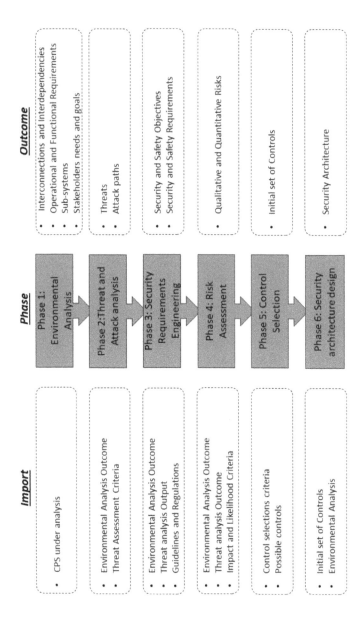

Figure 2.6 Security controls selection process.

As an example, the values of the control selection criteria for the spoofing threat against the AIS are as follows:

C1: Navigational CPS;

C2: Integrity and availability: These are derived from the security requirements that were established in [21].

C3: Spoofing/Tampering/DoS: These derive from the threat analysis results performed in [25] and [24].

C4: Encryption/Tamperproof hardware.

C5: High: This has been assessed within the process of attack path analysis, performed in [23].

C6: Very likely: This derives from the threat analysis performed within the risk assessment process in [24].

C7: Low: No alternative controls are already in place and lead to selecting the IA-3 control category of [40].

An example of a control that belongs to this category is the establishment and use of an authentication infrastructure for devices, such as the one proposed in [14, 13].

The application of the process described above to the three most vulnerable onboard systems of the unmanned ship (AIS, ECDIS, and GMDSS) results in identifying baseline security controls for each individual system. Some of these controls (Device Identification and Authentication (IA-3), Cryptographic Protection (SC-13), Denial of Service Protection (SC-5), Physical Access Control (PE-3), and Internal System Connections (CA-9)) are recommended for all systems, while others are recommended for two or only one of the studied systems. During the security architecture design phase, the controls identified for all systems will need to be reconsidered, consolidated, checked for applicability in the specific environment, conformance to guidelines, compliance to standards, etc.

As is typical with risk treatment strategies, the application of security controls does modify (reduce) the risk but does not eradicate it. To complete the risk treatment process, one needs to assess the effectiveness of the applied controls, consider the residual risk within the specific environmental and organizational context and possibly repeat the process until the residual risk falls below the accepted risk level. This process can be effectively performed when the whole security architecture of the unmanned ship has been determined; accordingly, this is also an item for possible future work.

One of the distinctive characteristics of CPSs is their ability to interconnect dynamically, sometimes to address scope beyond the originally intended one. This often results in emergent, hence unpredictable, behavior. In order to effectively secure CPSs in such situations, a dynamic assessment of cyber risk is recommended. The methodology in [24] cannot capture such behavior. However, it can be extended to this effect, along the lines followed in [22].

2.6 CONCLUSIONS

The time when fleets of unmanned ships will be sailing the oceans is now coming close. Notwithstanding the tremendous impact that such a development will have on the economy, the fact that it may unleash the significant potential for cyberattacks should also be acknowledged. Keeping in mind that efficient and effective cyber protection cannot occur as a result of patches but rather necessitates the development of systems that will be secure by design, the importance of designing security architectures for the unmanned ship becomes apparent. A number of questions need to be answered and problems need to be solved before such a practically applicable and demonstrably secure architecture can be defined. In this chapter, we provided an overview of cybersecurity issues related to the concept of the unmanned ship and we presented research results that hopefully contribute towards addressing these issues. Still, much more research will be required before the goal can be achieved.

REFERENCES

1. *A Technical Specification for the Common Shore-Based System Architecture (CSSA).* Technical report, International Association of Marine Aids to Navigation and Lighthouse Authorities, 2015.
2. Saqib Ali, Taiseera Al Balushi, Zia Nadir, and Omar Khadeer Hussain. Risk management for cps security. In *Proceedings of Cyber Security for Cyber Physical Systems*, pages 11–34. Springer, Cham, 2018.
3. Malik Shahzad Kaleem Awan and Mohammed A. Al Ghamdi. Understanding the vulnerabilities in digital components of an integrated bridge system (IBS), *Journal of Marine Science and Engineering*, 7, 350, 2019.
4. Marco Balduzzi. AIS exposed understanding vulnerabilities & attacks 2.0. *Blackhat, Asia*, page 44, 2014.
5. Volker Bertram. Technologies for low-crew/no-crew ships. In *Forum Captain Computer IV*. Citeseer, 2002.
6. BIMCO, CLIA, ICS, INTERCARGO, INTERMANAGER, INTER-TANKO, IUMI, OCIMF, and WORLD SHIPPING COUNCIL. The guidelines on cyber security onboard ships v3.0, 2018.
7. Victor Bolbot, Gerasimos Theotokatos, Evangelos Boulougouris, and Dracos Vassalos. Safety related cyber-attacks identification and assessment for autonomous inland ships. In *Proceedings of the International Seminar on Safety and Security of Autonomous Vessels (ISSAV)*, 2019.
8. CEN-CENELEC-ETSI Smart Grid Coordination Group. *Smart Grid Reference Architecture*. Technical report, 2012.
9. DNV-GL. The revolt, a new inspirational ship concept, 2015. https://www.dnvgl.com/technology-innovation/revolt/index.html
10. Federal Office for Information Security. It-grundschutz-catalogues: 13th version, 2013. https://enos.itcollege.ee/~valdo/bsieng/en/gstoolhtml/allgemein/einstieg/01001.html
11. Andrzej Felski and Karolina Zwolak. The ocean-going autonomous ship—challenges and threats, *Journal of Marine Science and Engineering*, 8(1), 41, 2020.

12. Oliver Fitton, Daniel Prince, Basil Germond, and Mark Lacy. *The Future of Maritime Cyber Security*. Technical report, 2015.
13. Athanasios Goudosis and Sokratis Katsikas. Secure ais with identity-based authentication and encryption, *Transnav: International Journal on Marine Navigation and Safety of Sea Transportation*, 14(2), 287–298, 2020.
14. Athanassios Goudossis and Sokratis K. Katsikas. Towards a secure automatic identification system (AIS), *Journal of Marine Science and Technology*, 24(2), 410–423, 2019.
15. Government of Spain, Ministry of Finance and Public Administration. *Magerit – version 3.0 Methodology for Information Systems Risk Analysis and Management*, pages 1–109, 2014.
16. International Maritime Organization. *MSC 85/26/add.1, Annex 20 Strategy for the Development and Implementation of E-navigation*. Technical report, 2009.
17. International Maritime Organization (IMO). e-Navigation. http://www.imo.org/en/OurWork/Safety/Navigation/Pages/ eNavigation.aspx [accessed 10-10-2019].
18. Joint Task Force. Control baselines for information systems and organizations. *NIST Special Publication, 800–53B*, 2020.
19. Joint Task Force. Security and privacy controls for federal information systems and organizations. *NIST Special Publication, 800–53*, Revision 5, 2020.
20. Sokratis K. Katsikas. Cyber security of the autonomous ship. In *Proceedings of the 3rd ACM Workshop on Cyber-Physical System Security*, pages 55–56. ACM, 2017.
21. Georgios Kavallieratos, Vasiliki Diamantopoulou, and Sokratis Katsikas. Shipping 4.0: Security requirements for the cyber-enabled ship, *IEEE Transactions on Industrial Informatics*, 16(10), 6617–6625, 2020.
22. Georgios Kavallieratos, Vasileios Gkioulos, and Sokratis K Katsikas. Threat analysis in dynamic environments: The case of the smart home. In *Proceedings of the 15th International Conference on Distributed Computing in Sensor Systems (DCOSS)*, pages 234–240, 2019.
23. Georgios Kavallieratos and Sokratis Katsikas. Attack path analysis for cyber-physical systems. In *Proceedings of CyberICPS 2020*. Springer, 2020.
24. Georgios Kavallieratos and Sokratis Katsikas. Managing cyber security risks of the cyber-enabled ship, *Journal of Marine Science and Engineering*, 8(10), 768, 2020.
25. Georgios Kavallieratos, Sokratis Katsikas, and Vasileios Gkioulos. Cyber-attacks against the autonomous ship. In *Proceedings of the SECPRE, CyberICPS 2018*. Lecture Notes in Computer Science, Vol. 11387, pages 20–36. Springer, 2018.
26. Georgios Kavallieratos, Sokratis Katsikas, and Vasileios Gkioulos. Modelling shipping 4.0: A reference architecture for the cyber-enabled ship. In *Asian Conference on Intelligent Information and Database Systems*, pages 202–217. Springer, 2020.
27. Georgios Kavallieratos, Sokratis Katsikas, and Vasileios Gkioulos. Safesec tropos: Joint security and safety requirements elicitation, *Computer Standards & Interfaces*, 70, 103429, 2020.

28. Mass Soldal Lund, Odd Sveinung Hareide, and Øyvind Jøsok. An attack on an integrated navigation system, *The Journal of the Ocean Technology*, 12, 23–27, 2017.

29. Microsoft. Chapter 3 – Threat modeling, 2010. [online] https://docs.microso ft.com/en-us/previous-versions/msp-n-p/ff648644(v=pandp.10)?redirectedfro m=MSDN

30. Haralambos Mouratidis and Paolo Giorgini. Secure tropos: A security- oriented extension of the tropos methodology, *International Journal of Software Engineering and Knowledge Engineering*, 17(02), 285–309, 2007.

31. MUNIN. Maritime unmanned navigation through intelligence in networks, 2016. http://www.unmanned-ship.org/munin/

32. NCSR 1–28. *Report to the Maritime Safety Committee, International Maritime Organization, Sub-committee on Navigation Communications and Search and Rescue.* Technical report, 2014.

33. Norwegian University of Science and Technology. Autoferry-autonomous all-electric passenger ferries for urban water transport. https://www.ntnu.edu/ autoferry. [Online; accessed 19-10-2020].

34. International Maritime Organization. IMO takes first steps to address autonomous ships. http://www.imo.org/en/mediacentre/pressbriefings/pages/08 -msc-99-mass-scoping.aspx, 2018. [Online; accessed 19-10-2020].

35. Ørnulf Jan Rødseth and Hans-Christoph Burmeister. Risk assessment for an unmanned merchant ship, *TransNav, International Journal on Marine Navigation and Safety Od Sea Transportation*, 9(3), 357–364, 2015.

36. Rolls-Royce. Remote and autonomous ship-the next steps, 2016.

37. Rolf Schönknecht. *Schiffe und Schiffahrt von Morgen*. VEB Verlag Technik, Berlin, 1973.

38. Adam Shostack. *Threat Modeling: Designing for Security*. Wiley Publishing, 1st edition, 2014.

39. Bilhanan Silverajan, Mert Ocak, and Benjamin Nagel. Cybersecurity attacks and defences for unmanned smart ships. In *Proceedings of the 2018 IEEE International Conference on Internet of Things (iThings) and IEEE Green Computing and Communications (GreenCom) and IEEE Cyber, Physical and Social Computing (CPSCom) and IEEE Smart Data (SmartData)*, pages 15–20, 2018.

40. Keith Stouffer, Victoria Pillitteri, Abrams Marshall, and Adam Hahn. Guide to industrial control systems (ics) security, *NIST Special Publication*, 800(82), 247, 2015.

41. Boris Svilicic, Junzo Kamahara, Jasmin Celic, and Johan Bolmsten. Assessing ship cyber risks: A framework and case study of ecdis security, *WMU Journal of Maritime Affairs*, 18, 509–520, 2019.

42. Boris Svilicic, Igor Rudan, Alen Jugović, and Damir Zec. A study on cyber security threats in a shipboard integrated navigational system, *Journal of Marine Science and Engineering*, 7, 364, 2019.

43. Kimberly Tam and Kevin Jones. Cyber-risk assessment for autonomous ships. In *International Conference on Cyber Security and Protection of Digital Services (Cyber Security)*, pages 1–8. IEEE, 2018.

44. Kimberly Tam and Kevin Jones. Macra: A model-based framework for maritime cyber-risk assessment, *WMU Journal of Maritime Affairs*, 18(1), 129–163, 2019.

45. Yongjing Wang, Yi Wang, and Xiaoliang Feng. Ship security relative integrated navigation with injected fault measurement attack and unknown statistical property noises, *Journal of Marine Science and Engineering*, 8, 305, 2020.

46. Benjamin Weinert, Axel Hahn, and Oliver Norkus. A domain-specific architecture framework for the maritime domain. In Heinrich C. Mayr and Martin Pinzger, eds., *Informatik 2016*, pages 773–784, Bonn, 2016. Gesellschaft f ür Informatik e.V.

47. Yara. Yara birkeland status, 2020. https://www.yara.com/news-and-media/press-kits/yara-birkeland-press-kit/ [Online; accessed 19-10-2020].

48. Ben You, Yunpeng Zhang, and Liang-Chieh Cheng. Review on cyberse- curity risk assessment and evaluation and their approaches on maritime transportation. In *Proceedings of the 30th Annual Conference of International Chinese Transportation Professionals Association*, 2017.

Chapter 3

Agile Incident Response in Industrial Control Environments

Helge Janicke, Richard Smith, Leandros Maglaras, Allan Cook, Ying He, and Fenia Ferra

3.1 INTRODUCTION

Industrial control system (ICS) refers to a group of process automation technologies, such as supervisory control and data acquisition (SCADA) systems and distributed control systems (DCS), which unfortunately have been subjected to a growing number of attacks in recent years [19]. A US executive order signed in 2013 stated that the "cyber threat to critical infrastructure continues to grow and represents one of the most serious national security challenges we must confront" [24]. This infrastructure is typically underpinned by industrial control systems (ICSs) that automate and manage electromechanical devices to provide services essential to a nation's wellbeing and prosperity, and as such, any antagonistic action against these represents a significant threat to the continued security of a country [27]. ICSs often use operating systems, applications, and procedures that may be considered unconventional by contemporary IT professionals and have operational requirements that include the management of processes that, if not executed in a predictable manner, may result in injury, loss of life, damage to the environment, as well as serious financial issues such as production losses that may have a negative impact on a nation's economy [27, 17, 10, 21, 9].

Naedele [23] argues that the costs involved in ICS security are prohibitive, especially within critical systems, when the perceived risks to an organization or infrastructure cannot be adequately quantified and a business case is not satisfactorily articulated. This often leads to an underdeveloped incident response capability in the deployed operational ICS [18, 6].

For many years, project management methodologies followed a linear design, such as the waterfall method [26], where one phase could not start until the previous phase was completed, and once complete that phase would not be revisited without significant cost. The main example of this is the capture of requirements, and any change to requirements proved costly and often led to delays, increased costs, or project failure [28]. As software became more complex and customer requirements for a quicker delivery and deployment cycle increased, it became obvious that in many cases

DOI: 10.1201/9781003109952-3

a more flexible and adaptive approach was required. This eventually led to the publishing of the Agile Manifesto [20], which defines the four core values for Agile development as:

1. Individuals and interactions over processes and tools
2. Working software over comprehensive documentation
3. Customer collaboration over contract negotiation
4. Responding to change over following a plan

By adopting the 4 values, along with the 12 principles also presented in the Agile manifesto, software teams were able to reduce the time required to bring products to market and facilitated rapidly changing requirements throughout the project lifecycle [16]. The adoption of Agile methods has increased rapidly in the 18 years since the publication of the manifesto, with some surveys indicating that 97% of respondents now use some form of Agile practice [15]. This innovative approach is geared towards environments where change is constant and the objectives and priorities change rapidly [12]. By adopting Agile tools and techniques, the proposed approach facilitates the security incident.

Rigid procedural incident response processes are increasing the predictability of the defense efforts and make it more difficult to protect the remaining infrastructure and business functions in the context of fast-pivoting and multi-pronged cyberattacks. Especially when incident response (IR) crosses information technology (IT)/operational technology (OT) boundaries, communication between stakeholders, often from different disciplines and organizational hierarchies, is frequently impeded and situational awareness is decreased. Agile approaches, on the other hand, welcome changing requirements and are driven by value and the understanding of the system by a cross-functional team that can manage conflicting stakeholder requirements. This approach is therefore geared to environments where change is constant and the environment and objectives are not clearly identified or defined. This proposal advocates the integration and evaluation of Agile methods and practices used in, e.g. Scrum and Kanban, to provide a security incident response team with the ability to respond quickly to changes while maintaining the focus on the business and its value chain. By its very nature incident response needs to be adaptive to the highly dynamic nature of cyberattacks and anticipate further exploitation paths of the adversaries [13] and requires a cross-disciplinary team effort to respond effectively.

3.2 COMPLYING WITH LEGAL REQUIREMENTS AND GUIDANCE FOR OPERATORS

The network and information security directive (NISD) requires operators of essential services (OESs) and digital service providers (DSPs) to notify the relevant authority of security incidents having a significant impact on the continuity of the essential services they provide without "undue delay" [18]. In the UK this timeframe is defined as no later than 72 hours after an organization becomes aware that an incident has occurred.

In the UK, the obligations of an OES include taking "appropriate and proportionate technical and organizational measures to manage risks posed to the security of the network and information systems on which their essential service relies". They must "notify the designated competent authority about any incident which has a significant impact on the continuity of the essential service which that OES provides". The NIS Directive allows member states to set their thresholds for financial penalties. In the UK, the Information Commissioner's Office can impose fines of up to £17 million. Any Agile approach to incident management has to be compliant with the European regulations and national laws in order to make sure that the organization will not be exposed to any fines. Recently cybersecurity maturity assessment frameworks either tailored to the NIS Directive requirements [8] or integrating several regulations [3, 2] were introduced. These frameworks could be used either as self-assessment tools from the organizations or as audit tools from the national competent authorities. An important question that needs to be answered is how these frameworks can be adapted in order to be efficient when Agile approaches are used especially in incident management.

3.3 CURRENT ISSUES IN MANAGING INCIDENTS IN INDUSTRIAL CONTROL ENVIRONMENTS

Thematic analysis, as described by Braun and Clarke [5], has been used to analyze the interviews of 18 incident response professionals to identify key pressure points and areas where Agile techniques can add value. The research indicated:

- How incidents may vary in volume and impact and how this influences IR and its effectiveness. Most professionals noted that they are mainly prepared to deal with common incidents, and when it comes to incidents of higher sophistication and scale they are often struggling to deal with. They mentioned that insider threats are common, and they result from inconsistencies and fallacies in policies, i.e. access to certain systems, removing access to ex-employees, etc. Moreover, they noted that investigations and IR are commonly economic driven, which is a factor that might influence or limit IR's effectiveness.
- There is an overload and at the same time a lack of information available. More precisely, there is an extreme volume of information to be digested (information digestion), while it seems that quite often there is a lack of information about systems and how systems work, which is commonly attributed to how old and complex OT systems might

be, as well as the lack of people having the appropriate expertise being available.

- The IR teams are focused on individual tasks and responsibilities, instead of team aims and goals, while there is often a lack of OT personnel in the operation rooms.
- There is a lack of communication between departments and IT and OT experts. This was also the case when third-party companies were involved. Third-party companies may be located in different countries, making communication even more challenging.
- Playbooks, as well as certain tools and techniques, are being used. Some of the tools and techniques involved are antivirus, forensic software, network monitoring, log files, etc. With regard to playbooks, while most professionals said that they do use them in actual practice, they noted that playbooks' effectiveness is questionable and mainly IT-focused. Hotwashes were mentioned by a small number of professionals as being part of their practices. According to them, hotwashes are a highly effective add-on to their practices.
- That their approach is commonly adaptive, but only when a need for adaptation was identified. Professionals noted that they do follow a consistent approach with common cases, and they only adapt in more sophisticated cases when there is a need for changes.
- That out of working hours is common within IR.
- They use certain metrics and methods for the evaluation of their work, which varied. However, they noted that both metrics and defining success might be challenging.
- That media and external communication is a great concern. It seems that there is a reluctance on sharing information of incidents with the authorities or talking to the media; while external communication is always being dealt with by people higher in the hierarchy.

3.4 AGILE APPROACH TO INCIDENT MANAGEMENT

The Agile method has been proved to be useful in the context of IT incident response [11]; however, it has not been effectively utilized within the ICS domain. This section explores how Agile can be integrated into ICS incident response, through mapping the four Agile values to the unique characteristics of ICS.

Agile values individuals and interactions over processes and tools. ICS highly values individuals' expertise. The individuals responsible for operating and maintaining the ICS are required to have diversified knowledge to understand the interdependencies between complex systems. ICS systems involve not only control system and IT systems security but also physical security that requires the individuals to understand the links between safety and security [4]. The ultimate target for cyberattacks is usually the safety systems; however, these systems do not usually consider deliberate failures of components in the design. Individuals' expertise and judgment are therefore essential factors affecting incident response decision-making in ICS. Incident handling cannot solely rely on pre-defined processes and tools [25].

Agile values working software over comprehensive documentation. Instead of comprehensive documentation, working software has become the primary measure of progress. During security incident investigation, a large amount of security-related information has been gathered such as log files, indicators, precursors, and incident reports. These are important deliverables that can be used for learning and preventing future attacks in the "follow-up" phase of incident response. However, the security professionals are overwhelmed by this information and not able to properly review and learn from previous incidents. There are some efforts to visualize security knowledge using security-assurance approaches [14]; however, working software (i.e. deliverables) should be considered for incident learning and sharing purposes [1].

Agile values customer collaboration over contract negotiation. ICS incident response calls for coordinated efforts between different stakeholders, such as management, the controls engineers and operators, the IT department, as well as other roles in the organization [4]. As the cultures of control engineering and IT are often significantly different, cross-cultural understanding and collaboration will be the key to a coordinated incident response [1]. In addition, most control systems are interconnected or have interdependencies, and most control systems' security attacks targeting critical national infrastructure are coordinated, which again emphasizes the importance of coordinated incident response in ICS.

Agile values responding to change by following a plan. Agile aims to equip the security incident response team with the capability to respond quickly to changes. Ideally, the incident response should be adaptive to highly dynamic cyberattacks and anticipate further exploitation paths of the adversaries; however, following a pre-defined plan will increase the predictability of the organizations' defense efforts. Frequent software patching and updates are not suitable for ICS as system availability is highly prioritized and ICS processes are always continuous in nature [29, 22]. A simulation environment is needed that can accurately model the ICS and evaluate the impact of the patches and system updates.

To aid incident response teams in adopting Agile methodologies, a number of techniques can be adapted from the software domain. These techniques reinforce the core values and principles of Agile methodology, greatly impacting the situational awareness of team members (see Figure 3.1). Some of the core techniques are included below:

- Sprints – rather than take a linear approach, sprints are a time-boxed iteration during which events take place with the goal of producing business value sooner. Sprints alter the operating procedures of

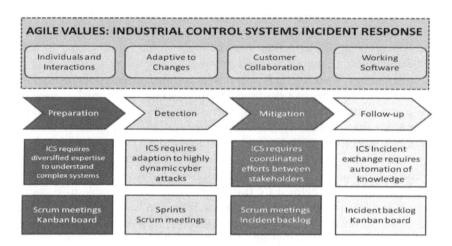

Figure 3.1 An Agile ICS incident response decision framework.

teams, work is better distributed and estimated along with increased communication. As the nature of an incident changes rapidly, sprints enable the incident response team to better identify and adapt to the threat and become proactive in identifying the optimal defensive effort.

- Stand-up meetings (Scrum meetings) – daily stand-up meetings with the entire team present. These meetings should take no more than 15 minutes but include the key actions from the most recent sprint. The meetings facilitate greater visibility and information sharing within the team, reducing wasted effort and working at cross-purposes. These meetings provide an opportunity for the control engineers to provide technical expertise into more ICS aspects impacting the current investigation and response. In an IR context, more frequent stand-up meetings may be required, depending on the nature of the incident. Other Scrum meetings, such as planning, review, and retrospectives are also applicable in shortened cycle times.
- Incident backlog – all activities are split into items that need to be completed to successfully manage the incident. These items should be *detailed* appropriately, *evolving* over time, *estimated, prioritized* (DEEP), and can then be grouped together clubbing similar incident backlog items into themes, such as forensic investigation, log analysis, and so on. Self-organization is an essential aspect of Agile team behaviors, and the collaborative approach to managing the tasks during an incident is essential to maximize the successful response. The incident backlog is owned by a single person who is responsible for prioritizing the deliverables during the response. To support the self-organization, typically task boards are used to show the progress of the response activities.

- Task board (Kanban board) – a visualization tool designed to help optimize workflow and increase information sharing. All activities required to manage an incident are included with teams separating off those actions currently active and those actions that have been identified as complete. By ensuring all teams complete and update the board frequently the situational awareness of team members increases and the time required to integrate new team members is significantly reduced. These updates are typically linked to the stand-up meetings, and capture and guide verbal updates.

3.5 ASSESSMENT EVENT

In order to assess the capabilities of the Agile techniques a Red vs Blue assessment exercise was performed over the period of three days in September 2019 at De Montfort's campus in Leicester, UK. The event utilized De Montfort University's (DMU) CYRAN cyber range, a hybrid cyber range providing both virtual and physical systems for the sandboxed environment. To increase the realism of the scenario a number of pieces of operational technologies were incorporated into the range. Before the commencement of the engagement, the Blue team participants were trained in the use of Agile and allowed familiarization time to allow themselves to understand the network and systems they would be defending. Both teams were provided with scenario documentation providing background and contextual information of the event. This included specific rules of engagement and objectives for each side.

3.5.1 The Scenario

The Maritime Scenario for Event1 was chosen as that of a port undergoing a sophisticated, multi-faceted cyberattack. Due to the availability of equipment, this scenario will make use of the Rolls Royce ship bus testbed. There will be three separate networks involved in the scenario:

- Enterprise network
- Operational technology of the port
- Ship bus network

The Blue team will be tasked with defending elements on all of these networks. Each network will comprise multiple machines, with realistic traffic generation included to ensure that any Red team actions are not immediately apparent.

3.5.2 Blue Team Composition

The Blue team comprised 16 individuals from across industry and government. As with a real incident team, the membership fluctuated during the event based upon the availability of individuals. A variety of skill sets were represented, with Security Operations Analysts the most prevalent.

During the event, the Blue team participants occupied one of three roles: incident owner (IO), scrum master (SM), or Team Member

- Incident Owner – a participant from the industry. This participant had traditional managerial and military squad command experience. Adoption of Agile techniques varied throughout the exercises. During the early phases, they took a more passive role and focused on strategic management of the engagement. As the scenario progressed and indicators of compromise became more apparent they took greater control of meetings and task allocation.
- Scrum Master – a participant from the military. The participant was used to a low level of command and had no previous experience of the role. He performed the tasks well and controlled the Scrum meetings at the start of the exercise but as the scenario unfolded he took more of a passive role as the IO asserted his leadership style.
- Team Members – participants from industry, military, and government. A number of participants on the Blue team had a military background. This demographic meant that an unconscious cognitive bias towards a certain modus operandi was introduced, that of a hierarchical, top-down approach. During the early phases of the exercise, a flatter team structure was deployed and team members were able to self-select the majority of tasks performed. As the exercise progressed and tasks became more complex, team members became more focused on specific types of tasks, often those they had the greatest experience with, such as firewall configuration or threat hunting. It should be noted that by the end of the exercise every team member had volunteered to complete a task in an area they had no familiarity with.

AIR4ICS aims to create a framework that will integrate into the existing operating procedures of CERTs, providing added value wherever possible rather than force a paradigm shift on teams immediately. To that end, the roles of the incident owner and Scrum master do not necessarily strictly follow the approach found in Agile software engineering. The incident owner will fulfill the role of the traditional IR manager and is thus required to maintain strategic oversight of the incident; at the same time, they are able to allocate the resources of the team as appropriate. They will also be responsible for ensuring that any threat intelligence received is identified and integrated into the response. The Scrum master will be responsible for maintaining situational awareness of the team and leading the Scrum and sprint meetings. Their key focus will be on communication within the team; they will be responsible for ensuring that the incident backlog and Scrum board are maintained and up-to-date. They also act as the facilitator for arranging any breakout meetings that need to take place between team members.

3.5.3 Agile Methodologies

The methodologies adopted by the Blue team are detailed below. Feedback was obtained from participants through questionnaires and discussion sessions to identify best practices.

3.5.3.1 Sprints

To best represent the timeframes of a real incident within the allotted time, sprints lasted 3 hours. Despite the increasing pressure of events as the scenario progressed, sprint planning and retrospectives were utilized throughout. One of the key elements highlighted by the focus group was the sprint concept: participants identified the opportunity to compartmentalize timings and to take time to analyze the situation as a whole as particularly beneficial.

3.5.3.2 Sprint Planning

During the early exchanges sprint planning meetings were open and communication between the different participants was observed. The Scrum master kept the discussions moving and participants were able to choose the tasks that they felt most comfortable with. In the later stages of the event, the incident owner took more direct control of the meetings and the discussions became situation updates around specific tasks. As a consequence, tasks were allocated to individuals based upon the criticality of the engagement.

3.5.3.3 Sprint Retrospectives

All participants attended sprint retrospectives. These were used as a hotwash of the previous 3 hours. The inclusion of the learning matrix (see Section 1.5.5.3) encouraged greater participation of all team members in the discussion. These sessions allowed the participants to identify their task priorities for the next sprint based upon their experience of the previous sprint.

3.5.3.4 Scrum Meetings

Scrum meetings lasting 15 minutes took place regularly throughout the event. On day 1 Scrums took place every 30 minutes, with 4 Scrum meetings per sprint. Participants' feedback indicated that while useful, 30 minutes was insufficient time to complete some of the more complex tasks.

On days 2 and 3, one Scrum meeting per sprint was removed and the time between Scrums extended to 45 minutes. After shifting to longer sessions, all participants agreed that the Scrum meetings were useful and allowed them to have a more informed picture as to the overall engagement. This is an artifact of the reduced timescales of the event. In a real incident, it is envisaged that Scrum meetings would take place daily or in rapidly changing engagements twice daily. The timing of the Scrum meeting should be often enough to ensure that all team members retain good situational awareness of the incident response but are not so onerous that it negatively impacts engagement.

3.5.4 Task Allocation

Agile facilitates the dynamic allocation of tasks to allow the quick reallocation of resources in response to the developing situation.

3.5.4.1 Self-Selection of Tasks

Self-allocation of tasks, chosen from the incident backlog, occurred during sprint planning meetings. Participants were able to choose the key tasks that they felt best fit their individual skill sets or interests. This enabled the Blue team to make good initial progress during the preparation day. As the scenario progressed, the IR team reverted to a more familiar hierarchical structure. This was identified as partially due to increased delegation from the incident owner and partially due to a lack of confidence in acting outside their own specialty when the timely results became crucial. The incident owner directly allocated tasks in the sprint where no one volunteered. The fear of failure was identified as a driving factor for the decisions of the participants, highlighting the importance of training exercises for personal development. Without the pressure stimuli of clear indicators of compromise, participants were more willing to engage with unfamiliar technologies and increase their base understanding.

3.5.4.2 T-Shaped Team

On days 1 and 2 participants with operational technology knowledge were embedded within the IR team. On these days the OT specialist not only was used to investigate but also acted as a coordinator for other team members who had chosen to work on the OT infrastructure protection elements. By combining the skill sets of the team members, it allowed the OT specialist to take a more strategic role, while providing the analysts with enough information to draw informed conclusions from the available network traffic. The requirement for a greater breadth of knowledge was highlighted during the event. A participant unfamiliar with OT deleted the SCADA logs on the warehouse air conditioning system as they mistook regular traffic for noise. Because of the large number of records they were unable to recognize the useful information included within them. This led to evidence of Red team actions, such as the creation of a new system user, to be lost.

3.5.5 Agile Tools

The following tools were utilized by the participants as part of the sprint lifecycle to aid their situational awareness and decision-making.

3.5.5.1 Incident Backlog

The initial incident backlog was created on the preparation day. This incorporated both high-level tasks, designed for further segregation as further information became available, and atomized tasks that could be assigned immediately. This dynamic resource was routinely used and updated as necessary throughout the incident. To aid strategic planning all tasks were prioritized, although it was noted that estimates of effort were treated as abstract rather than definitive estimations of the required effort for the task.

As the event progressed and new information/infrastructure became available, such as the arrival of the MV Black Pearl and the new challenges presented, the incident backlog was updated accordingly. The incident backlog was viewed as a useful strategic planning tool, allowing participants to identify current and future tasks quickly and easily.

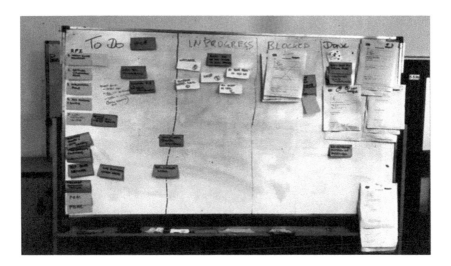

Figure 3.2 Scrum board from AIR4ICS event.

3.5.5.2 Scrum Board

The Scrum board provided a dynamic focal point for Scrum meetings and was used extensively (See Figure 3.2). Participants added new tasks into the to-do section as and when they arose. Tasks were migrated to the appropriate phase area during the Scrum meeting by the responsible team member. This pattern was adopted naturally, and team members were able to manipulate the task board at any point but were often focused on completing their tasks and content to wait for the interruption of the Scrum meeting. This approach limited the situational understanding of other team members as it no longer presented an accurate representation of work. Therefore, as the exercise progressed, the IO and SM became more proactive in updating tasks as necessary outside of Scrum meetings.

All participants felt that the Scrum board was beneficial during the fast-paced event. It allowed them to improve their efficiency, by better structuring their own tasks, identifying dependencies, and removing bottlenecks in information sharing due to participant availability.

Figure 3.3 Learning matrix example.

3.5.5.3 Learning Matrix

Participants agreed that the learning matrix was a useful tool in the retrospective (See Figure 3.3). All participants were able to provide information in one of the four quadrants:

- What went well
- What went badly
- Any star performers
- Any ideas for the next phase

Ideas were collated into themes with the top five selected via open discussion. This vital reflection allowed the Blue team to identify new operational methods, focus their efforts on the greatest perceived risk, and highlight any issues that required attention. By utilizing anonymous sticky notes as the communication method, it allowed input from team members that might not otherwise have contributed to the sprint retrospective.

3.5.6 Event Questionnaires

Questionnaires were completed by each participant as part of every sprint retrospective. These questionnaires were designed to assess the mental load, trust, and situational awareness of each participant. The key findings are summarized below:

a. The study's earlier findings (interviews with practitioners) have been supported by the initial findings from the questionnaire designed by the research team looking at the current practices and challenges in IR for industrial control systems.
b. Decision-making style: there was an increased thoroughness, control, hesitancy, and idealism after Agile training and practice.
c. Team decision-making: a slight increase in the scores after Agile training and practice.
d. Positive and negative effects: there was an increase in positive after the training, but there was also an increase in negative effects for some elements.
e. Team interpersonal trust: There was an increase of propensity to trust, perceived trustworthiness, cooperative behaviors, and a decrease in monitoring behaviors.

3.6 DISCUSSION AND CONCLUSIONS

ICS incident response differs from traditional IT incident response. While there is some crossover, many IR practices in IT cannot be directly applied in ICS. Because of this a new approach is required, one that can adapt quickly and promote communication between stakeholders. The interview responses of industry professionals have been thematically analyzed with key themes emerging such as the criticality of communication and situational awareness. The four Agile values have been mapped into the context of ICS incident response to meet those requirements along with a number of tools to aid IR teams in the field. Proper incident response can improve technical attribution in relation to ICS [7].

Future research will focus on business case studies on whether the integration of Agile values can improve ICS IR procedure through the implementation of exploratory industrial case studies. Future research also includes the selection and evaluation of specific Agile techniques such as Scrum or Kanban to address challenges in ICS IR in line with the coordination of multiple teams and stakeholders in Scrum teams and introduce IR coordinators to facilitate best practice within incident response teams, playing the role of a Scrum master.

3.7 GLOSSARY

Incident Response: An organized approach to addressing and managing the aftermath of a security breach or cyberattack.
Agile: A set of methods and practices where solutions evolve through collaboration between self-organizing, cross-functional teams.
ICS: A general term that encompasses several types of control systems and associated instrumentation used for industrial process control.
Sprint: A short, time-boxed period when a development team works to complete a set amount of work.
NISD: The Directive on security of network and information systems.

REFERENCES

1. Atif Ahmad, Justin Hadgkiss, and Anthonie B. Ruighaver. Incident response teams–challenges in supporting the organisational security function, *Computers & Security*, 31(5), 643–652, 2012.
2. Opeoluwa Ore Akinsanya, Maria Papadaki, and Lingfen Sun. Towards a maturity model for health-care cloud security (m2hcs), *Information & Computer Security*, 2019.
3. Aliyu Aliyu, Leandros Maglaras, Ying He, Iryna Yevseyeva, Eerke Boiten, Allan Cook, and Helge Janicke. A holistic cybersecurity maturity assessment framework for higher education institutions in the united kingdom, *Applied Sciences*, 10(10), 3660, 2020.
4. Ryan K. Baggett and Brian K. Simpkins. *Homeland Security and Critical Infrastructure Protection*. ABC-CLIO, 2018.
5. Virginia Braun and Victoria Clarke. Using thematic analysis in psychology, *Qualitative research in psychology*, 3(2), 77–101, 2006.

6. Allan Cook, Helge Janicke, Leandros Maglaras, and Richard Smith. An assessment of the application of it security mechanisms to industrial control systems, *International Journal of Internet Technology and Secured Transactions*, 7(2), 144–174, 2017.

7. Allan Cook, Andrew Nicholson, Helge Janicke, Leandros A. Maglaras, and Richard Smith. Attribution of cyber attacks on industrial control systems, *EAI Endorsed Transactions on Industrial Networks & Intelligent Syststems*, 3(7), e3, 2016.

8. George Drivas, Argyro Chatzopoulou, Leandros Maglaras, Costas Lambrinoudakis, Allan Cook, and Helge Janicke. A nis directive compliant cybersecurity maturity assessment framework. arXiv preprint arXiv:2004.10411, 2020.

9. Thomas Dubendorfer, Arno Wagner, and Bernhard Plattner. An eco- nomic damage model for large-scale internet attacks. In *13th IEEE International Workshops on Enabling Technologies: Infrastructure for Collaborative Enterprises*, pages 223–228. IEEE, 2004.

10. Wei Gao and Thomas H. Morris. On cyber attacks and signature based intrusion detection for modbus based industrial control systems, *Journal of Digital Forensics, Security and Law*, 9(1), 3, 2014.

11. George Grispos, William Bradley Glisson, and Tim Storer. Rethinking security incident response: The integration of agile principles. arXiv preprint arXiv:1408.2431, 2014.

12. Steve Harrison, Antonis Tzounis, Leandros A. Maglaras, Francois Siewe, Richard Smith, and Helge Janicke. A security evaluation framework for UK e-goverment services agile software development. arXiv preprint arXiv:1604.02368, 2016.

13. Ying He and Helge Janicke. Towards agile industrial control systems incident response. In *3rd International Symposium for ICS & SCADA Cyber Security Research (ICS-CSR 2015)*, no. 3, pages 95–98, 2015.

14. Ying He, Chris Johnson, Yu Lu, and Yixia Lin. Improving the information security management: An industrial study in the privacy of electronic patient records. In *27th International Symposium on Computer-Based Medical Systems*, pages 525–526. IEEE, 2014.

15. John Jeremiah. Survey: Is agile the new norm. *Noudettu osoitteesta: techbeacon.com* website: https://techbeacon. com/app-devtesting/survey-agile-new-norm, 2015.

16. Mikael Lindvall, Dirk Muthig, Aldo Dagnino, Christina Wallin, Michael Stupperich, David Kiefer, John May, and Tuomo Kahkonen. Agile software development in large organizations, *Computer*, 37(12), 26–34, 2004.

17. Javier Lopez, Cristina Alcaraz, and Rodrigo Roman. Smart control of operational threats in control substations, *Computers & Security*, 38, 14–27, 2013.

18. Leandros Maglaras, George Drivas, Kleanthis Noou, and Stylianos Rallis. Nis directive: The case of greece, *EAI Endorsed Transactions on Security and Safety*, 4(14), 2018.

19. Leandros A. Maglaras, Ki-Hyung Kim, Helge Janicke, Mohamed Amine Ferrag, Stylianos Rallis, Pavlina Fragkou, Athanasios Maglaras, and Tiago J. Cruz. Cyber security of critical infrastructures, *Ict Express*, 4(1), 42–45, 2018.

20. Agile Manifesto. Agile manifesto, *Haettu*, 14, 2012, 2001.

21. Robert Mitchell and Ing-Ray Chen. A survey of intrusion detection techniques for cyber-physical systems, *ACM Computing Surveys (CSUR)*, 46(4), 1–29, 2014.
22. Roberto Mugavero, Stanislav Abaimov, Federico Benolli, and Valentina Sabato. Cyber security vulnerability management in cbrn industrial control systems (ics). *International Journal of Information Systems for Crisis Response and Management (IJISCRAM)*, 10(2), 49–78, 2018.
23. Martin Naedele. Addressing it security for critical control systems. In *40th Annual Hawaii International Conference on System Sciences (HICSS'07)*, pages 115–115. IEEE, 2007.
24. Barack Obama. Executive order 13636: Improving critical infrastructure cybersecurity, *Federal Register*, 78(33), 11739, 2013.
25. Adrian Pauna, Konstantinos Moulinos, Matina Lakka, J. May, and T. Tryfonas. *Can We Learn from Scada Security Incidents*. White Paper, European Union Agency for Network and Information Security, Heraklion, Crete, Greece, 2013.
26. Winston W. Royce. Managing the development of large software systems: Concepts and techniques. In *Proceedings of the 9th International Conference on Software Engineering*, pages 328–338, 1987.
27. Keith Stouffer, Joe Falco, and Karen Scarfone. Guide to industrial control systems (ics) security, *NIST Special Publication*, 800(82), 16–16, 2011.
28. Brenda Whittaker. What went wrong? Unsuccessful information technology projects, *Information Management & Computer Security*, 1999.
29. Shinya Yamamoto, Takashi Hamaguchi, Sun Jing, Ichiro Koshijima, and Yoshihiro Hashimoto. A hot-backup system for backup and restore of ics to recover from cyber-attacks. In *Advances in Human Factors, Software, and Systems Engineering*, edited by Goonetilleke, Ravindra S., Karwowski, Waldemar, pages 45–53. Springer, 2016. Proceedings of the AHFE 2016 International Conference on Physical Ergonomics and Human Factors, July 27–31, 2016, Walt Disney World®, Florida, USA.

Chapter 4

Multi-Stage Threat Modeling and Security Monitoring in 5GCN

Robert Pell, Sotiris Moschoyiannis, and Emmanouil Panaousis

The fifth generation of mobile networks (5G) promises a range of new capabilities, including higher data rates and more connected users. To support the new capabilities and use cases, the 5G Core Network (5GCN) will be dynamic and reconfigurable in nature to deal with the demand. It is these improvements that also introduce issues for traditional security-monitoring methods and techniques that need to adapt to the new network architecture. The increased data volumes and dynamic network architecture mean an approach is required to focus security-monitoring resources where it is most needed and react to network changes in real time. When considering multi-stage threat scenarios, a coordinated, centralized approach to security monitoring is required for the early detection of attacks that may affect different parts of the network. In this chapter, we identify potential solutions for overcoming these challenges, which begins by identifying the threats to the 5G networks to determine suitable security-monitoring placement in the 5GCN.

4.1 INTRODUCTION

Security analysis of computer networks has become a vital tool to identify security risks, evaluate vulnerabilities, and guide the decisions on protecting the network. In recent years, networks have grown in complexity leading to the development of security models to conduct effective security analysis [1]. A prime example of the evolution in network complexity is the 5G mobile network. 5G will incorporate a range of new technologies including software-defined networking (SDN), network function virtualization (NFV), multi-access edge computing, and transition to a cloud-based service. All of these technologies provide the capability for 5G networks to meet the performance requirements and support a variety of new use cases, but they also introduce an increased attack surface and a range of new threats.

The 5GCN architecture is still under development and is currently in the specification stage [2]. Specific details and industry-wide deployments

DOI: 10.1201/9781003109952-4

of the 5GCN may not be realized for several years, but the overarching architecture and the key components of the 5GCN are defined as shown in Figure 4.1. The key building blocks are demonstrated in this diagram, which are the focus of various threat assessments to date. The building blocks of the 5GCN inherit many existing technologies and there are plenty of examples of virtualized, cloud-based deployments existing across different industries. What makes the 5GCN a unique challenge from a security perspective is the radical transition from the previous generation of mobile networks. The transition includes the introduction of network slicing (NS), the move away from centralized hardware and unique interfaces to different user equipment (UE), third-party applications, and other mobile network service providers. Each of these interfaces is critical for providing the required functionality of telecommunication networks but they also introduce an attack surface beyond traditional enterprise networks. Surrounding the issues of security relating to the individual technology enablers there is plenty of literature that evaluates the security risks of each [3]. The biggest challenge now for industry and researchers is evaluating the holistic security risks to the 5GCN when these technologies are combined. This includes the trust boundaries both within the 5GCN and with the external services interfacing with the core network. The network architecture and vulnerabilities form the basis of traditional vulnerability-based security risk assessments. Given the current maturity of the 5GCN, this poses a significant issue in that traditional security risk assessments are not well-suited for the current state of development and alternative approaches, including

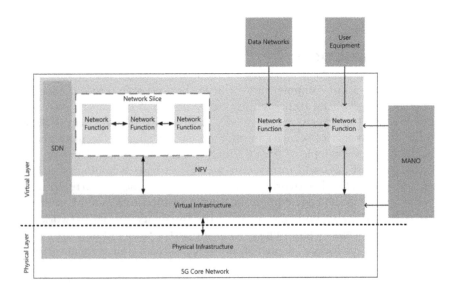

Figure 4.1 Overview of the 5G network architecture.

threat-based risk assessments, may be more suitable. A suitable security model for 5G networks should take a holistic view of the various new and existing threats to telecommunication service providers. Particularly when considering multi-stage attack scenarios, a suitable model should consider the chain of attack steps and the consequences on the network state of each step and overall.

Such a challenge requires consideration of the attackers' end goal, the threat of a network intrusion, and every attack step in between. One of the most well-recognized cybersecurity frameworks is that of the National Institute of Standards and Technology (NIST) [4]. The NIST framework core comprises five stages to manage cybersecurity risk, which are *identify, protect, detect, respond,* and *recover.* With threat-based risk assessments, the first step of the process involves the identification of threats, which helps to define the requirements for protecting the network and detection. The process for attack simulation and threat analysis (PASTA) is a risk-centric threat modeling framework [5] that consists of seven stages in which threat analysis is included in step 4. In PASTA, threat analysis includes the generation of probabilistic attack scenarios that would include the modeling of multi-stage attacks. Our first focus is on identifying suitable security monitoring within the 5GCN through threat identification and decomposition in line with the NIST framework and the threat analysis step of the PASTA framework. In the following subsections, we apply these frameworks in the context of 5G networks. Starting with the identification of threats to the 5GCN, we review relevant literature applicable to threat identification, evaluation of probabilistic attack scenarios, and the current approaches to modeling multi-stage attack scenarios.

In this chapter, we propose a framework for modeling threats for the purpose of identifying security-monitoring requirements in the 5GCN that includes sensor placement and detection methods through threat decomposition and threat modeling using graphs.

The remainder of this chapter is structured as follows; in Section 1.2, we present the related work in 5GCN threat assessments and modeling of multi-stage attack scenarios. In Section 1.3, we propose and demonstrate a method of modeling multi-stage attack threat scenarios using graphs applicable to the 5GCN. In Section 1.4, we describe how threat graphs can be used to provide decision support on security monitoring through sensor placement and how this can be used for the detection of multi-stage attack threat scenarios. Finally, Section 1.5 of this chapter outlines the open research challenges and future work.

4.2 RELATED WORK

In this section, we review the literature relating to the 5GCN threats and approaches towards multi-stage attack modeling.

4.2.1 5GCN Threats

With the introduction of new technologies to the 5GCN, several 5G threat assessments have been produced [3, 6, 7, 8]. In these works, threats are evaluated with respect to the new technologies that are introduced in 5G mobile networks, including SDN, NFV, and the new service-based architecture (SBA) within the 5G core. With a focus on the SDN and NFV technologies, [9] identifies the threats to NFV components such as firewalls and intrusion detection systems (IDS) and the interfaces between the architectural layers of the data, control, and application planes introduced by SDN. One of the biggest transitions within the 5GCN is the introduction of the SBA. In this architecture, the network functions (NFs) communicate using HTTP/2, which introduces openness and flexibility, but the commonality of the protocol introduces several new threats [7]. An EU report on the threat landscape for 5G networks [8] provides a taxonomy of threats and identifies which of the 5GCN infrastructure components are at risk of each threat scenario. Table 4.1 provides a summary of the 5G network threats identified in the current literature.

4.2.2 Multi-Stage Attack Modeling

The 5GCN threats that have been identified in the literature can be considered an abstract representation of an adversary's goal realized by a multi-stage attack scenario. Initially, an adversary would be required to gain access to the core network followed by several attack steps in order to achieve some goals as demonstrated by the threats in Table 4.1. Attack graphs have been researched as a solution for modeling multi-stage attacks

Table 4.1 The Key Threats Identified to the 5GCN

Threat description	[8]	[3]	[6]	[7]
Flooding attack of a NF	✓	✓	✓	✓
Eavesdropping the SBI	✓		✓	
Gaining access to data on a NF	✓		✓	✓
Installation of malware on NF environment	✓		✓	
Modification of signaling traffic	✓	✓		✓
Modification of application data	✓			✓
Modification of configuration data	✓			✓
API vulnerability exploit	✓	✓		
Exploit of network protocol	✓	✓		
SDN controller attack	✓	✓	✓	
Abuse of Lawful Interception function	✓			
Roaming scenario attacks	✓	✓	✓	

and quantifying security risk [10, 11]. Attack graphs can be useful at both the design phase [12] and for real-time intrusion detection through alert correlation [13, 14, 15]. The process of automatically generating attack graphs when there is a change to the network topology or on the discovery of new vulnerabilities [16] has become critical for many modern networks due to their dynamic nature – a feature present in the 5GCN. As attack graphs have proved valuable tools for conducting a security risk analysis, several tools have emerged [17, 18, 19] for the automatic attack graph generation. Although drawbacks have been identified relating to readability and generation time, it is widely agreed the output proves a valuable tool for modeling attack scenarios.

Attack graphs usually rely on knowledge of the network topology and known vulnerabilities within the network to identify the potential attack steps an attacker may take to achieve a specific goal. Less common than attack graphs for security risk analysis are threat graphs. Threat graphs have been used to conduct risk assessments for enterprise networks [20] and to evaluate the impact of threats on the security objectives of an organization to help evaluate the effect of security controls [21]. Although more abstract than attack graphs, threat graphs encompass a range of additional threats beyond software and hardware vulnerability exploits.

More specific to 5G networks, the authors of [22] present a graph model for multi-stage attack scenarios relating to the critical assets of the hierarchical network architecture of the 5GCN. In this work, an automated attack and a defense framework are proposed based on the attacker's actions. Although vulnerabilities are generalized in this model rather than hardware- or software-specific ones, it does nonetheless rely on knowledge of vulnerabilities in the 5G network. As with many other approaches, any technique that focuses on software vulnerabilities to model multi-stage attacks tends to overlook other types of threats such as insider threats, zero-day vulnerabilities, or supply chain threats, to name a few.

4.3 THREAT MODELING OF THE 5GCN

With reference to some of the well-established threat modeling frameworks such as the NIST framework for improving critical infrastructure [4] and the process for attack simulation and threat analysis (PASTA) we identify some of the key activities as part of our modeling framework and outline the hybrid approach to threat modeling for the 5GCN.

Identify: This set of activities form part of the identification process that includes identification of the key assets and components of the network, high-level threat scenarios, network interactions such as interfaces and data flows, and network boundaries. The outputs of this process include identification of the network attack surface, potential attack paths within the network, and attack vectors.

Threat Decomposition: An important part of identifying the security-monitoring requirements for threat detection is understanding the particular threat events associated with each threat scenario. This includes where within the network an attack could be launched and which components of the network may be targeted. We provide an example of the threat decomposition process in a later section.

Modeling Threats with Graphs: We propose the use of graphs to model threats in the 5GCN for mapping threat sources to threat targets. For the proposed model, threat scenarios and 5GCN components represent graph nodes where edges between nodes represent possible threat sources and targets. We provide a further definition of the graph model in Section 1.3.3.

4.3.1 Identification

For modeling threats and the associated multi-stage attacks, we first require an understanding of the network topology. In traditional models, this will include knowledge of specific software, services, and hardware, but this approach is not suitable for the 5GCN, given the maturity of development. Additionally, it is anticipated that various service providers will likely use different vendors and therefore there is no single representative 5GCN deployment we can refer to. For this reason, we propose using the high-level network architecture according to the latest 3GPP specification for providing the baseline architecture as shown in Figure 4.1. For our 5GCN model, we define the following:

Components represent a group of assets that belong to one of the subsystems of the 5GCN, providing some overarching functionality. These are the management and orchestration (MANO), SDN, NFV, and cloud infrastructure consisting of both the physical (PI) and virtual infrastructures (VI) and the application layer virtualized network functions of the SBA.

Threat Scenario is a set of threat events associated with one or more threat sources and targets.

Threat Event can be considered as a specific attack step contributing to some undesired outcome of a threat scenario.

Threat Source is the term used for the network component from where a threat event is launched.

Threat Target is the term used for the network component that is targeted by a threat event.

In the following subsection, we provide further details of the process of threat decomposition of threat scenarios into the threat events, source, and target.

4.3.2 Threat Decomposition

The process of threat decomposition involves taking the threat scenarios identified in the literature to produce a set of threat events and assigning the potential source and targets within the 5GCN. We provide a working example of the process as follows:

> **Threat Scenario:** *Application programming interface (API) vulnerability exploit*
>
> **Threat Events:** *SQL injection, buffer overflow, remote code execution*
> **Threat Source:** *External networks*
> **Threat Target:** *Network Functions, MANO*

In this example, the threat *API vulnerability exploit* as identified in the literature can be realized through the use of several different threat events, each of which is a technique an attacker may use to exploit the public-facing APIs provided to the 5GCN. Both the MANO and some of the 5GCN network functions such as the network exposure function (NEF), Access Management Function, and Security Edge Protection Proxy provide a public-facing API and therefore are potential targets of this threat scenario. These components provide an interface for external networks and systems to interact with the 5GCN, and so in this example, the potential threat source is the external networks.

Beyond helping to guide decisions on security-monitoring requirements for the 5GCN, the process of threat decomposition also helps to identify, if detected, which stage of a multi-stage attack the threat event belongs to. Although the derived threat events are not as specific as known vulnerability exploits, which are used in some security risk assessments, they do provide an abstract representation of attack steps. This approach shares similarities with the MITRE ATT&CK framework, which provides a set of techniques, tactics, and procedures (TTP) commonly used by adversaries targeting enterprise networks. The MITRE ATT&CK framework[1] defines a tactic as the goal or aim of each attack step and techniques as the method or "how" the tactic is achieved. In the process, we describe the threat events that can be thought of as similar to techniques, i.e., how the threat scenario is realized. The tactics defined in the MITRE ATT&CK framework represent the 12 different stages associated with multi-stage attack scenarios typical of advanced persistent threat (APT) campaigns. Although beyond the scope of our work, the process of assigning a specific technique or threat event to a tactic group can help in the detection of APT multi-stage attacks. We discuss related work using this approach in the concluding section of this chapter.

4.3.3 Modeling 5GCN Threats as Graphs

As a tool for modeling multi-stage attacks, attack graphs can be utilized to map the relationship between attack steps to network infrastructure. Rather than using graphs to map attack steps with respect to vulnerability exploits, we investigate the use of graphs for modeling threat scenarios relating to the 5GCN infrastructure.

Threat scenarios can be mapped to the network infrastructure and graph edges between different components can help to identify where in the network security sensors should be placed in order to detect a threat event. A cyber threat can be defined as *the possibility of a malicious attempt to damage or disrupt a computer network or system.* We extend this concept to include a source and target of a threat with regard to the network components. In the context of the 5GCN, this relates to the key components we have identified. Any threat scenario T can be defined as a tuple $T = (src, dst, scenario)$, where src is the component from where the malicious action originates and dst is the destination or the component being targeted by the threat $scenario$. As a simplistic example, $T = (\text{External Network, NEF, API Exploit})$ describes the threat of exploiting the API of the NEF from an external network. We can model the 5GCN threats in graph form.

Definition 1. Threat Graph Given a set of threat scenarios $t \in T$, a set of 5GCN infrastructure components $c \in C$, a threat source $T_s \subseteq C \times T$ and a threat target $T_t \subseteq T \times C$ a threat graph G is a directed graph $G = (C \cup T, T_s \cup T_t)$, where $C \cup T$ is the vertex set and $T_s \cup T_t$ the set of edges. $\cup$

An important feature of the threat graph model is the relationship between multi-stage attack steps. A component node of the graph can serve as both a threat target and, if that attack step is successful, provide a platform for further attacks originating from the compromised component. As a result, this component will then become a threat source represented by the outbound edges in the graph. Likewise, the inbound edges of a network component node represent is a threat target. This concept plays a key role in the detection of multi-stage attacks. For our threat graph model, we assume the attacker starts outside of the 5GCN, and as such, the initial node of the graph is represented by the external network node. Graph edges starting from the external network represent the first step of a multi-stage attack and each proceeding edge from a 5GCN component to a threat scenario represents $1 + n$ attack steps.

4.3.4 A 5GCN Threat Graph Example

With the graph representation of threats and the relationship between 5GCN infrastructure components, we can represent the progression of a multi-stage attack scenario. The example threat graph in Figure 4.2

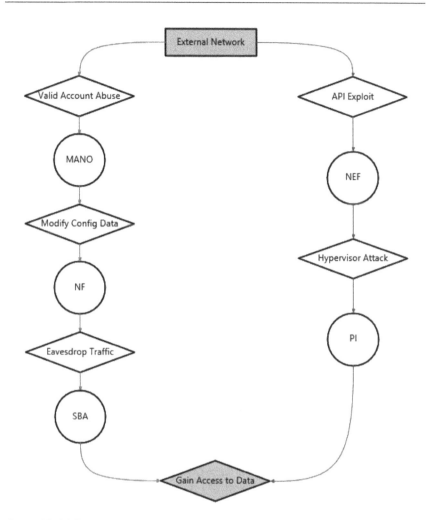

Figure 4.2 5GCN threat graph.

demonstrates how the threats identified in the literature can be related to the 5GCN components.

From the example threat graph, we identify two multi-stage attack scenarios and explain how these are represented on the graph.

Threat Scenario 1

1. An attacker gains credentials for the MANO component.
2. The adversary is able to make configuration changes that introduce a malicious NF into the SBA.
3. The malicious NF begins to harvest sensitive data by eavesdropping on the SBA.

Threat Scenario 2

1. An attacker exploits a vulnerability in the API of the NEF.
2. The attacker establishes a remote connection to the NEF of the 5GCN.
3. The attacker exploits a vulnerability in the hypervisor and gains access to the PI.
4. The adversary is able to access memory storing data for all of the NFs in the SBA.

In the above scenarios, the threat graph demonstrates the steps an attacker may take by moving laterally between the 5GCN components. This approach provides a holistic view of how an adversary may attack the different key components in a multi-step threat scenario without only focusing on the security events relating to the individual components in isolation. Scenario 1, highlighted by the red edges, and Scenario 2, highlighted by the blue edges, show how an adversary can attack the 5GCN through different attack vectors with the same goal of gaining access to sensitive data. With regard to security-monitoring placement, we can see where an attack may originate and which components could be targeted and so are provided with guidance on sensor placement to detect threat events. In Section 1.4, we further discuss security-monitoring requirements using the example threat graph for reference.

4.4 GRAPH-BASED SECURITY MONITORING FOR THE 5GCN INFRASTRUCTURE

Effective security monitoring within a network includes two important aspects: (1) knowing where in the network the security monitoring should be applied and (2) what type of security monitoring is required. With traffic volume and the number of connected devices in the 5G network anticipated to surpass levels previously seen, traditional approaches to security monitoring may not be suitable. Analysis of the network for applying security monitoring may quickly become outdated due to the dynamic, reconfigurable nature of the core network, and techniques such as deep packet inspection (DPI) of traffic for detection of threats will need to be applied only where and when required. Due to the large amounts of data transiting the 5G network, many existing DPI tools would not be able to process the results in real time and may even miss suspicious packets. In this chapter, we have described a process involving threat decomposition for mapping threats to 5GCN components using graphs to identify where in the network security monitoring should be placed to detect threat events. The process of threat decomposition also provides identification of threat events, which gives further guidance on the methods to detect them. The last stage of the framework is to provide a set of security-monitoring requirements that can be translated into a set of rules applied to the 5GCN capable of providing effective security monitoring despite the challenges posed by the dynamic nature and high data throughput.

When considering the security monitoring of specific threats, examples include the use of anti-virus software for detecting malware signatures or firewalls that can monitor traffic flows, which can be used to detect malicious connections within the network. In most cases, the type of security monitoring is guided by knowing what type of attack technique is used. The placement of security sensors within the network by contrast relies on knowledge of the network architecture, identification of the critical assets, and the threats posed to those assets. As previously explained, modeling these threats in the form of a graph provides a way of doing this for providing security-monitoring requirements by identifying which threats apply to specific 5GCN components. When it comes to security monitoring and specifically intrusion detection systems (IDS), there are two types that can be applied. The first is host-based IDS (HIDS), which, as the name suggests, are responsible for the security monitoring of a specific host. With reference to the 5GCN architecture, this could include the physical and virtual hosts within the network on which components such as the VNF, SDN, and MANO reside. The second type of security monitoring is network-based IDS (NIDS) and is focused on monitoring traffic and connections within the network. In the context of the 5GCN and the threat graph produced traffic-based security, monitoring is important for the detection of threat events between two different 5GCN components. The threat graph 1.2 provides a mapping between threat events and the *at-risk* 5GCN network components for identifying *where* security monitoring is required. To understand *what* type of monitoring is required in these locations, we further evaluate the threat events and identify network parameters to be monitored.

Threat Scenario: *Flooding attack of an NF*
Security Monitoring: Traffic volumes, network connections, resource usage, and error codes.
Description: There are several threat events that could contribute to a flooding attack of an NF. The detection of this threat type relies on identifying abnormal traffic flows between the threat source and target components, which could include an increase in volume generated by user equipment such as a botnet attack or through an innocent or malicious NF generating additional traffic. In both scenarios, monitoring traffic volumes and any error codes that may result from illegitimate HTTP/2 traffic can help identify this threat.

Threat Scenario: *Eavesdropping the SBI*
Security Monitoring: n/a
Description: Directly detecting an NF that is eavesdropping is a difficult task. Instead, it is advised to monitor the symptoms of eavesdropping such as data collection of intercepted communication through abnormal file sizes or types. Additionally, monitoring registered NFs for suspicious behavior can help identify malicious NFs registered in the SBA.

Threat Scenario: *Gaining access to data on an NF*
Security Monitoring: Monitor access to data repositories.
Description: A lot of sensitive data in the 5GCN is stored in data repositories. Detection of an adversary accessing the data will rely on monitoring access, particularly, attempted access that is denied by the system. Properties such as frequency of access and size of data requests should be monitored for abnormalities.

Threat Scenario: *Installation of malware on NF environment*
Security Monitoring: Anti-virus software monitor system logs of new software and monitor behaviors such as resource usage and system calls for anomalies.
Description: In most cases, the use of anti-virus software is deemed adequate in the detection of malware. When considering APTs and the efforts taken to remain undetected, the use of any malware is likely to take additional efforts to evade defenses. An adversary may disguise malware in applications or executables, deploy zero-day attacks, or even introduce a malicious NF to the 5GCN, which could bypass anti-virus software. Therefore, in addition to anti-virus software, it may be necessary to monitor the installation of new applications or software and the behavior of them to identify any malicious side effects.

Threat Scenario: *Modification of application data*
Security Monitoring: Monitor system logs.
Description: Modification of application data may be an intended action, but it could also indicate malicious activity. Although not definitively a signal of malicious activity, system logs should be used to raise alerts when application data is modified, including information such as the user that made changes.

Threat Scenario: *Modification of configuration data*
Security Monitoring: Monitor system logs.
Description: Modification of configuration data within the 5GCN is anticipated to be a normal behavior. Routing tables, network slicing, and virtualized network functions will be reconfigurable and dynamic in nature to support the network demands. Adversaries may take advantage of this feature for redirection of traffic or to introduce vulnerabilities to the configuration of NFs.

Threat Scenario: *API vulnerability exploit*
Security Monitoring: Monitor application logs.
Description: Monitoring logs of the public-facing applications providing APIs for behavioral abnormalities may help to detect attempted or successful exploits. With large volumes of traffic anticipated within the 5GCN, DPI may not be effective for real-time analysis. The use of application firewalls can be deployed to detect invalid inputs as an indicator of attempted exploits.

Threat Scenario: *SDN controller attack*
Security Monitoring: Monitor system logs, resource usage, and access, traffic flows.
Description: The SDN controller plays a critical role in the 5GCN. Attacks on the SDN controller range from DoS-type attacks, malicious configuration changes to redirect traffic, and gaining knowledge of routing tables. A range of monitoring should be used to not only detect changes but also monitor symptoms of any malicious activity.

Threat Scenario: *Abuse of lawful interception (LI) function*
Security Monitoring: Monitor the use of the LI function.
Description: Monitoring abuse of the LI function is not an easy task. Monitoring when the LI function is used and verifying it with the relevant authorities is the most reliable method of detection. With regard to LI function being used via a visited mobile, network operator maintaining a whitelist or blacklist of trusted/untrusted visited networks may help to identify the misuse.

Threat Scenario: *Roaming scenario attacks*
Security Monitoring: Monitor blacklisted networks and correlate user location tracking.
Description: There are several threat events posed by the roaming scenario threat. There are several methods that could be used to detect roaming scenario abuse, including maintaining a blacklist of fraudulent visited network requests and geographical tracking of the user equipment to check if the location matches the expected location of a user.

The detection methods identified provide ways of generating alerts of potentially suspicious behavior. In many cases, these alerts could be innocent and normal operations, but the more threat events that are detected and then correlated, the probability of detecting a multi-stage attack increases while the false positive rate of detection should be reduced. Many alerts such as suspicious user login activity or reconfiguration of the network are expected to be detected. We discuss the process of alert filtering and correlation in Section 1.5 of this chapter.

4.5 OPEN RESEARCH CHALLENGES AND FUTURE WORK

In this chapter, we describe a framework for the detection of multi-stage attacks on 5G networks and in particular the 5GCN. The framework takes a three-stage approach to translate high-level threat scenarios and models these as threat events against the 5GCN infrastructure components using graphs. In this section, we discuss the challenges and future work for further developing the framework for the detection of APTs in 5G networks.

4.5.1 Detection of Multi-Stage Attack Scenarios

Different approaches have been evaluated for detecting multi-stage attacks based on security alerts. The merits of correlating security alerts to the "attack lifecycle" involving the multiple tactic groups are presented in [23]. The idea is that during a multi-stage attack, the different tactics would be deployed in chronological order, starting with a network intrusion and usually resulting in some data being exfiltrated from the network. An attacker would deploy tactics, as identified in the MITRE ATT&CK framework, to remain undetected while moving laterally around the network, gaining the required privileges to gain access, and gather data before finally transferring it out of the network, sometimes by establishing command and control node to hide the process. Through this chronology of events, it is possible to correlate security alerts by the order in which they occur and to which tactic group they belong. If there is a security event that could indicate a suspicious user login followed by some events relating to a malicious configuration change within the network by the same user account, there is a potential for these two events to be related. This concept, as with many attack graph models, assumes a prerequisite action or state to occur beforehand. In the case of the threat graph, this same assumption exists. If we consider the threat of a signaling attack in the service-based interface (SBI), where one NF is a source and another is the target, we assume the source component has been compromised and under the control of the attacker.

In addition to relating security events based on the order in which they occur and to which tactic group they belong, the threat source and target can be used to further correlate security events. When a security alert is generated, the source, destination, and alert types can be translated into the nodes and connecting edges of the threat graph. If we consider an alert $A = (src, dest, alert)$, this can be translated into the connection from a threat source $(component, threat)$ to the threat target $(threat, component')$ where $component = src$, $threat = alert$, and $component' = dest$ and matches can be found through a graph traversal.

Through this process of security alert correlation, we propose the following steps for the detection of multi-stage attacks:

- **Chronology of Events:** This step involves sorting the security alerts by the order in which they occur.
- **Identification of Attack Tactic:** Once security alerts have been ordered, each event is related to a specific attack stage aligned to the tactic group they belong.
- **Relating Events to 5GCN Infrastructure:** Finally, the filtered security alerts are correlated based on the network infrastructure components, which are the source or target. This stage of correlation looks to identify components that are first targeted by an attack that later become the source of an attack step.

The threefold approach to security alert filtering and correlation may provide a solution to issues relating to overlooked security alerts. Security alerts analyzed in isolation may not provide a holistic view of the multi-stage attack steps; however, when analyzed in the context of attack tactics and the infrastructure components affected, the process of linking different events becomes a useful tool.

4.5.2 A Centralized Threat Detection Engine

The process of decomposing threats, linking the threats to the 5GCN infrastructure components, and identifying suitable security-monitoring requirements for the placement and detection of threat events is the first step, which can be conducted without detailed network data. To evaluate the feasibility and performance of detecting threats in a centralized manner requires the various vendors of MANO, SDN, NFV, and cloud computing to provide the security-monitoring data suggested in a common way. There are multiple vendors who provide solutions such as virtualization software suitable for deployment in 5G networks and each of them may have different security-monitoring capabilities for their products. Access to any security-monitoring data for the purpose of threat detection requires this to be made available for the analysis of a centralized threat detection engine.

The future development based on the framework described will rely on collating the security-monitoring data, including system logs and traffic flows being made available by vendors. In order to test the process described for analyzing security alerts, a quality set of data will be required consisting of both genuine and false positive alerts to measure the effectiveness of the process.

4.5.3 A 5G Network TTP Matrix

In the framework proposed, we describe how threat scenarios can be decomposed into threat events that represent the techniques that the security-monitoring system should be capable of detecting. The process of detecting threat events will rely heavily on a full and comprehensive list of adversarial techniques used to attack 5G networks. The MITRE ATT&CK framework for enterprise networks is the result of threat intelligence based on real-world observations. It may be possible to provide a similar TTP framework for 5G networks but this would require a similar level of cooperation between mobile networks to disclose information about network attacks, which may prove challenging. The threats that have been identified in the literature relating to the new 5G technologies provide a platform for collating the different techniques applied to 5G networks, which could prove valuable future work for the initial development of such a framework but remains an open research challenge.

NOTE

1. https://attack.mitre.org/matrices/enterprise/

REFERENCES

1. D. Bodeau, C. McCollum, and D. Fox. *Cyber Threat Modeling: Survey, Assessment, and Representative Framework.* The Homeland Security Systems Engineering and Development Institute, Technical report, 2018.
2. TS:ETSI. Ts 23.501, system architecture for the 5g system. Specification release 15, 3rd Generation Partnership Project, 2018.
3. Rabia Khan, Pardeep Kumar, Dushantha Nalin K. Jayakody, and Madhusanka Liyanage. A survey on security and privacy of 5g technologies: Potential solutions, recent advancements and future directions, *IEEE Communications Surveys & Tutorials*, 22(1), 196–248, 2019.
4. Adam Sedgewick. *Framework for Improving Critical Infrastructure cybersecurity, Version 1.0.* Technical report, 2014.
5. Tony UcedaVelez and Marco M. Morana. *Risk Centric Threat Modeling.* Wiley Online Library, 2015.
6. Ijaz Ahmad, Tanesh Kumar, Madhusanka Liyanage, Jude Okwuibe, Mika Ylianttila, and Andrei Gurtov. Overview of 5g security challenges and solutions, *IEEE Communications Standards Magazine*, 2(1), 36–43, 2018.
7. Hans Christian Rudolph, Andreas Kunz, Luigi Lo Iacono, and Hoai Viet Nguyen. Security challenges of the 3gpp 5g service based architecture, *IEEE Communications Standards Magazine*, 3(1), 60–65, 2019.
8. *Enisa Threat Landscape for 5g Networks.* Report, European Union Agency for Cybersecurity, 2019.
9. Min Chen, Yongfeng Qian, Shiwen Mao, Wan Tang, and Ximin Yang. Software-defined mobile networks security, *Mobile Networks and Applications*, 21(5), 729–743, 2016.
10. Vivek Shandilya, Chris B. Simmons, and Sajjan Shiva. Use of attack graphs in security systems, *Journal of Computer Networks and Communications*, 2014, 1–14, 2014.
11. Steven Noel, Sushil Jajodia, Lingyu Wang, and Anoop Singhal. Measuring security risk of networks using attack graphs, *International Journal of Next-Generation Computing*, 1(1), 135–147, 2010.
12. Suvajit Gupta and Joel Winstead. Using attack graphs to design systems, *IEEE Security & Privacy*, 5(4), 80–83, 2007.
13. Lingyu Wang, Anyi Liu, and Sushil Jajodia. Using attack graphs for correlating, hypothesizing, and predicting intrusion alerts, *Computer Communications*, 29(15), 2917–2933, 2006.
14. Seyed Hossein Ahmadinejad, Saeed Jalili, and Mahdi Abadi. A hybrid model for correlating alerts of known and unknown attack scenarios and updating attack graphs, *Computer Networks*, 55(9), 2221–2240, 2011.

15. Chun-Jen Chung, Pankaj Khatkar, Tianyi Xing, Jeongkeun Lee, and Dijiang Huang. Nice: Network intrusion detection and countermeasure selection in virtual network systems, *IEEE Transactions on Dependable and Secure Computing*, 10(4), 198–211, 2013.

16. Oleg Sheyner, Joshua Haines, Somesh Jha, Richard Lippmann, and Jeannette M. Wing. Automated generation and analysis of attack graphs. In *Proceedings 2002 IEEE Symposium on Security and Privacy*, pages 273–284. IEEE, 2002.

17. Xinming Ou, Sudhakar Govindavajhala, and Andrew W. Appel. Mulval: A logic-based network security analyzer. In *USENIX Security Symposium*, Vol. 8, pages 113–128. USENIX, Baltimore, MD, 2005.

18. Sushil Jajodia, Steven Noel, and Brian O'berry. Topological analysis of network attack vulnerability. In Vipin Kumar, Jaideep Srivastava, and Aleksandar Lazarevic (eds), *Managing Cyber Threats*, pages 247–266. Springer, 2005.

19. Kyle Ingols, Richard Lippmann, and Keith Piwowarski. Practical attack graph generation for network defense. In *22nd Annual Computer Security Applications Conference (ACSAC'06)*, pages 121–130. IEEE, 2006.

20. Richard P. Lippmann and James F. Riordan. Threat-based risk assessment for enterprise networks, *Lincoln Laboratory Journal*, 22(1), 33–45, 2016.

21. Ruth Breu, Frank Innerhofer-Oberperfler, and Artsiom Yautsiukhin. Quantitative assessment of enterprise security system. In *Third International Conference on Availability, Reliability and Security*, pages 921–928. IEEE, 2008.

22. Zhihong Tian, Yanbin Sun, Shen Su, Mohan Li, Xiaojiang Du, and Mohsen Guizani. Automated attack and defense framework for 5g security on physical and logical layers. arXiv preprint arXiv:1902.04009, 2019.

23. Ibrahim Ghafir, Mohammad Hammoudeh, Vaclav Prenosil, Liangxiu Han, Robert Hegarty, Khaled Rabie, and Francisco J. Aparicio-Navarro. Detection of advanced persistent threat using machine-learning correlation analysis, *Future Generation Computer Systems*, 89, 349–359, 2018.

Chapter 5

Blockchain Technology for 6G Communication Networks

A Vision for the Future

Othmane Friha and Mohamed Amine Ferrag

The limits of 5g networks that have been recognized with the continued deployment of 5g networks prompted the exploratory research into the sixth generation of wireless communications technologies (6G). Blockchain is an emerging technology that is expected to solve many problems associated with the lack of trust, and it is regarded as one of the key features of 6G mobile networks. In this chapter, we will first give the reader a clear introduction to the subject, by providing an overview of this technology in terms of its fundamental components and the relationships between them. Second, the link between cryptography and blockchain technology is made clearer by reviewing some of the techniques used in this technology, together with its implementation in the blockchain environment. Moreover, we discuss a very important aspect of the subject, namely the consensus mechanism, by which the parties reach an agreement on the data to be published in the network. Also, we examine some of the main challenges facing the 6G networks, together with some of the blockchain-based solutions in both infrastructure and application levels. Finally, we close the chapter by highlighting the challenges of open research in today's blockchain technology.

5.1 INTRODUCTION

Interest in blockchain technology increased initially with the introduction of cryptocurrencies such as Bitcoin [1]; however, its potential goes far beyond this when considering its key characteristics, including system distribution, data persistence, logs traceability, and records immutability [49]. The global market size for blockchain technology is expected to reach $57,641.3 million by 2025, with a compound annual growth rate (CAGR) of 69.4%, between 2019 and 2025, according to a new study [3]. This fast growth is driven by rising demand for this technology in all sectors, from finance, media, telecommunications, transportation, healthcare and utilities, consumer and industrial goods, to many others [7].

Telecommunications networks are facing the challenge of providing the ultimate service level requirements, such as ultra-high data rates and critical

DOI: 10.1201/9781003109952-5

security features for future applications. As 5G systems are being deployed, the limitations of the system concerning its initial vision as an enabler of the internet of everything (IoE) is constantly being revealed [44, 27, 41], researchers across the world are getting interested in what 6G could be [47]. 6G is intended to power the future of a smart, ubiquitous, connected, and data-intensive IoE, and to revolutionize the way wireless technologies evolve from "connected things" to "connected intelligence" [30]. It is also being considered for 6G to follow the enormous growth expected in mobile traffic, estimated at 607 Exabyte/month by 2025 and 5016 Exabyte/month by 2030 [45], to power emerging applications such as virtual reality, remote surgery, holographic communications, wireless brain-computer interaction (BCI), etc. 6G will likely benefit from many of the technologies of 5G, however, additional new technologies will certainly be needed to take it to the next level [44]. Currently, the preliminary design of 6G is under development [41, 30, 44], and efforts to configure potential techniques to meet the above vision are still in their early stages [47]. Blockchain technology is considered as one of the key enablers for 6G mobile networks [27, 41, 47]. As a result, it is essential to investigate its background details, the potential opportunities, and the challenges anticipated with its implementation.

5.1.1 Blockchain Overview

The blockchain system can be thought of as a distributed electronic ledger, in which all committed transactions are grouped into batches, encoded into a Merkle tree, and stored in blocks that are linked together to form a chain of blocks [23]. The block is considered valid and added to the chain if there is an agreement among the majority of nodes on the validity of transactions. Each block integrates the hash of the previous block, which enables the integrity confirmation of the blockchain iteratively back to the genesis block [22].

5.1.1.1 Blockchain Technology Architecture

Blockchain technology can be broken down into four main layers, which are the things layer, network layer, blockchain composite layer, and application layer, as presented in Figure 5.1.

- *Things layer:* includes virtual clusters that contain smart things that generate, transmit, capture, and/or aggregate data [23].
- *Network layer:* responsible for forwarding data to upper layers, using many features, including routing protocols, network security, and networking technologies, such as software defined networking (SDN) and network function virtualization (NFV).

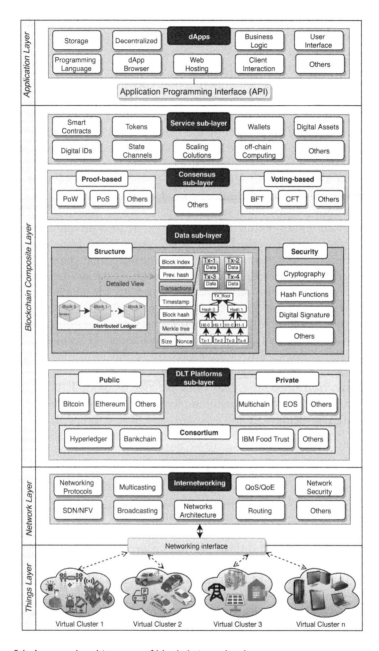

Figure 5.1 A general architecture of blockchain technology.

- *Blockchain composite layer:* comprises four sub-layers that form the core of the blockchain system [14]: (1) *DLT platform sub-layer:* consists of both specific and general-purpose blockchain platforms that are used to develop DLT-based systems. There are three types of blockchain systems [50], and the first type is public or permissionless, where anyone can send and view transactions and participate in the execution of a consensus protocol. Public blockchains currently dominate the global distributed ledgers that exist today. The second type is private or permissioned, where no one can join the system without being invited by the administrators. Private blockchains are partially decentralized systems, due to a well-defined management hierarchy; however, they are distributed, considering that many nodes save the chain copy locally. The last type is federated or consortium blockchain, which combines features from both public and private chain types. The platform is governed by multiple organizations instead of a single organization for private blockchains, meaning that there are equally powerful parties acting as validators; (2) *Data sub-layer:* includes the blockchain data structure together with the related techniques for generating and securing those blocks; (3) *Consensus sub-layer:* incorporates different protocols used between peers in the system to reach an agreement and validate transactions. (4) *Service sub-layer:* provides various features to blockchain applications, including smart contracts, tokens, and off-chain computing.
- *Application layer:* the final principal tier of blockchain technology concentrates on the successful implementation of blockchain solutions in different fields.

5.2 BLOCKCHAIN AND CRYPTOGRAPHY

While the chain data appears to be pretty safe to date, total security is never fully assured. Cryptography is a fundamental component for securing any blockchain system, as it can be used to enable secure transactions without the help of trusted third parties, ensure tamper-proof distributed records, and provide strong peer-to-peer (P2P) authentication of the system [49]. The main objective of blockchain-used cryptography is to ensure that a specific security property is maintained where it should be throughout each layer of the technology [39]. This section discusses some of the cryptography techniques used in blockchain technology as a means of achieving specific security properties.

5.2.1 Confidentiality

A confidential system is one in which there is a mechanism to ensure that only authorized persons can access sensitive information, which is kept separate from those who are not. One of the ways to achieve this in many systems in general and blockchain systems, in particular, is to use security mechanisms such as symmetric and asymmetric cryptography.

- *Symmetric cryptography* is the simplest well-known kind of encryption, which involves a single secret key to encrypt and decrypt information. An example of such mechanisms is the Advanced Encryption Standard (AES) with different key sizes from 128 to 256 bits, which is used in Hyperledger Fabric permissioned blockchain to protect smart contracts confidentiality [8]. Symmetric cryptography is also used in Internet of Things (IoT)-based blockchain applications where light and efficient security is needed, for example, between devices in blockchain-based IoT-based applications [22].
- *Asymmetric cryptography* also known as public-key cryptography uses two keys rather than one, compared to the first mechanism. The first key is publicly available, while the second is a private one. Even though symmetric cryptography is more fast and lightweight, asymmetric encryption is considered more secure since there is no need to share keys, as the public key is already publicly available. For example, consider an electronic wallet, where the public key is used to receive cryptocurrencies and check the balance on the blockchain, while the private key is used to access and spend coins. Also, secret sharing modules are being used in different Bitcoin wallets to protect the private keys of holders [39]. Rivest-Shamir-Adleman (RSA) and the elliptic curve cryptography (ECC) are the most widely used asymmetric-key algorithms for blockchains [13]. In RSA, the challenge of getting the plaintext back from the ciphertext and the public key lies in the difficulty of factoring the huge product of two prime numbers, whereas the same is more difficult for ECC since it needs to find the discrete logarithm of a random elliptic curve element from a publicly known base point and this problem is known as the elliptic curve discrete logarithm problem (ECDLP).

5.2.2 Integrity

Integrity is the certainty that information is reliable and accurate. Because of its design, blockchain technology is inherently robust against data modification, which means that if any data is added to the distributed ledger, it can neither be modified nor be deleted, thanks to the cryptographic techniques used in the implementation, including cryptographic hash functions, Merkle Trees, and digital signatures.

- *Hash functions* are cryptographic methods that map input of arbitrary size to an output of fixed size, according to properties such as collision resistance, preimage resistance, and second preimage resistance. Blockchain makes use of hash functions for a variety of purposes as linking blocks together using hash index pointer to the previous block in the chain, to verify if the data have been tampered with or not, as shown in Figure 5.2, solving cryptographic puzzles as in Bitcoin's proof of work (PoW) consensus, generating and shortening addresses, and in digests of signature messages [39]. SHA256 is a Secure Hash Algorithm-2 cryptographic hash function that has a digest length of 256 bits used twice in Bitcoin [1], and the output is called SHA256d, where SHA256d(msg) = SHA256(SHA256(msg)).

- *Merkle tree* is a data structure used to store transactions and their hashes in a hierarchical format [50]. The hashes of the child nodes are merged into the header of the parent node and the process is repeated iteratively until the final node, known as the Merkel root, is reached. At this root node, all information of the entire tree is stored as a fingerprint.

  The most common form of the Merkle tree is the binary tree shown in Figure 5.2.

- *Digital signature* uses asymmetric cryptographic algorithms and certificates to ensure data authenticity and protection against forgery by allowing peer signatures for the creation of fingerprints and/or time-stamps, as well as ensuring non-repudiation among users in the block-chain network. The commonly used types of digital signature schemes in blockchain networks are a variant of the elliptic curve digital signature algorithm (ECDSA). The ECDSA curve secp256k1 [2] is widely used in DLT-based platforms [18], including Bitcoin, Ethereum, and Hyperledger.

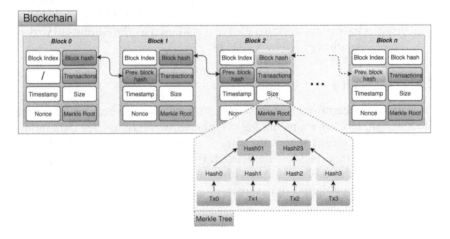

Figure 5.2 Chain blocks data structure.

5.2.3 Availability

In blockchain technology, availability means that there is guaranteed reliable and secure access to information by any authorized party. Because of the P2P nature and a large number of distributed nodes in the network that are running continuously, the blockchain technology is operationally robust and has no single point of failure, which renders it more resistant to distributed denial-of-service (DDoS) attacks [38]. When one node is down, the other nodes in the network can still access the data, since all nodes always retain a full copy of the ledger. Agreement between network peers for synchronizing or updating the registry is a key element in the blockchain, which is done through consensus mechanisms, which we will discuss in detail in the following section.

5.2.4 Privacy

Crypto-based privacy-preserving techniques enable users to become more anonymous and manage their data in the blockchain technology [9]; we address two, in particular, access controls and zero-knowledge proof.

- *Access control* ensures that information or resource access is selectively restricted based on certain conditions or policies; this access can be either data access, i.e., read or write authorization, or network access, i.e., blockchain membership [39]. Access controls used in blockchain to enforce data and users' privacy includes (1) role-based access control (RBAC): depending on its role, each entity in the blockchain system has its access rights. RBAC is used in many blockchain applications, including private healthcare blockchain [48]; (2) attribute-based access control (ABAC): access control rules are built according to the attribute model structure; these attributes can be user-, environment- or object-specific. In [17], ABAC is used to provide privacy in IoT systems; (3) organization-based access control (OrBAC): defines the permission for a subject to act on an object. In [35], OrBAC is used to provide fair access to IoT-based blockchain applications.
- *Zero-knowledge proof (ZKP)* is a cryptographic protocol that enables the proving party to provide proof to another entity, the verifier, that a particular statement is true, without disclosing any information beyond the fact that the proof itself is correct [9]. Zerocoin uses ZKP to preserves the privacy of users in the cryptocurrency platform [32].

5.3 CONSENSUS MECHANISM

Consensus mechanisms help distributed or decentralized systems containing unreliable nodes to solve the consensus problem, which is used to reach an agreement on a single data value or state without relying on a central authority. This section offers important insights to understand the consensus problem and the solutions developed over the years, within both the traditional and newer blockchain systems.

5.3.1 The Consensus Problem

Reaching agreement in a distributed and faulty environment is called the consensus problem and it is one of the main challenges in the areas concerning fault-tolerant distributed computing and cryptographic protocols, and has been largely studied through the literature, starting with the Byzantine agreement of Pease, Shostak, and Lamport [29, 37], where N nodes try to agree on a fixed value of a fixed domain V, regardless of the malevolent actions of several malicious actors T, each node Pn initiates the consensus protocol with an initial setting v V, each protocol round should satisfy the following conditions except for a negligible probability [26]: (1) *Termination:* each honest node decides a value; (2) *Agreement:* if honest nodes P_i and P_j decide v and w, respectively, then $v = w$; (3) *Validity:* if all honest nodes initially have the value v, then all honest nodes agree on v. Consensus protocol quality is measured by various metrics: *resilience*, which is the number of malicious nodes that the protocol can tolerate, expressed as (T/N); *the running time* of the least number of cycles by which honest nodes terminates; and *the communication complexity*, being the worst cumulative bits/messages count during protocol execution [26].

5.3.1.1 Ledger Consensus

Also called the Nakamoto consensus [1], it is a problem where a set of nodes continuously works together to validate transaction entries and incorporate them into a shared data structure called a ledger. The goal of ledger consensus is to ensure a unique view of the ledger for everyone who requests to see it. The two fundamental characteristics that a ledger consensus protocol must meet are consistency and liveness, where consistency guarantees that all parties have the same view of the transaction log, while liveness guarantees that transactions are incorporated quickly [26]. Figure 5.3 illustrates an example of transaction validation throughout a blockchain network, in which peer A wants to send a transaction to peer B, so it broadcasts it over the P2P network, now all honest nodes validate the transaction, and then append it with other transactions to form a valid block and add it to the ledger.

5.3.2 Blockchain Consensus Algorithms

Blockchain's principal contribution is the consensus algorithm, which decides how the agreement is reached about adding a new block amongst all the nodes of the verification network. According to *Nguyen* and *Kim* [33],

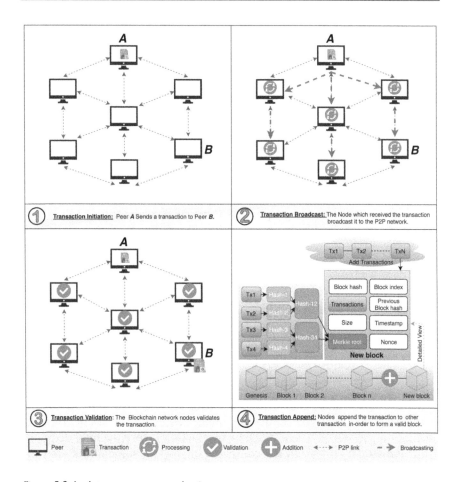

Figure 5.3 Ledger consensus mechanism.

blockchain consensus algorithms fall into two major classes: the first one is the proof-based consensus algorithms, which are commonly used in public blockchains, while the second class is for voting-based consensus algorithms, that are widely used in the private and consortium blockchains.

5.3.2.1 Proof-Based Algorithms

In this class, the verifying nodes are obliged to show proof that they are more qualified than others to obtain the right to add a new block to the chain and to earn the reward [33]. Proof of work (PoW) and proof of stake (PoS) represent the two popular algorithms of this class.

- *Proof of work (PoW):* this is the first and the famous consensus mechanism, which was designed by Satoshi Nakamoto, for the Bitcoin platform [1], but is also widely used by other cryptocurrencies. The PoW algorithm can be described as a mathematical answer to a mathematical problem, requiring extensive work (or mining), yet it is generally straightforward to verify the answer once it is obtained, the minor node that solves the puzzle will be permitted to append the new block of the transaction and receive compensation for it [23]. The mining process is highly computationally intensive, so a strong hash rate is a critical factor in allowing miners to compute the hash, which in turn allows them to earn the rewards.

- *Proof of stake (PoS):* in contrast to the PoW algorithm, PoS has a low computational cost for validators and is based on the participants' coins, in that it requires the users to prove that they have several coins for validating any additional blocks and obtaining the reward [23]. There are currently two popular types of PoS consensus [33]: PoS in its raw forms, such as the one used in Nextcoin [4], and the type that merges PoS and PoW, introduced in [28].

- *Others:* consensus algorithms belong to this class including, *proof of authority (PoA)*, where validators rely on their reputations to validate blocks, *proof of importance (PoI)*, where the proof is the importance score of the validators, *proof of burn (PoB)*, where miners are allowed to write blocks if they prove that they have burned (or destroyed) some coins, and *proof of capacity (PoC)*, which enables mining nodes according to the available space on their hard drives [23].

5.3.2.2 Voting-based Algorithms

In this class, the verifying nodes are obliged to share the results of their verification process on a new block or transaction before the final decision. While individual nodes run the consensus algorithm, some nodes are subject to various bad situations, including subversion, where nodes send different results to other nodes, as well as crash cases, where nodes are unable to send their results to other nodes, which complicate the final decision-making. According to these bad situations, voting-based consensus algorithms may be divided into two main types [33]:

- *Byzantine fault tolerance based consensus:* consensus algorithms in this type could avoid cases of crashed nodes and subverted nodes, but with the assumption that within N nodes, at least $(2N/3 + 1)$ nodes should be functioning normally [33]. A good example of this type is the practical byzantine fault tolerance (PBFT) consensus proposed by Miguel Castro and Barbara Liskov in 1999 [12]; it delivers reliable properties in a synced mode that takes replicas for tolerating Byzantine faults at the same time. New blocks are created within one round. At each round, there is a primary node chosen following certain rules, which is in charge of the order of the transaction; thus the entire procedure can be divided into three phases: pre-prepared,

prepared, and commit [23]. During each phase, a node enters the next phase if it has received the votes of more than (2/3) of all the nodes, requiring each node to be known to the entire network [50].

- *Crash fault tolerance based consensus:* consensus algorithms in this type could only avoid the case of crashed nodes, with the assumption that within N nodes, at least $(N/2 + 1)$ nodes should be functioning normally [33]. RAFT is a consensus algorithm that establishes strong governance in the network, where the leadership voting process is based on random timers; the algorithm mirrors the transactions for all participating nodes by ensuring that each node produces the same sequence of transactions locally while tolerating $(N/2)$ crashed nodes of the total N nodes [10].

5.4 BLOCKCHAIN FOR 6G NETWORKS

Even though the age of the 5G network is not yet fully mature, it is clear that the limitations in 5G technology require us to start researching 6G networks early, which has already begun in Q1 2019 during the first global 6G summit in Finland, where international communications experts released the first 6G white paper [46], in addition to the UK government's plans to invest in technologies suitable for use in 6G networks, and many other initiatives of the research community around the globe [41, 30]. According to Wang et al. [46], the strongest parts in the 6G study that has been conducted to date include distributed artificial intelligence (AI), intelligent radio, real-time intelligent edge, and 3D intercoms, where the technologies associated with these key components comprise, among others, terahertz (THz) technology, blockchain technology, and molecular communications, which will be used to attain the main key requirements such as high data rates of at least 1 Tbps with less than 1 ms latency, permit devices high-speed mobility (up to 1000 km/h), operating in the GHz to THz frequency range, and enabling IoE by supporting an extensive range of objects [41, 27]. In this section, we discuss some of the potential challenges that 6G networks may face, together with possible solutions provided by one of the key technologies mentioned above, namely blockchain technology, at both the network infrastructure level and the application level.

5.4.1 Challenges in 6G

Research in 6G is still in its very early stages; therefore many issues have yet to be addressed [47, 41] and some of the potential challenges of the future of 6G network development includes:

- *Security:* Network security is a fundamental concern for 6G wireless networks. Apart from traditional physical layer security, additional layers of security, such as integrated network security, should be considered jointly. Hence, emerging security solutions, involving low complexity and higher security rates, need to be studied more intensively [47, 46]. Future 6g infrastructure technologies such as IoE will carry significant threat surfaces for wireless connectivity, such as the increased risk of DDoS attacks due to the huge number of interconnected devices [25]. Besides, the massive volume of data generated by future systems will require sophisticated access control mechanisms to prevent unauthorized manipulation [27].

- *Scalability:* The emergence of new concepts such as massive machine-to-machine communications (mMTC) and ultra-reliable and low latency communications (uRLLC), together with billions of interconnected devices, will make it difficult to scale the design of 6G systems to handle massive traffic demand [27].
- *Resources as a Service:* The shift toward service-oriented and integrated resource distribution (also known as RaaS), driven by the evolution of SDN and NFV technologies, introduced the concept of network slicing, which can deliver powerful virtualization capability that enables multiple virtual networks over the top of a shared physical infrastructure [44]. However, since the network is getting increasingly complex and heterogenerous and network softwarization alone is not enough, 6G is expected to move toward network intelligentization [30].
- *Stringent hardware constraints:* 6G networks are expected to virtualize the medium access control (MAC) and physical layer (PHY) components as they presently necessitate specific hardware implementations, and build distributed platforms with minimal antenna size and processing [30]. However, since companies have spent years miniaturizing today's large high-frequency transmitters and receivers (i.e., mmWave components), for the terahertz band, the challenge may be more difficult [47]. 6G will also be AI-driven and will require more computing power to execute AI algorithms and to adopt security standards, which will be more difficult due to the resource constraints of the devices [44, 27].

5.4.2 Blockchain-Based Solutions

Blockchain technology provides powerful solutions to address most of today's limitations, including support for 6G networks infrastructure and future applications [27], and in this sub-section, we discuss some of the solutions offered.

5.4.2.1 Infrastructure Solutions

It is possible to leverage the blockchain technology within the 6G infrastructure itself to improve performance or to enable new features [27]. These include:

- *High-security features:* As discussed in the previous sections, blockchain technology can meet a variety of security needs that 6G services can use to ensure trust and security for the complex security requirements that future networks will impose. For instance, in blockchain-based privacy preservation systems, frameworks based on a blockchain guarantees the integrity of the information exchanged over the network, DDoS prevention mechanisms, authentication, access control, distributed key management, and transparent immutable log for network events auditing [34, 27, 46]. This will result in higher performance and more secure 6G network services, as well as increased growth in blockchain-based applications, resulting in a favorable feedback cycle [34].
- *Smart resource management:* One major challenge with the huge connectivity that needs to be envisioned in future telecommunications environments is the management of network resources, where the compatibility of these management services must be effectively implemented with large-scale 6G networks [27]. Spectrum management ensures that several user classes can securely share the same frequency ranges, allowing the radio spectrum available for communications to be used more efficiently [47]. Through spectrum sharing, the main user arranges leases so that other users can use its spectrum. Blockchain technology can provide additional security for spectrum sharing by preventing tampering with lease records [34]. Besides, smart contracts can provide self-organized network capabilities for 6G [27], and blockchain-based network decentralization has the potential to simplify network management, improve network performance, and secure data sharing [46, 27].
- *Edge AI:* Recent research focus has moved toward edge caching and Fog Radio Access Networks (fog-RANs), where content is held nearer to the users' devices, enabling very low latency communications and power consumption [44]. Blockchains can be used in these implementations to ensure reliable coordination and transparent resource accounting [27].
- *Subscription business model:* Blockchains have the potential to facilitate the billing process in the absence of a centralized infrastructure, resulting in an architecture that is more flexible and efficient than traditional systems. Also, the service level agreement (SLA) management, the agreement between the service provider and the customer on specific aspects of the service, is an important system requirement since 6G networks are expected to serve a very wide range of use cases with various service levels guarantees. The blockchains permit secure, decentralized management of SLAs in these complex conditions [27].

5.4.2.2 Emerging Applications

While famous applications of blockchain technology reside in the financial sector, many blockchain-based applications are applied in various other fields well beyond cryptocurrencies [49, 11]. We briefly describe some applications of blockchain in six basic domains, namely finance, healthcare, industry, governance, education, and the IoT.

- *Finance:* Blockchains significantly contribute to financial innovation through providing essential technology for the Fintech revolution, especially in currencies and payments, where the needs of safe and smart transactions are taken into account, all without requiring third-parties involvement [7]. The application of blockchain technology in the financial sector includes, among others, the following branches: banking, insurance, asset management, capital markets, and trade [11].
- *Healthcare:* Research in Blockchain-based healthcare solutions is growing rapidly; although still in its infancy, the subject is now established as an academic field, having achieved significant growth in the number and quality of publications over the past few years; solutions currently being studied include: electronic health record (EHR) systems, personal health record (PHR) systems, clinical trial systems, automated diagnostic service for patients, administrative systems, knowledge infrastructures, population health management systems, Remote surgery, and pharma supply-chains [40].
- *Industry:* Blockchain technology improves supply chain data management solutions [15, 16, 42], by increasing transparency and accountability, resulting in a reduction in the risk of counterfeiting and gray markets [11]. It also offers the ability to engage business consumers in the energy market [20] and enable the creation of energy communities, to reduce costs and enable new business models and markets, by better handling complexity, security, and ownership management of grids [11].
- *Governance:* Historically, governments have been charged with the responsibility of managing and preserving the official records of citizens and/or enterprises, and since blockchain-based applications are reliable, automated, and secure for handling public documents, they can potentially prevent fraud and enhance the effectiveness of government services [11, 36], including citizenship/user services [21, 5] and e-voting services [43].
- *Education:* A growing number of blockchain-based applications have been developed for use in educational contexts, but only a subset of them has been launched publicly [6, 11], and most of them are mainly used to deliver and validate academic certificates, share students' competencies and experiences, and assess their professional capacity [6].
- *Internet of things (IoT):* Blockchain technology applies to nearly all areas of IoT [19], with the main concept of delivering secure and auditable data exchange in context-sensitive scenarios with numerous

interconnected smart devices [11]. Its applications in the IoT include, among others, the Internet of Vehicles (IoV), Internet of Energy (IoE), Internet of Cloud (IoC), Internet of Healthcare Things (IoHT), connected robotics, and autonomous systems [22, 41, 24].

- *Other applications:* including augmented reality (AR), virtual reality (VR), and mixed reality (MR) technologies, all of which are part of the extended reality (XR) concept, referring to both the merged real-virtual environments and human-computer interactions produced by information technology (IT), wireless brain-computer interaction (BCI) technology where human physiological signals are wirelessly communicated with a computer system for interpretation [46, 41], and many other futuristic applications will benefit from the 6G network infrastructure and the blockchain technology by exploiting their advantages [47, 27].

5.5 DISCUSSION

Sixth-generation networks are expected to outperform previous generations and meet the requirements of future services and applications, such as ubiquitous AI-based IoE. Blockchain technology is a key enabler of IoE, as it establishes trust between end-to-end connected systems without the need for trusted intermediaries [34], and provides both infrastructure and application solutions for future 6th generation networks. However, there remain open issues in the implementation of the current blockchain technologies that need to be dealt with.

5.5.1 Open Research Issues

Here we explore some of the key potential problems that can constrain the widespread adoption and use of blockchain technology for the future of 6G networks.

- *Security:* There are several security issues to be considered in the current implementation of blockchain technology [19, 31, 34], all of which can be transferred to 6G if it is incorporated as a core technology. Blockchain common risks include, but are not limited to, *the majority vulnerability:* also known as the 51% Vulnerability that can be used to control the whole blockchain network [19]. For example, in PoW-based consensus blockchains, it can be launched if the hashing power of a node is greater than 50% of the total hashing power of the entire blockchain, while the same thing in PoS-based consensus blockchains if a stack value held by a node is greater than 50% of the total blockchain [31]. If this happened, an attacker could freely manipulate and modify the ledger; *Double spending attack:* where an attacker can exploit the time between the execution and confirmation of two transactions to quickly use the same cryptocurrency several times [31]; *Transaction privacy leakage:* Blockchain is built on transparent transactions. User privacy is therefore at risk in systems based on blockchain [19, 34]; *Smart contract vulnerabilities:* Smart contracts, as programs operating in the blocking chain, offer automatic control; however, they have security vulnerabilities at different points, including source code-based, blockchain mechanism-based, and Virtual machine-based [31]; *Combined Attacks:* Resisting combined attacks while taking into account the feasibility of implementing the solution, remains a problem [19].

- *Latency:* In future networks, the targeted end-to-end latency is less than 1-ms [41]. Thus, the performance of a blockchain-based application can be limiting in terms of latency, since it necessitates forced delays with significant amounts of information transmitted and shared among participants. Even though some private blockchains reach 20,000 transactions per second (TPS), the case for public ones is much less, as in the Bitcoin protocol that performs 7 TPS, and 10 min latency for each block confirmation [34]. Billions of smart devices with their massive transaction needs to be projected for 6G will certainly deepen the challenge. Efficient blockchain architectures, techniques, consensus algorithms, etc., are therefore needed.

- *Standardization and interoperability:* IoE is broader than IoT because it seeks to intelligently and transparently connect things, processes, and people [27]. Ensuring interoperability between different blockchains is needed to enable IoE, but it remains a challenge that must be taken up and overcome by researchers. For the widespread adoption of a global chain in the 6G, local and international standardization is required.

5.6 CONCLUSION

In this chapter, we first provided a comprehensive introduction to blockchain technology in terms of its fundamental components and the relationships between them. Secondly, we reviewed some of the cryptographic techniques used in this technology, along with their implementation. Besides, we discussed a major aspect of the topic, specifically the consensus mechanism. Moreover, we explored some of the main challenges facing 6G networks, together with blockchain-based solutions. Finally, we wrap up this chapter by highlighting the challenges of open research in current blockchain technology.

REFERENCES

1. Satoshi Nakamoto. Bitcoin: A peer-to-peer electronic cash system. Available at: https://bitcoin.org/bitcoin.pdf, 2009.
2. Ecdsa secp256k1. Available at: http://www.secg.org/sec2-v2.pdf, last accessed 2020-09-25.
3. Global blockchain technology market report, 2019. Available at: https://www.grandviewresearch.com/press-release/global-blockchain-technology-market, last accessed 2020-10-08.
4. Whitepaper: Nxt. Available at: https://nxtwiki.org/wiki/Whitepaper:Nxt, last accessed 2020-10-04.
5. Walid Al-Saqaf and Nicolas Seidler. Blockchain technology for social impact: Opportunities and challenges ahead, *Journal of Cyber Policy*, 2(3), 338–354, 2017.
6. Ali Alammary, Samah Alhazmi, Marwah Almasri, and Saira Gillani. Blockchain-based applications in education: A systematic review, *Applied Sciences*, 9(12), 2400, 2019.
7. Omar Ali, Mustafa Ally, Yogesh Dwivedi, et al. The state of play of blockchain technology in the financial services sector: A systematic literature review, *International Journal of Information Management*, 54, 102199, 2020.
8. Elli Androulaki, Artem Barger, Vita Bortnikov, Christian Cachin, Konstantinos Christidis, Angelo De Caro, David Enyeart, Christopher Ferris, Gennady Laventman, Yacov Manevich, et al. Hyperledger fabric: A distributed operating system for permissioned blockchains. In *Proceedings of the Thirteenth EuroSys Conference*, pages 1–15, 2018.
9. Jorge Bernal Bernabe, Jose Luis Canovas, Jose L. Hernandez-Ramos, Rafael Torres Moreno, and Antonio Skarmeta. Privacy-preserving solutions for blockchain: Review and challenges, *IEEE Access*, 7, 164908–164940, 2019.
10. Christian Cachin and Marko Vukolić. Blockchain consensus protocols in the wild. arXiv preprint arXiv:1707.01873, 2017.
11. Fran Casino, Thomas K. Dasaklis, and Constantinos Patsakis. A systematic literature review of blockchain-based applications: Current status, classification and open issues, *Telematics and Informatics*, 36, 55–81, 2019.
12. Miguel Castro, Barbara Liskov, et al. Practical byzantine fault tolerance. In *OSDI*, Vol. 99, USENIX, pages 173–186, 1999.
13. Sonali Chandel, Wenxuan Cao, Zijing Sun, Jiayi Yang, Bailu Zhang, and Tian-Yi Ni. A multi-dimensional adversary analysis of rsa and ecc in blockchain encryption. In *Future of Information and Communication Conference*, pages 988–1003. Springer, 2019.
14. Hong-Ning Dai, Zibin Zheng, and Yan Zhang. Blockchain for internet of things: A survey, *IEEE Internet of Things Journal*, 6(5), 8076–8094, 2019.
15. Abdelouahid Derhab, Mohamed Guerroumi, Abdu Gumaei, Leandros Maglaras, Mohamed Amine Ferrag, Mithun Mukherjee, and Farrukh Aslam Khan. Blockchain and random subspace learning-based ids for sdn-enabled industrial iot security, *Sensors*, 19(14), 3119, 2019.

16. Abdelouahid Derhab, Mohamed Guerroumi, Leandros Maglaras, Mohamed Amine Ferrag, Mithun Mukherjee, and Farrukh Aslam Khan. Bloster: Blockchain-based system for detection of fraudulent rules in software-defined networks. In *6th International Symposium for ICS & SCADA Cyber Security Research*, no. 6, pages 38–40, 2019.

17. Sheng Ding, Jin Cao, Chen Li, Kai Fan, and Hui Li. A novel attribute-based access control scheme using blockchain for iot, *IEEE Access*, 7, 38431–38441, 2019.

18. Weidong Fang, Wei Chen, Wuxiong Zhang, Jun Pei, Weiwei Gao, and Guohui Wang. Digital signature scheme for information non-repudiation in blockchain: A state of the art review, *EURASIP Journal on Wireless Communications and Networking*, 2020(1), 1–15, 2020.

19. Mohamed Amine Ferrag, Makhlouf Derdour, Mithun Mukherjee, Abdelouahid Derhab, Leandros Maglaras, and Helge Janicke. Blockchain technologies for the internet of things: Research issues and challenges, *IEEE Internet of Things Journal*, 6(2), 2188– 2204, 2018.

20. Mohamed Amine Ferrag and Leandros Maglaras. Deepcoin: A novel deep learning and blockchain-based energy exchange framework for smart grids, *IEEE Transactions on Engineering Management*, 67(4), 1285–1297, 2019.

21. Mohamed Amine Ferrag and Leandros Maglaras. Deliverycoin: An ids and blockchain-based delivery framework for drone-delivered services, *Computers*, 8(3), 58, 2019.

22. Mohamed Amine Ferrag, Leandros Maglaras, and Helge Janicke. Blockchain and its role in the internet of things. In Androniki Kavoura, Efstathios Kefallonitis, and Apostolos Giovanis (eds), *Strategic Innovative Marketing and Tourism*, pages 1029–1038. Springer, 2019. 7th ICSIMAT, Athenian Riviera, Greece, 2018.

23. Mohamed Amine Ferrag, Lei Shu, Xing Yang, Abdelouahid Derhab, and Leandros Maglaras. Security and privacy for green iot-based agriculture: Review, blockchain solutions, and challenges, *IEEE Access*, 8, 32031–32053, 2020.

24. Othmane Friha, Mohamed Amine Ferrag, Lei Shu, Leandros Maglaras, and Xiaochan Wang. Internet of things for the future of smart agriculture: A comprehensive survey of emerging technologies. *IEEE/CAA Journal of Automatica Sinica*, 8, 1, 2021.

25. Othmane Friha, Mohamed Amine Ferrag, Lei Shu, and Mehdi Nafa. A robust security framework based on blockchain and sdn for fog computing enabled agricultural internet of things. In *International Conference on Internet of Things and Intelligent Applications (ITIA)*, pages 1–5. IEEE, 2020.

26. Juan Garay and Aggelos Kiayias. Sok: A consensus taxonomy in the blockchain era. In *Cryptographers' Track at the RSA Conference*, pages 284–318. Springer, 2020.

27. Tharaka Hewa, Gürkan Gür, Anshuman Kalla, Mika Ylianttila, An Bracken, and Mad- husanka Liyanage. The role of blockchain in 6g: Challenges, opportunities and research directions. In *2nd 6G Wireless Summit (6G SUMMIT)*, pages 1–5. IEEE, 2020.

28. Sunny King and Scott Nadal. Ppcoin: Peer-to-peer crypto-currency with proof-of-stake.self-published paper, August, 19, 1, 2012.

29. Leslie Lamport, Robert Shostak, and Marshall Pease. The byzantine generals problem, *ACM Transactions Programming Languages and Syststems*, 4(3), 382–401, July 1982.

30. Khaled B. Letaief, Wei Chen, Yuanming Shi, Jun Zhang, and Ying-Jun Angela Zhang. The roadmap to 6g: Ai empowered wireless networks, *IEEE Communications Magazine*, 57(8), 84–90, 2019.

31. Xiaoqi Li, Peng Jiang, Ting Chen, Xiapu Luo, and Qiaoyan Wen. A survey on the security of blockchain systems, *Future Generation Computer Systems*, 107, 841–853, 2020.

32. Ian Miers, Christina Garman, Matthew Green, and Aviel D. Rubin. Zerocoin: Anony-mous distributed e-cash from bitcoin. In *IEEE Symposium on Security and Privacy*, pages 397–411. IEEE, 2013.

33. Giang-Truong Nguyen and Kyungbaek Kim. A survey about consensus algorithms used in blockchain, *Journal of Information Processing Systems*, 14(1), 101–128, 2018.

34. Tri Nguyen, Ngoc Tran, Lauri Loven, Juha Partala, M-Tahar Kechadi, and Susanna Pirttikangas. Privacy-aware blockchain innovation for 6g: Challenges and opportunities. In *2nd 6G Wireless Summit (6G SUMMIT)*, pages 1–5. IEEE, 2020.

35. Aafaf Ouaddah, Anas Abou Elkalam, and Abdellah Ait Ouahman. Fairaccess: A new blockchain-based access control framework for the internet of things, *Security and Communication Networks*, 9(18), 5943–5964, 2016.

36. Adrian-Tudor Panescu and Vasile Manta. Smart contracts for research data rights management over the ethereum blockchain network, *Science & Technology Libraries*, 37(3), 235–245, 2018.

37. M. Pease, R. Shostak, and L. Lamport. Reaching agreement in the presence of faults, *Journal of the ACM*, 27(2), 228–234, 1980, April.

38. Eric Piscini and Lory Kehoe. Blockchain & cyber security. Let's discuss. *Deloitte*, 2017.

39. Mayank Raikwar, Danilo Gligoroski, and Katina Kralevska. Sok of used cryptography in blockchain, *IEEE Access*, 7, 148550–148575, 2019.

40. Juan M. Roman-Belmonte, Hortensia De la Corte-Rodriguez, and E Carlos Rodriguez-Merchan. How blockchain technology can change medicine, *Postgraduate Medicine*, 130(4), 420–427, 2018.

41. Walid Saad, Mehdi Bennis, and Mingzhe Chen. A vision of 6g wireless systems: Applications, trends, technologies, and open research problems, *IEEE Network*, 34(3), 134–142, 2019.

42. Sara Saberi, Mahtab Kouhizadeh, Joseph Sarkis, and Lejia Shen. Blockchain technology and its relationships to sustainable supply chain management, *International Journal of Production Research*, 57(7), 2117–2135, 2019.

43. Yash Soni, Leandros Maglaras, and Mohamed Amine Ferrag. Blockchain based voting systems. *ACPI*, 2020.

44. Faisal Tariq, Muhammad R. A. Khandaker, Kai-Kit Wong, Muhammad A. Imran, Mehdi Bennis, and Merouane Debbah. A speculative study on 6g, *IEEE Wireless Communications*, 27(4), 118–125, 2020.

45. IT Union. *Imt Traffic Estimates for the Years 2020 to 2030*. Report ITU, pages 2370, 2015.

46. Minghao Wang, Tianqing Zhu, Tao Zhang, Jun Zhang, Shui Yu, and Wanlei Zhou. Security and privacy in 6g networks: New areas and new challenges, *Digital Communications and Networks*, 6(3), 281–291, 2020.
47. Ping Yang, Yue Xiao, Ming Xiao, and Shaoqian Li. 6g wireless communications: Vision and potential techniques, *IEEE Network*, 33(4), 70–75, 2019.
48. Xiao Yue, Huiju Wang, Dawei Jin, Mingqiang Li, and Wei Jiang. Healthcare data gateways: found healthcare intelligence on blockchain with novel privacy risk control, *Journal of medical systems*, 40(10), 218, 2016.
49. Zibin Zheng, Shaoan Xie, Hong-Ning Dai, Xiangping Chen, and Huaimin Wang. Blockchain challenges and opportunities: A survey, *International Journal of Web and Grid Services*, 14(4), 352–375, 2018.
50. Zibin Zheng, Shaoan Xie, Hongning Dai, Xiangping Chen, and Huaimin Wang. An overview of blockchain technology: Architecture, consensus, and future trends. In *IEEE International Congress on Big Data (BigData Congress)*, pages 557–564. IEEE, 2017.

Chapter 6

Securing Components on a 5G Core

*Jorge Proença, Vasco Pereira, Daniel Fernandes,
Marco Sequeira, Pedro Quitério, André Gomes,
Paulo Simões, Tiago Cruz, and Luís Cordeiro*

6.1 INTRODUCTION

Compared with the previous generations of wireless communication networks (4G), a 5G network provides a great increase in data rates with improved Quality of Service (QoS), exceptionally low latency (Ahmad, et al., 2017), and high device density. This will allow not only a great number of handheld devices but also to massively connect Internet of Things (IoT) devices, machine-to-machine (M2M), and cyber-physical systems (CPS). Considering the new application scenarios made possible by 5G networks and the increase in types of services and connected devices (in variety and number), the threat landscape has grown extensively for this new network generation.

6.1.1 Security across Previous Generations

Each generation of wireless mobile networks had security issues. The first generation (1G) was known to have challenges of interception and cloning due to their analog nature. The second generation (2G) became digital and brought some security features provided by User Equipment (UE) anonymity, authentication, signaling, and user data protection. However, it had some security issues, such as only having one-way authentication (UE didn't authenticate the operator), and was vulnerable to message spamming, unwanted broadcast, and injection of false information (Ahmad, et al., 2017) (Ahmad, et al., 2019). Also, the encryption algorithms were reverse engineered, resulting in the cipher algorithms being subjected to several attacks (Cattaneo, Maio, & Petrillo, 2013) (Golić, 1997). Furthermore, it was not capable of being upgraded to improve its security. The third generation (3G) brought higher data rates and new services. IP-based communication started to be part of the infrastructure as well. Although 3G has significantly improved its security (with the five sets of security features specified in TS33.102 (3GPP, 1999)), it still had some noticeable flaws, such as IP-based vulnerabilities. With the arrival of the 4G, IP communication expanded to more points of the mobile network, which increased IP traffic-induced security risks. Ahmad et al. details the main security mechanisms and challenges of wireless technologies from 1G to 4G (Ahmad, et al., 2019).

6.1.2 Structure of the M5G Project

The 5G mobilizer (M5G) is a 36-month project, which was started in 2018, bringing together industrial and academic partners, aiming at the research and development of future products and solutions to be integrated into the fifth generation of mobile networks (5G). The products are divided into four main areas: network edge, network core, machine-to-machine (M2M), and human communication.

The project is divided into different areas, and the proof of concept (PoC) presented in this chapter is related to the development of products and services of the 5G network core. The PoC is part of a broader security framework (out of the scope of this chapter).

6.1.3 The Need to Secure the 5G Core

The core components of the 5G infrastructure may have to deal with a high number of threats and security concerns. The traffic is expected to have a huge increase compared with the previous generation, and there are estimates that the signalling traffic may increase 50% faster than the data traffic (Nokia, 2012). The signalling plane can be overwhelmed by a huge number of infected IoT devices in an attempt to disrupt service via a DoS attack or to gain unauthorized access (Ahmad, et al., 2019) (NGMN Alliance, 2016). As software-defined networks (SDNs) and network function virtualization (NFV) are expected to be used in the core network to provide flexibility and scalability of services, they also may compromise security if not well addressed.

6.1.4 Proposal

The present proposal is included in the security framework of the M5G project and focuses on the detection of security attacks to 5G core components. Specifically, it includes two distinct components: an application intrusion detection and prevention system (AppIDPS), and an event processing and visualization platform (EPVP) composed by an Event Collector, and a Dashboard. To validate it, the network exposure function (NEF) from a typical 5G core is used as an example. Figure 6.1 illustrates the main components of a typical 5G network plus the main components of the PoC (AppIDPS and Event Collector). In this scenario, the AppIDPS analyses the requests and responses of the NEF to detect unwanted activity. Any suspicious activity detected by the AppIDPS will trigger a security event that is

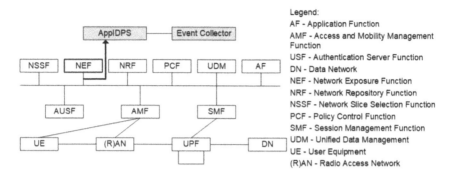

Figure 6.1 Components of the 5G system, plus PoC components – adapted from (ETSI, 2020).

further processed by the EPVP and displayed to security personnel through a dashboard.

6.1.5 Chapter Structure

The remaining of the chapter is divided into the following structure. Section 6.2 provides an overview of the security in 5G. Section 6.3 describes the related work published within the academic community. Section 6.4 details the architecture and components of the PoC presented here. Section 6.5 contains the results of component testing and the integration scenario. Section 6.6 concludes the chapter.

6.2 SECURITY IN 5G

This section overviews the current state of security in 5G and research efforts that are related to the PoC addressed in this chapter.

6.2.1 Security Architecture of 5G Networks

Security challenges in 5G have a broad spectrum, as the service diversity has significantly increased from previous generations, along with some paradigm changes in the network architecture. The 5G specification was designed to tackle these new challenges. Virtualization is expected to be widely adopted as well as multi-tenancy support, which can bring new security issues if not addressed carefully. Examples of such technologies are SDN, NFV, Mobile Edge Computing, and Massive Multiple Input Multiple Output (Ahmad, et al., 2019). The NGMN (NGMN Alliance, 2015) lists recommendations for 5G, as well as points out some limitations (Liyanage, Ahmad, Abro, Gurtov, & Ylianttila, 2018): flash network traffic, security of radio interface keys, user plane integrity, mandated network security, consistency in subscriber level security policies, and DoS attacks on the infrastructure.

The security in 5G is based on a vision with three main principles: supreme built-in security, flexible security mechanisms, and automation (Liyanage, Ahmad, Abro, Gurtov, & Ylianttila, 2018). Furthermore, it follows a security architecture as defined in Int. Telecommun Union (2005) and 3GPP (2018) to provide a systematic approach, resulting in a security framework divided into six main domains, which are (1) Network Access Security, (2) Network Domain Security, (3) User Domain Security, (4) Application Domain Security, (5) Service-Based Architecture Domain Security, and (6) Visibility and Configurability Security.

6.2.2 Current Research

The security aspects of 5G have been getting the attention of the research community. As a general overview, Cao et al. (Cao, et al., 2019) discuss security aspects of 5G networks related to the UE access and handover methods, including security in Internet of Things (IoT), Device to Device, Vehicle to Everything, and network slicing. The authors also list possible solutions for each use case and describe some open issues for future research. In this fifth generation, the authentication between UE and the network uses the evolved packet system based authentication and key agreement (EPS-AKA) introduced in Long Term Evolution (LTE) because although it introduces some communication overhead and latency, it does not have any security vulnerabilities so far. A threat model classifying attacks in the 4G and 5G networks was proposed by Ferrag et al. (Ferrag, Maglaras, Argyriou, Kosmanos, & Janicke, 2018) in a paper discussing the existing surveys for 4G and 5G wireless mobile networks security. They classify the attacks into four categories: privacy, integrity, availability, and authentication.

The security of 5G networks will also depend on which options are made in different implementations. A considerably wide range of possibilities in the specification allows configuration options that may leave the network with security breaches that increase the network's vulnerability to attacks (Jover & Marojevic, 2019). For example, null encryption and null authentication are still supported, and valid network configurations might use them. Another example is in function chain configuration as described by Li et al. (Li, et al., 2018) in which they've proposed a rule management framework to implement security rule configuration with anomaly resolution. There are also mechanisms that may only be useful with global cooperation, which is unlikely to happen. This cooperation would be needed to guarantee security against pre-authentication message exploits, and each Universal Subscriber Identity Module would have to include the public keys from all the network operators available worldwide without exception, which would be extremely difficult (if not impossible) to achieve.

6.3 RELATED WORK

The security of the 5G infrastructure has been the subject of research in the academic community. To address the security of the SDN-based network use in 5G, Luo et al. (Luo, Wu, Li, Guo, & Pei, 2015) have proposed a vulnerability assessment for SDN-based Mobile Network using attack graph algorithm and analytic hierarchy process (AHP). A security architecture for 5G is proposed by Arfaoui et al. (Arfaoui, et al., 2018), following the security architecture of X.805 from ITU-T. They present it as a methodology for secure instantiation of systems based on (1) domain separation, (2) classification of strata through a high-level view of protocols, data, and functions that are related to each other in a common threat environment, (3) security realms, and (4) security control classes. Another security architecture for 5G networks proposed in Fang, Qian, and Hu (2017) was tested in scenarios of handover procedure and signalling load analysis. They point out four security domains defined in the 3GPP security architecture for 5G networks: (1) network access security, (2) network domain security, (3) user domain security, and (4) application domain security.

Deployment and configuration of the security services can also determine the overall security of a system. The 5G architecture can be composed by chaining different functions together. This may also apply to its security systems. Rules configuring a security system can have an impact on security if the rules are misconfigured. Different systems can have different rules, and chaining components with different rules will increase this risk. Li et al. (Li, et al., 2018) proposed a rule management framework to reduce the risk of rule misconfiguration in a security function chain environment, which will, in turn, minimize security breaches in security architecture.

Using a 5G-based vehicular networking environment, a software-defined dynamic security defense is proposed by Xu, Dong, Ota, Wu, and Li (2019) for 5G software-defined vehicular networks. This proposal dynamically generates and deploys security strategies in a software-defined way after evaluating the security level of the current system. The security is evaluated following three aspects of information security: confidentiality, integrity, and availability. A mathematical model is used to assess security using a hybrid decision-making model based on fuzzy AHP and Technique for Order of Preference by Similarity to Ideal Solution. The dynamic security policies are then generated and applied using software-defined networking.

In this chapter, the authors have a different approach to increase the security of a 5G network as they provide an active approach in detecting unwanted or malicious activity in the 5G core components. The PoC presented here is composed of an applicational IDPS (AppIDPS) and an event processing and visualization platform (EPVP). The main role of the AppIDPS is to detect unwanted activities in requests made to the modules of the 5G network core.

6.4 ARCHITECTURE AND COMPONENTS

The components of the proposed PoC are shown in Figure 6.2 and are a subset of the more complete security architecture of the M5G core. The NEF will be used as the core component to protect, and its activity will be monitored by the AppIDPS. For context purposes, Figure 6.2 also includes other components that may send events to the EPVP, such as the Domain Name System IDPS, the Honeynet, and the Vulnerability Assessment Scanner, which are not addressed in this chapter.

6.4.1 Event Processing and Visualization Platform

The EPVP receives security events from several 5G core nodes and presents them to an operator in a simple, easy-to-understand web interface. It is tasked with receiving, processing, logging, and presenting the processed security event data and respective node metrics to the network manager. It follows a microservice-oriented architecture and is built upon three main components/microservices: a Kafka cluster, which takes care of event forwarding and centralization; a Middleware, where pre-processing and data treatment functions are applied, together with some calculations of node-specific data; and a Web UI (Dashboard), necessary for outputting the treated information to the security operator. The deployment of the EPVP is done using Docker-based containers, which simplify the management and deployment processes. Docker[1] was also chosen with scalability in mind, complementing the easily scalable Kafka[2] services.

The architecture (Figure 6.3) was designed for optimal event processing. By separating the web interface and data processing into different

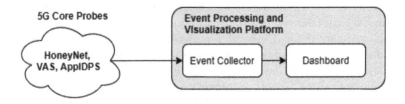

Figure 6.2 M5G security framework's basic architecture.

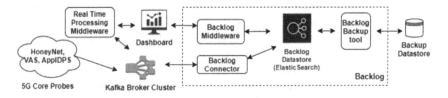

Figure 6.3 EPVP internal architecture and its connection to the 5G core probes.

components, we can achieve higher throughput numbers and better overall performance, effectively separating the workload without compromising data integrity, while keeping all data relevant and up-to-date. There is also a datastore, which was created specifically to store older events, directly reducing the resource usage at the Middleware. Those events can then be looked up by the user at the web interface.

The events received are transmitted in a JSON format, using a common data model that specifies message structure and variable limits. It has some generic fields that are common to all components and metadata fields that are extensible to allow it to be custom fitted.

6.4.2 AppIDPS

The AppIDPS was developed as an extra layer of security at the applicational level. It analyzes information from the selected secured components and the requests processed by their APIs to detect threats from malicious entities. AppIDPS has rule-based algorithms to allow detection of emerging threats and report them to the EPVP.

6.4.2.1 Internal View

The AppIDPS gathers information from other services, through specific APIs, to perform the security analysis. A general perspective of the AppIDPS is depicted in Figure 6.4.

The internal architecture of the AppIDPS includes diverse elements: (1) scalable component to gather information from Network Functions (NFs) and Application Functions (AFs) that aim to be secured; (2) correlation component to perform the security analysis based on a set of

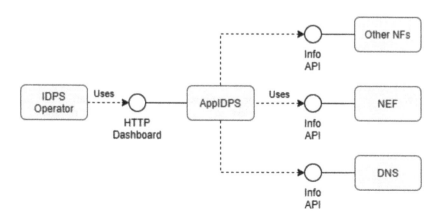

Figure 6.4 AppIDPS – general perspective.

rules and security algorithms to detect security flaws and attacks using the information provided; (3) security server component that assures the signalling between the different components are secured and performs the integration with external dashboards; (4) real-time database components that are responsible for providing the information in real-time to support the security analysis of the correlation components. The internal view is pictured in Figure 6.5 and the main internal components are described in Table 6.1.

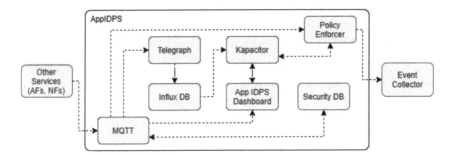

Figure 6.5 ApplDPS – internal view.

Table 6.1 App IDPS Component Description

Component	Component description
Policy enforcer	Applies policies in response to certain events and keeps a record of applied policies in its internal database.
MQTT	MQTT is an ISO standard publish-subscribe-based messaging protocol. This component is the broker for such messages and allows receiving and sending data from/to external components.
Telegraph	An agent to collect and report both metrics and data. Its plugins allow interaction with multiple data sources. In this case, it receives data from MQTT and feeds the InfluxDB with the collected data.
InfluxDB	Time series database optimized for fast, high-availability storage and retrieval of time series data. It stores large quantities of monitoring data from the Telegraph.
Kapacitor	Data processing engine to process data from InfluxDB with custom logic or user-defined functions to process alerts with dynamic thresholds, match metrics for patterns, compute statistical anomalies, and perform specific actions based on these alerts like dynamic load rebalancing.
Dashboard	Allows human interaction with the system, and the definition of rules and policies. It also handles situations that the automatic system cannot handle by itself.
SecurityDB	Database with ACLs to provide access control to MQTT server and its topics. It also includes AAA (Authentication, Authorization, and Accounting) for the MQTT server and the Dashboard.

6.4.2.2 Metrics and Policy Messages

Probes send metrics to AppIDPS and receive policies whenever actions take place. Messages are sent using JSON and the MQTT protocol. The information that is sent for analysis includes diverse items and contains both a common header and a body with app-specific information. The fields in the common header are the source IP of the application client, access timestamp, network function ID, and network function type (according to 3GPP specifications). As for policies, the body format is also defined by each app.

6.4.3 NEF

The NEF is a 5G standard component that exposes an API of network services and capabilities in a developer-friendly manner. The NEF used in this PoC was developed in Python following the 3GPP OpenAPI specifications. The internal components of NEF include (1) the API worker itself, running as a stateless RESTful service that can be easily scaled out/in; (2) the load balancer that sits in front of the API and has a dual purpose of distributing load among existing API workers and blocking requests from malicious entities (this reflects the existing integration with AppIDPS, which receives information from a security probe located in the NEF that is analyzing all the requests); (3) a database containing all the exchanges and subscriptions performed by each NEF client (AF). Scaling policies are based on an external orchestrator based on metrics and performance indicators gathered by a NEF internal monitoring agent. Scaling out is done by launching additional API workers and notifying the load balancer.

6.5 FIRST RESULTS

The subsections of this chapter will describe the tests made to the EPVP, AppIDPS, and NEF, as well as a global integration scenario.

6.5.1 Event Processing and Visualization Platform Tests

Considering the EPVP architecture previously described, there is a key component that needs to be tested, given the possibility of bottlenecking incoming data, the Middleware. As for the Kafka Broker(s), its performance has been already studied in the academic community (L. Bougé, Costan and Noach 2017), so it will not be tested individually. The tests conducted on the Middleware include the average processing time of an event, as well as integrity testing to verify its robustness when dealing with invalid or wrongful data. All tests were conducted on a VMWare Virtual Machine with 4 vCPU(s) – Intel Xeon X5660 @ 2.80GHz, 16 GB of DDR RAM, and 40 GB of SSD storage.

The Middleware and Dashboard components work together to funnel the data consumed from the Kafka Brokers into easy-to-understand visual elements for the end user's interpretation of the 5G core network security behavior over time. While the Middleware collects and treats the incoming events, there is a limit to how much data it can store at a given time. The data is kept in memory to be easily and quickly accessed by the WebUI via WebSocket. However, with increasing amounts of data, the number of events to be kept in memory without affecting performance had to be studied, allowing the optimization of the Dashboard user experience without consuming excessive resources.

The Middleware recalculates metrics that consider the whole set of in-memory events when a new event arrives. The tests regarding the average event processing time at the Middleware had the goal of estimating the maximum number of events the Middleware should keep at any given time without noticeably affecting processing speed when recalculating metrics. Once that limit is reached, the Middleware starts discarding the older events. Since the data is kept in array data structures, to be easily accessed by the Dashboard, larger amounts of data directly correlate to slower array cycle times. These tests were run under different values (10000, 25000, 50000, 75000, and 100000) for the maximum number of events kept at a time (Middleware buffer), and processing time samples were then taken (see Figure 6.6) and compared. Events were generated randomly, using a synthetic event generator, effectively simulating a live event feed, while imposing the different buffer capacities listed previously. Each set was repeated three times for each buffer capacity value. Since NodeJS (the programming language this component is based on) is inherently single-threaded, the buffer is filled in a sequential order, with events arriving at the Middleware via a Kafka Consumer module, which directly consumes events from the Kafka Broker. The event is then processed and sent to the Dashboard along with the necessary visual data corresponding to that event. A copy of the event is also stored in memory at the Middleware.

The results for the capacity test show increases in average processing time (Figure 6.7) by up to 16 times with event buffer sizes above fifty thousand events. Increasing the buffer size translates into a rapid growth in average

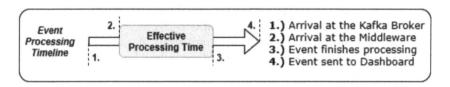

Figure 6.6 Event processing timeline.

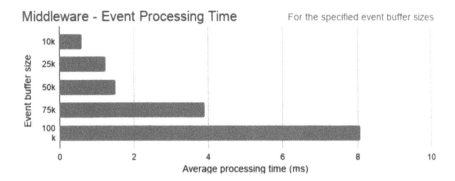

Figure 6.7 Effective processing time test for each "buffer" capacity threshold proposed.

event processing time, which adds overhead to the system for each incoming event. This overhead is partially explained by the limitations of NodeJS itself (mainly the lack of multithread support – which means there is no parallel event processing), and also by the size of the buffer array, in which operations requiring iteration throughout the array become significantly slower at larger sizes. Therefore, based on the results obtained, it is advised to keep the buffer size less than or equal to seventy-five thousand entries to ensure optimal Middleware event processing time. This test helped find a good ratio between how much data should be kept in the Middleware and the time it takes to process an event. However, it is also important to note that a solution for the problem is implemented: a side application to store/retrieve older events to/from disk, for the sake of data logging and to look up old events via the Dashboard itself, solving the problem of keeping all data in memory. This way, the Middleware can keep relevant new data and all the metrics obtained from it in memory, while still providing a way for the user to look up older events.

Robustness Middleware tests were also made. The tests were split into two categories: (1) message structure – validates the integrity of the JSON tuple message and its structure, as well as presence of the mandatory fields and (2) message contents – validates the JSON message fields. All events tested were correctly identified as valid or invalid.

6.5.2 Network Exposure Function Tests

The NEF was tested to assess its performance and scaling capacity. The tests were performed using a different number of AFs (Application Functions) sending continuous requests, in two specific scenarios, with one and two NEF instances. The tests had a duration of 210 seconds for each variation. The results in Figure 6.8 show that total requests processed are similar when using one NEF instance for a different number of AF instances running.

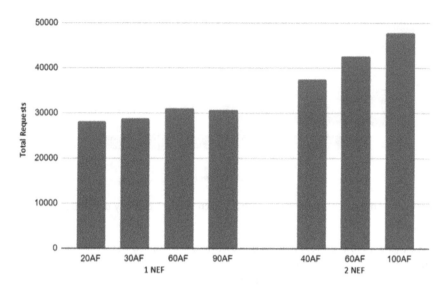

Figure 6.8 NEF request handling.

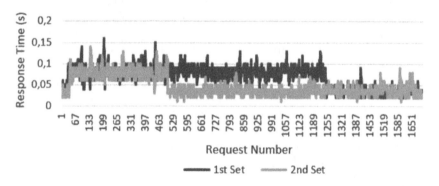

Figure 6.9 NEF response time with attack block.

This shows that the NEF is always at the maximum processing capability. When increasing to two NEF instances, we can observe an increase of the average of requests, showing an effective performance gain in increasing the number of NEF instances.

The NEF was also tested in order to assess the effectiveness of security measures implemented through the AppIDPS. In this scenario, the AppIDPS receives data from the NEF in predefined time intervals, which are analyzed to detect attacks. Whenever these attacks are detected, the AppIDPS provides feedback to the NEF, informing about the attack's origin, which is then used to trigger a block action against requests from the malicious IP address. In Figure 6.9, two experiences were made where it is observable the impact of the block action when the attack is detected, as the response time

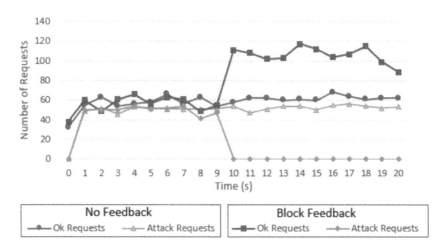

Figure 6.10 Number of requests processed by the NEF with and without AppIDPS feedback.

in both sets drops to nearly half when compared to the response time during the attack. In Figure 6.10, it is possible to understand that the number of valid requests processed increases after the attack is blocked in the scenario where the AppIDPS provides feedback, in contrast with the scenario where no feedback is given.

6.5.3 Integration Scenario

An integration scenario was designed and implemented using the proposed PoC. The application scenario uses a device called BodyKit, which interacts with the 5G infrastructure to change network parameters such as delivery priority. The BodyKit is a wearable device to be worn in emergency scenarios by emergency personnel such as firefighters or the police. It enhances current Command and Control Center capabilities by providing field data that increases situational awareness for emergency response situations, including advanced 2-way voice, video communications, and a large array of data collected from environmental (e.g., gas, smoke, temperature, humidity, location) and biosensors (e.g., electrocardiogram, respiration rate, blood pressure, heart rate, body temperature). It also has automated alarms that include the detection of man-down events and the presence of adverse and dangerous atmospheric environmental conditions such as high temperatures and toxic levels of gases. All the information sent to the 5G network is prioritized according to its Quality of Service (QoS) profile. In order to accomplish that, the BodyKit server interacts with the 5G Core via Network Exposure Function (NEF), requesting the desired QoS profile for each flow at the Policy Control Function.

In this scenario, the BodyKit is being used and requests a change through the NEF component. At some point, an attacker interacts with the system, sending unauthorized requests to the NEF, which could compromise the actions of the BodyKit by changing network parameters or triggering a Denial of Service (DoS) by overloading the NEF component. The requests targeting the NEF are analyzed by the AppIDPS and an anomalous NEF request pattern is detected. In response, the AppIDPS sends a security event to the EPVP, which is displayed in a dashboard to be analyzed by a security employee that acts accordingly.

6.5.3.1 Testbed Description

The integration scenario is set up in a testbed and the services are deployed in Virtual Machines (VMs), with their interactions following the diagram illustrated in Figure 6.11.

A description of the components illustrated can be found in Table 6.2.

6.5.3.2 Dashboard

The security of the 5G core is monitored through a dashboard as shown in Figure 6.12. The Dashboard presents a total count of the events by severity, presents the list of events received, and also enables the security operator to access each event detail. Access to older events in the Backlog Datastore is also possible.

6.6 CONCLUSION

In this chapter, the authors designed and implemented a proof of concept (PoC) of architecture to improve the security of 5G core components using the 5G network exposure function (NEF) as an example. A testbed was

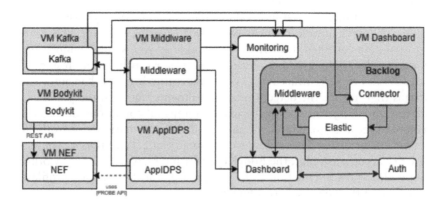

Figure 6.11 Testbed for the integration scenario.

Table 6.2 Component Description

Component	Description
ApplDPS VM	Contains Tick Stack (Telegraph, Influx, Cronograf, and Kapacitor), Postgres, and eMQTT. It uses the Probe API to obtain data from NEF.
BodyKit VM	Runs the services that make requests to NEF by REST API.
Dashboard	Web interface aiming to act as a centralized monitoring station for all other core 5G components, as well as the internal Event Collector elements. It receives processed real-time data from the Middleware.
Kafka	Kafka Broker handles the event collection and forwarding downstream to the different Event Collector components.
NEF	This VM runs NEF service and Probe.
Middleware	Processes data from a Kafka Broker into metrics to send to the Dashboard.
Dashboard VM	Contains all elements needed for the web dashboard.
Auth	Handles Dashboard user authentication, role assignment, and access permissions.
Monitoring	Collects monitoring data from other Event Collector components through the use of NetData agents and sends it to the Dashboard.
Backlog	Contains the elements that work together to provide a DB connection for the user at the Dashboard, which can use it to query old DB data: **Middleware** – Connects to the web Dashboard and allows users to search the DB for older data that has been stored for data permanency reasons. It sends requests downstream to the Elasticsearch database. **Elastic** – DB element where events are stored and used for future searches by the user at the web Dashboard. **Connector** – Consumes data directly from the Kafka Broker to avoid extra processing overhead at the Middleware and stores it in the Elasticsearch Database for future lookups by the user.

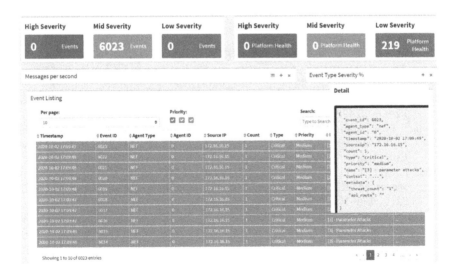

Figure 6.12 EPVP operator dashboard.

created, and the NEF was the target of attacks that were detected by an AppIDPS, generating security events that were processed and shown to a security operator. Future work will improve the performance and integration tests, extending the number of core components monitored. Scalability will also be addressed.

ACKNOWLEDGMENTS

This work was supported by the European Regional Development Fund (FEDER) through the Regional Operational Programme of Lisbon (POR LISBOA 2020) and the Competitiveness and Internationalization Operational Programme (COMPETE 2020) of the Portugal 2020 framework (Project 5G with Nr. 024539 (POCI-01-0247- FEDER-024539)).

NOTES

1. https://www.docker.com/
2. https://kafka.apache.org/

REFERENCES

3GPP. *3G Security; Security Architecture.* 3GPP, 1999.
3GPP. Security architecture and procedures for 5G system, release 15, TS 33.501. EGPP, 2018.
Ahmad, I., Kumar, T., Liyanage, M., Okwuibe, J., Ylianttila, M., and Gurtov, A. 5G security: Analysis of threats and solutions. In *IEEE Conference on Standards for Communications and Networking (CSCN)*, Helsinki, Finland, 2017.
Ahmad, I., Shahabuddin, S., Kumar, T., Okwuibe, J., Gurtov, A., and Ylianttila, M. Security for 5G and beyond, *IEEE Communications Surveys & Tutorials*, 21(4), 3682–3722, 2019.
Arfaoui, G., Bisson, P., Blom, R., Borgaonkar, R., Englund, H., Félix, E., . . . Zahariev, A. A security architecture for 5G networks, *IEEE Access*, 6, 22466–22479, 2018.
Bougé, L., Costan, A., and Le Noac'h, P. A performance evaluation of Apache Kafka in support of big data streaming applications. In *IEEE International Conference on Big Data*. Boston, MA, 2017.
Cao, J., Ma, M., Li, H., Ma, R., Sun, Y., Yu, P., and Xiong, L. A survey on security aspects for 3GPP 5G Networks, *IEEE Communications Surveys & Tutorials*, 22(1), 170–195, 2019.
Cattaneo, G., Maio, G. D., and Petrillo, U. F. Security issues and attacks on the GSM Standard: A review, *Journal of Universal Computer Science*, 19(16), 2437–2452, 2013.

ETSI. 5G; System architecture for the 5G System (5GS). 3GPP TS 23.501 version 15.8.0 Release 15, 2020.

Fang, D., Qian, Y., and Hu, R. Q. Security for 5G mobile wireless networks, *IEEE Access*, 6, 4850–4874, 2017.

Ferrag, M. A., Maglaras, L. A., Argyriou, A., Kosmanos, D., and Janicke, H. Security for 4G and 5G cellular networks, *Journal of Network and Computer Applications*, 101, 55–82, 2018.

Golić, J. D. Cryptanalysis of alleged A5 Stream Cipher. In *International Conference on the Theory and Applications of Cryptographic Techniques*, 1997.

Int. Telecommun Union. *Security Architecture for Systems Providing End-to-End Communications*. Geneva: ITU-Recommendation X.805, 2005.

Jover, R. P. and Marojevic, V. Security and protocol exploit analysis of the 5G specifications, *IEEE Access*, 7, 24956–24963, 2019.

Li, G., Zhou, H., Feng, B., Li, G., Zhang, H., and Hu, T. Rule anomaly-free mechanism of security function chaining in 5G, *IEEE Access*, 6, 13653–13662, 2018.

Liyanage, M., Ahmad, I., Abro, A. B., Gurtov, A., and Ylianttila, M. *A Comprehensive Guide to 5G Security*. Wiley, 2018.

Luo, S., Wu, J., Li, J., Guo, L., and Pei, B. Toward vulnerability assessment for 5G mobile communication networks. In *IEEE International Conference on Smart City/SocialCom/SustainCom (SmartCity)*, Chengdu, China, 2015.

NGMN Alliance. Next Generation Mobile Networks (NGMN) 5G White Paper, 2015.

NGMN Alliance. *5G Security Recommendations*. Frankfurt, Germany, 2016.

Nokia. A signaling storm is gathering - Is your packet core ready? Retrieved August 2020 from https://www.nokia.com/blog/a-signaling-storm-is-gathering-is-your-packet-core-ready, 2012.

Xu, H., Dong, M., Ota, K., Wu, J., and Li, J. Toward software defined dynamic defense as a service for 5G-enabled vehicular networks. In *International Conference on Internet of Things (iThings) and IEEE Green Computing and Communications (GreenCom) and IEEE Cyber, Physical and Social Computing (CPSCom) and IEEE Smart Data (SmartData)*, Atlanta, GA, USA, 2019.

Chapter 7

RF Jamming Attacks and Countermeasures in Wireless Vehicular Networks

Dimitrios Kosmanos and Antonios Argyriou

7.1 INTRODUCTION

With the continued integration of automated vehicles onto the roadways, the interaction between human-driven vehicles and automated vehicles is extremely important [29]. Mixed traffic behavior is imminent, as technology and auto-manufacturing companies are publicizing their autonomous technology. However, autonomous vehicle control imposes very strict security requirements for the wireless communication channels [14] which are used by a fleet of vehicles [8]. The deployment of connected autonomous vehicles (CAVs) is considered the key factor to enhance road safety, increase infrastructure efficiency, and reduce fuel consumption in intelligent transportation systems (ITS). The connected vehicles often exchange cooperative awareness messages (CAMs) to coordinate their movement using the Inter-Vehicle Communication [19]. These messages are transmitted several times per second using dedicated short range communication (DSRC) and wireless access in vehicular environments (WAVE) technology, based on the IEEE 802.11p standard.

Wireless communications, however, are vulnerable to a wide range of attacks [13], [11]. A Denial of Service (DoS) attack is particularly hard to be detected in a Vehicular Ad-Hoc Network (VANET) environment due to the constant and rapid changes in topology and the high mobility of the vehicles. Even more difficult can be the detection of the presence of an unintentional interference in the area and its separation with a malicious jammer who tries to interfere and affect the wireless communication between two legitimate vehicles. radio frequency (RF) jamming is a kind of DoS attack in which a malicious node can use it to disrupt the transmission between the nodes of a wireless network [30], [25], as most nodes use one single frequency band.

Over the last few years, there have been several experimental approaches for jamming detection [4], [13], [30]. Only a small portion of them uses machine learning techniques [30]. Specifically, the authors in [30], [10] examine closely the adoption of machine learning techniques for jamming detection. However, none of the above works that propose

DOI: 10.1201/9781003109952-7

machine-learning-based schemes have investigated a feature that takes into account the moving pattern of the RF jammer in combination with other features from the passive wireless communication between transmitter and receiver.

In this book chapter, we introduce a cross-layer intrusion detection system (IDS) that is based on supervised learning algorithms k-Nearest Neighbors (*KNN*), random forests (*RaFo*), and a data fusion method that combines the outcomes of the two classification algorithms. In order to enhance the detection accuracy of the proposed cross-layer intrusion detection system (IDS), an Application (APP) layer metric is introduced, namely the variations of relative speed (*VRS*) as an extra feature for classification combined with other features from the physical (PHY) or media access control (MAC) layer (such as the received signal strength indicator (RSSI), the signal to interference and noise ratio (SINR), and the packet delivery ratio (PDR) for training and testing. Specifically, we propose the use of RF signals for estimating the relative speed between the jammer and the receiver in the PHY layer and use the variations of it as an extra feature in the classification process. We investigate how the proposed *V RS* metric between the jammer and the receiver can enhance the detection accuracy of different types of RF jamming attacks. With the combination of the *KNN V RS*, *RaFo V RS* classification algorithms, we are able to efficiently detect various cases of DoS jamming attacks, differentiate them from cases of unintentional interference as well as foresee a potential danger successfully and act accordingly. We evaluate the proposed IDS under different "smart" jamming strategies and a different number of interfering nodes in the area.

7.1.1 Motivation

A subcategory of related papers uses single-input-multiple-output (SIMO) [38] or multiple-input-multiple-output (MIMO) [20] techniques for suppressing RF jamming effects at the PHY layer. Therefore, there is a need for completely passive methods without additional hardware for detecting an RF jamming attack. This can be achieved using the proposed completely passive pilot-based scheme that is based on RF communication between the transmitter and the receiver being interfered with by a jammer in the area [17].

Moreover, the proposed *V RS* metric is combined with lower open systems interconnection (OSI) layers metrics leading to a cross-layer approach. This set of cross-layer features are utilized for the classification of different jamming scenarios. In the general case, jamming reduces the receiver SINR, a problem that can be addressed with classic communication algorithms. In several applications, however, the actual reason behind the reduction in the signal-to-noise ratio (SNR) and the PDR, and even more, the nature of the attack. It is difficult, however, to determine whether the reason for the SINR reduction is an RF jamming attack or unintentional interference. This is the main motivation for proposing the use of the VRS metric in our novel jamming detection scheme. Our results indicate that the proposed scheme can effectively differentiate the case of a jamming attack from that of an interfering wireless source. This is a crucial aspect of our system because these two problems should be solved differently, that is, in the case of interference, an interference cancellation (IC) scheme [3] is needed, or a spectral evasion (channel surfing, spatial retreats) scheme for jamming attacks. Many countermeasures have also been proposed to address the RF jamming issues from different technical perspectives. For example, frequency hopping techniques, such as frequency hopping spread spectrum (FHSS), direct sequence spread spectrum (DSSS), and Hybrid FHSS/DSSS [22], have been widely adopted to avoid the jamming interference by rapidly switching between frequencies, or spreading the signal in a much wider band to allow for greater resistance to unintentional and intentional interference.

Consequently, in this book chapter, we present novel RF jamming detection schemes that leverage new application-layer metrics, namely *the variations of relative speed*. Unlike current work, this new detection system is able to perfectly differentiate interference from malicious RF jamming. Additionally, it is able to distinguish the unique characteristics of each attack, especially when the proposed VRS metric is utilized among the other cross-layer features. The accuracy of the proposed detection method is about or over 90% under different evaluation parameters such as the interference level in the area, "smart" jamming strategies, and realistic values of the relative speed between the jammer and the receiver.

7.2 RF JAMMING ATTACKS IN VEHICULAR NETWORKS

RF jamming has been extensively studied in the context of classical 802.11 networks without accounting for the particularities of vehicle-to-vehicle (V2V) communications. Besides the differences in PHY design of 802.11p compared to other 802.11 amendments, the propagation conditions of VANETs are fundamentally different due to the rapidly changing vehicular environment. A lot of different jamming attacks have been studied in VANETs [24]. The two most important categories of RF jamming attacks are *constant jamming* and *reactive jamming*. Constant jamming transmits randomly generated data on the channel without checking the state of the channel (idle or not). The reactive jamming happens only when the attacker senses activity between two legitimate nodes on the channel. In [31], authors observe that constant, periodic, but also reactive RF jammer can hinder a lot the communication over large propagation areas, which would threaten road safety. Reactive jamming attacks reach a high jamming efficiency and can even improve to a significant extent the energy efficiency of the jammer in several application scenarios [38]. Also, they can easily and efficiently be implemented on commercially available off-the-shelf (COTS) hardware such as universal software radio peripheral (USRP) radios [38],[28],[5]. However, more importantly, reactive jamming attacks are harder to detect due to the "smart" attack model, which allows the jamming signal to be hidden behind wireless transmission activities performed by legitimate users [26]. By analyzing these articles, we can conclude that the jammer's speed is a crucial metric for all the techniques that try to suppress or detect the RF jamming attack in RF communications in VANETs.

7.3 RF JAMMING CLASSIFICATION USING RELATIVE SPEED ESTIMATION

The recent literature that deals with RF jamming attacks detection usually uses real-time MAC-based jamming detection methods to meet the requirements of safety applications in vehicular networks. These methods operate under either the realistic assumption of random jitter accompanying every CAM transmission [23] or the decision of the detector (monitor) depends on the historical observation of events in the V2V channel [6]. These detection methods differentiate three phenomena: contention collision, interference, and jamming attacks in communication. In [15] the authors propose a method for DoS attack detection in wireless sensor networks (WSNs). This method is first based on a clustering approach of the sensor nodes in which using every node's timestamp is proposed and second on the PDR calculated from one node to another node. All the above papers use threshold-based methods, in which a threshold value is estimated as a boundary to differentiate between a normal scenario and a jammed scenario (i.e., presence of jamming attack). However, estimating this threshold accurately is a necessary task that significantly affects the performance of the method in terms of the probability of detection. Last, N. I. Mowla et al. [27] propose a federated learning based on device jamming attack detection security architecture for flying ad-hoc network (FANET) with fairly good accuracy results in detecting the RF jamming attack.

Karagiannis et al. [16] propose an RF jamming attack detection scheme using unsupervised learning with clustering. The novelty of the above paper is that the relative speed metric is utilized between the jammer and the receiver, along with other parameters, in order to differentiate intentional from unintentional jamming as well as identify the unique characteristics of each jamming attack. However, this relative speed metric is obtained from the on-board wireless communication devices at the receiver vehicle and is not estimated through real signals obtained from the wireless medium.

We must mention here that the majority of the works that proposed machine-learning-based schemes use parameters only from the MAC or the PHY layer for training and testing without upper layer features in a cross-layer jamming detection approach to be used. Only the authors in [10] adopt a cross-layer approach for detecting and classifying different forms of RF jamming attacks. However, the estimated variations of the relative speed have not been considered as a classification feature. Our proposed system is the first in the literature that uses point-to-point RF communication in order to estimate the relative speed metric. Variations of relative speed are used for effectively differentiating interference from jamming, by distinguishing the unique characteristics of each attack. Moreover, we use a supervised learning scheme, for which input data is collected about the wireless communication between the transmitter and the receiver with or without the presence of a jammer.

7.3.1 System Model

Our system topology involves the receiver (R_x) that serves as the target of the jammer, another vehicle the transmitter (T_x) which sends the useful signal, and the jamming vehicle J_x that tries to intervene in the communication between R_x and T_x (in scenario B of Figure 7.1).

In the area, there is also an RF jammer that interferes with the V2V communication between T_x and R_x. This is a simple scenario in a rural area that is used for the initial verification of our system and the scalability of our proposed will be tested under a different range of node densities. In Figure 7.1, an Interference Scenario is presented in A in which we assume that no jammer is present in the considered topology. This scenario is important in order to be able to evaluate the efficiency of our method in differentiating jamming from interference. The vehicle travels, when, at some point, it passes through an area with significant RF interference that is caused by a road side unit (RSU). In B, a jamming situation is presented.

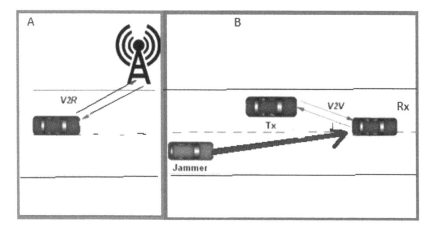

Figure 7.1 Considered topology in this chapter. In A, the interference only situation; in B, the jamming situation with the presence of a moving Jammer. Blue arrows represent LOS V2V wireless communication.

The traveling speed of R_x, namely u_{Rx}, is equal to the traveling speed of T_x, namely u_{Tx}. Upon spotting its target, the jammer begins following it and starts jamming either continuously or periodically (in order to stay undetected for as long as possible). This jamming behavior summarizes all the potential DoS jamming attacks.

For the representation of the wireless channel between T_x and R_x we use an advanced V2V stochastic model that takes into account the multipath effect in VANETs. The received signal at the receiver node is the legitimated transmit ted signal from the transmitter added by the jamming signal from the jammer through the stochastic wireless V2V channel and is modeled as the relation (2) in [17].

The relative speed metric (Δu) defined as the relative speed between the jammer and the receiver [16]:

$$\Delta u = \left| \vec{u}_{J_x} - \vec{u}_{R_x} \right| \tag{7.1}$$

where u_{J_x} and u_{R_x} are the speed of the jammer and the speed of the receiver, respectively.

In order to include the relative speed between the jammer and the receiver in the channel model of jammer-receiver (see the relation (11) in [17]), we write the Doppler frequency $f_{D,j}$ from the transmitted signal by the jammer as:

$$fD,j = \frac{\Delta u f_c \cos\phi}{c} \tag{7.2}$$

where f_c is the carrier frequency with a value of 5.9 GHz (which is the band dedicated to V2V communication). Also, $\cos \varphi_i$ is the incidence angle of departure (AOD) between the jammer and the receiver and c is the speed of light.

7.3.2 Jamming Attack Scenarios

We investigated three different attack scenarios – namely Interference Scenario, Smart Attack Scenario, and Constant Attack Scenario – each representing a jamming attack case that could affect a VANET in real life.

Interference: In the Interference Scenario, we assume that no jammer is present in the network. This scenario is useful for evaluating the efficiency of our method in differentiating jamming from interference. The vehicle travels, when, at some point, it passes through an area with significant RF interference that affects the communication with other vehicles or the RSU.

Smart Jamming: The Smart Attack Scenario models an intelligent jammer behavior [20]. This "smart" jammer is designed to start transmitting in a reactive way upon sensing energy above a certain threshold. We set the latter to 75 *dBm* as it is empirically determined to be an average threshold between jammer sensitivity and false transmission detection rate [35], [31]. Using this minimum threshold each ongoing transmission can be detected by the reactive jammer. In the case that the detected energy exceeds the threshold during a certain time span, the jammer starts its transmission for a duration of ($T_{duration} = 64\,\mu s$) in order to jam a substantial part of the packet header to prevent being decoded by the receiver. Specifically, a "smart" jammer starts following the victim vehicle, while transmitting a jamming signal. When the jammer reaches its target at a distance of about (8 10) *m*, it retreats to a different position in order to stay undetected and transmits in a reactive way as described above. The most common approach in literature [35] is when the jammer selects its optimal transmission power [9], thus achieving the same disrupt or thwart in the communication (DoS attack) without the need of changing its distance from the target. With our "smart" attack, we aim at affecting the communication of the T_x-R_x pair, with the jammer detection being more difficult, pointing out the importance of the proposed *V RS* metric for the detection accuracy results. For that reason, the "smart" jammer alters also its position with the aim of staying unde-tected. The rate of the jamming signal transmission can vary, representing different "smart" jamming strategies. We represent a jamming behavior that has the form of a periodic reactive jammer that increases its transmis-sion rate as it approaches the target so that the jammer remains undetected and increases its efficiency at the same time. We span the transmission rate of the reactive jammer in the interval [10,100] signals per detected 802.11p frame. This jamming behavior simulates the periodic jamming behavior only when the attacker detects that there is a 802.11p frame on the air. The reason that increases its transmission rate is to worsen the consequences of the RF jamming attack on the wireless communication between T_x and R_x. This type of "smart" jammer represents a form of a hybrid jamming behavior that combines reactive jamming with periodic jamming (since the periodic jamming attack only takes place for a short time). The periodic jamming signal is characterized by a 64 μs ON phase (the reactive jamming signal duration) and a 10 μs OFF/sleeping phase.

Constant Jamming: In the Constant Attack Scenario, we study the case of a jammer that follows the receiver while transmitting constantly at mini-mum power. When the jammer reaches its target, it begins transmitting constantly with its full power without any intention to stay undetected, as in the Smart Attack Scenario.

The **Constant** and the **Smart** jammer profiles in Figure 7.2 compare the time domain with a default 802.11p transmission. We observe that the **Smart** jamming attack is targeting the preamble and the physical layer con-vergence protocol (PLCP) header so that 802.11p cannot be decoded on the receiver.

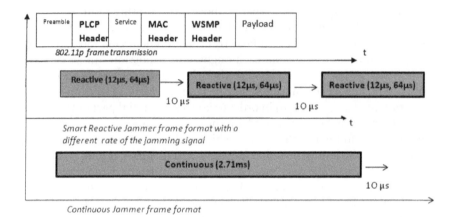

Figure 7.2 **Constant** and the **Smart** jammer profiles in the time domain compared with a default 802.11p transmission.

7.3.3 Estimation of Relative Speed Metric

In this section, we present the estimated relative speed (Δu) value that indicates the relative speed between the jammer and the victim's vehicle. Based on the obtained values, the $V\,RS$ metric is created and then used for classification.

In our system model, a fixed number of known pilot symbols are sent using the wireless IEEE 802.11p standard [25] over consecutive time instants from the transmitter to the receiver. At the same time, the jammer simultaneously transmits over consecutive time instants random jamming symbols to the receiver. Afterward, the combined channel between the T_x and the R_x, with the intervention of the J_x, is estimated using a minimum mean square error (MMSE) estimator [37]. Each one of the channel values between transmitter-receiver and jammer-receiver can be estimated with the elimination method for the linear system that is created after sending the specific pilot symbols at successive time instants (see equation (9) in [17]). By exploiting the Doppler effect to model the line of sight (LOS) channel h_2 between J_x-R_x and also the relative speed value being integrated into the Doppler frequency in (7.2), we can estimate the above relative speed value as described in [17].

7.3.4 The variations of relative speed ($V\,RS$) Algorithm

To make our detection method robust, except relying only on the physical and network layer metrics, we also use the $V\,RS$ metric that is derived from the application layer and can be efficiently estimated from the exchange of

RF signals. Our method uses this new metric as an extra feature in a cross-layer approach, so as to increase classification efficiency.

To generate the VRS metric for classification, we make three fundamental assumptions:

1. When the relative speed is equal to zero and remains unchanged, it indicates the existence of a constant jammer that follows the victim vehicle.
2. When the relative speed is not equal to zero and remains unchanged, it indicates the absence of a moving jammer as the relative speed is equal to the speed of the receiver and the speed of the jammer is equal to zero.
3. When the relative speed is not equal to zero for a period of time and then becomes zero while remaining unchanged, it indicates the existence of a jammer that begins following the target after reaching it.

7.3.5 Proposed IDS Based on Supervised Learning

The supervised learning methods that are used in this work are KNN [36] and Random Forests [21]. Both supervised learning techniques are very popular, with the KNN being robust against noisy training data like the ones obtained from a real-life urban environment and Random Forests being one of the most accurate algorithms, due to the fact that it reduces the chance of over-fitting (by averaging several trees, there is a significantly lower chance of over-fitting). Our detection scheme is currently based on offline training that leverages the use of a dataset of collected measurements in order to train the classifier. As mentioned earlier, our method uses the new VRS metric, as an extra feature in a cross-layer approach, along with other metrics from the physical layer for the classification process.

To avoid testing with "previously seen data", thus leading to biased classification results, we have to ensure that the training and testing sets are completely separated. So prior to presenting the classification results, we have to define the size of the training and testing sets as well as the total number of observations used, so as to make them more interpretable. To avoid over-fitting only 30% of the total number of the observations are used for training, while the remaining 70% for testing.

7.4 ENHANCING THE PROPOSED IDS WITH DATA FUSION TECHNIQUES

Each of the used supervised machine learning algorithms is able to generate accurate results when implemented independently. However, the combined use of these algorithms may help improve the overall performance of the proposed IDS. Different methodologies were evaluated to assess whether the classification results could be improved, for instance, by applying data fusion techniques.

Ensemble learning has been used to combine the outputs from different classification techniques [2]. Ensemble learning is the process in which multiple classifiers are strategically selected and combined in order to solve a particular computational intelligence problem. This method is primarily used to improve the classification performance of a model. One of the commonly used ensemble learning algorithms is known as bagging [12]. The idea of bagging is simple: we want to fit several independent models and "average" their predictions in order to obtain a model with a lower variance [33]. In this method, bootstrapped replicas of the training data for each classifier (*RaFo*, *KNN*) are used. Thus, for each instance of the testing dataset, the probability for each of the three classes examined is estimated separately from each classification algorithm. Since the intended output of the IDS is a combination of the two classification algorithms, the conditional probabilities are estimated for each class in the presented IDS using the Bayesian rule as a data fusion technique. During the last step of bagging, the majority voting combination rule is used in order to decide the final prediction of the detection system. The chart of Figure 7.3 represents all the steps for the proposed data fusion method between the *KNN* and the *RaFo* algorithm.

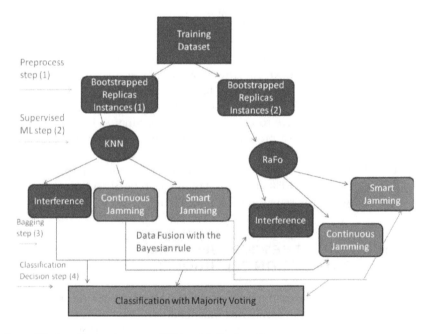

Figure 7.3 Data Fusion between *KNN* and *RaFo* algorithms.

7.5 SIMULATION AND PERFORMANCE EVALUATION

Regarding the details of our simulation setup, the speed of the vehicles involved in the legitimate communication (u_{Tx}, R_x) is in the range (15 to 25) m/s, the initial distance between the jammer and the pair of R_x-T_x ($dist_{initial}$) is 200 m, the distance that separates the receiver from the transmitter throughout the course of the simulation ($dist_{Tx}$, R_x) is 35 m as well as the power of all the transmitted signals (P_{Tx},J_x) is 100 mW and the reference distance ($dist_{ref}$) is 100 m with which the path loss component is estimated. Last, the minimum receiver sensitivity threshold is –85 dBm.

Each signal that is transmitted from both the jammer and the transmitter consists of streams that are 500 bits long. In all scenarios, the Transmission Rate of the transmitter is (TR_{Tx} =100 packets/s). Using a time sample of 0.1 s, we simulate the system for 100 s and obtain 1000 measurements.

We used Veins that combines the simulation of urban mobility (SUMO) and the OMNET++/VEINS [34]. SUMO is adopted as our traffic simulator and OMNET++ is used to simulate wireless communication. Furthermore, the GEMV (a geometry-based efficient propagation model for V2V) [7] tool was integrated into the VEINS network simulator for a more realistic simulation of the PHY layer [20]. Last, to set up and test our classification algorithms for the RF jamming attacks detection on the previously obtained data, we chose to use the programming language R [1]. Part of the Erlangen city (see the Evaluation Setup in [18]) is used for conducting the simulations.

7.5.1 Detection Performance under Different Δu Values

Our RF jamming attack detection system is based on offline training, using a dataset of measurements collected under a transmitter-receiver speed of 15 m/s or 25 m/s so as to train the classifier prior to its use for testing. We evaluate the proposed detection system using data measurements of a speed of 15 m/s or a higher speed at about 25 m/s. In Table 7.1, we summarize the

Table 7.1 Classification Accuracy Percentages While Training Lower and Higher Speed Measurements

	Train with 15 m/s	Train with 25 m/s
Test with 15 m/s (KNN)	82.27%	74.31%
Test with 15 m/s (RaFo)	80.04%	74.41%
Test with 25 m/s (KNN)	66.97%	94.46%
Test with 25 m/s (RaFo)	69.84%	94.61%

classification accuracy, exploiting the usage of the proposed VRS metric s an extra feature, achieved while training with measurements from a speed of 15 m/s and a speed of 25 m/s, respectively.

From these classification results, a basic conclusion can be made. There is an increase in the classification accuracy when the training is done using data from a higher speed. The higher classification accuracy comes from the fact that the increase in speed adversely influences the effects of jamming. More concretely, in the *Constant Attack Scenario* the jammer overtakes the sender-receiver pair faster and in the *Interference Scenario* the sender-receiver pair remains in the jamming area for a shorter period of time, and in the *Smart Attack Scenario* the jammer reaches its target faster, thus the gradual effect of the jamming observed at lower speeds is greatly reduced. All the above lead to a significant increase in the quality of the measurements obtained, hence leading to higher classification accuracy as well as to a better distinction between the different types of jammers affecting the communication.

In order to investigate how the proposed VRS metric affects the RF jamming attack detection in a two-class classification problem between the (*Smart Attack, Interference*) classes, the two investigated RF jamming scenarios (*Continuous Attack, Smart Attack*) are incorporated in one class. The measurements used in the training set are collected under a speed equal to 18 *m/s* while the measurements used in testing are collected under the same speed. We evaluated the performance of our attack detector by using a detection rate and receiver operating characteristic (ROC) curve in Figure 7.4a. In this figure, the influence of using the VRS feature to detect the RF jamming attack for each false positive rate (FPR) value is clear. The accuracy achieved for detecting the RF jamming attack using the *KNN* algorithm is 86% in the case that the VRS metric is used, while when the VRS metric is not used, the accuracy is 69% (see Figure 7.4a). Using the *RaFo* algorithm, the accuracy achieved for detecting the RF jamming attack is 88% when the VRS metric is used and 60% without it (see Figure 7.4b).

Consequently, the effect of the proposed VRS metric is more obvious when we use the *RaFo* algorithm.

We investigate now the detection rate of the proposed IDS in a multi-class problem in which all three classes (*Smart Attack, Continuous Attack, Interference*) are taken into account. We present the below *confusion matrices* in Tables 7.2 and 7.3 using the *KNN* algorithm depending on whether the VRS metric is used or not, where the rows represent classification output while the columns represent the ground truth. In these experiments, the measurements used in the training set are collected at a higher speed at about 20 m/s while the measurements used in testing are collected under the same speed.

We can observe that when the VRS metric is used among the other features for training and testing the supervised machine learning algorithms we have a perfect differentiation between the *Interference* and *RF Jamming*

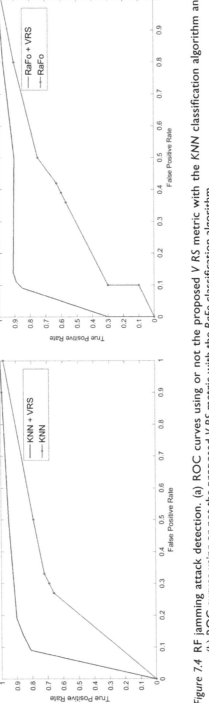

Figure 7.4 RF jamming attack detection. (a) ROC curves using or not the proposed *V RS* metric with the *KNN* classification algorithm and (b) ROC curves using or not the proposed *V RS* metric with the *RaFo* classification algorithm.

Table 7.2 Confusion Matrix Using the $V RS$ Metric among Features

Scenario	Interference	Smart attack	Constant attack
Interference	703	0	0
Smart attack	0	399	17
Constant attack	0	286	654

Table 7.3 Confusion Matrix without Using the $V RS$ Metric among Features

Scenario	Interference	Smart attack	Constant attack
Interference	688	2	3
Smart attack	1	411	30
Constant attack	14	272	638

cases while there are some misclassifications between the two forms of the RF jamming attacks (see Table 7.2). Specifically, the accuracy of the prediction model achieved in the case that the $V RS$ metric is used with the *KNN* algorithm is 85.28%, while when the $V RS$ is not used, the accuracy is 82.9%. On the other hand, using the *RaFo* algorithm, the accuracy achieved in the case that the $V RS$ metric is used is 91% and 86% without it.

Last, we want to investigate the accuracy achieved with the *RaFo* algorithm when the *"smart" jammer* differentiates its transmission rate as it approaches the target. As mentioned in Section 7.3.2 this jamming behavior has the form of a periodic reactive jammer that increases its transmission rate as it approaches the target so that the jammer remains undetected and increases its efficiency at the same time. We span the transmission rate of the reactive jammer in the interval [10,100] signals per detected 802.11p frame. In Figure 7.5, the accuracy results for detecting a reactive jamming attack are presented when the transmission range of the reactive jammer spans in the interval [10,100] signals per detected 802.11p frame.

When the jammer transmits 10 signals per detected 802.11p frame the accuracy that is achieved using the $V RS$ metric is 90% and 87.5% without using the proposed metric. On the other hand, when the jammer increases its transmission rate at about 100 signals per detected frame the accuracy decreases to 75% in the case that the $V RS$ metric is used and at about 62% without the proposed metric. This deterioration in accuracy results is due to the fact that when the jammer increases its transmission it approaches the continuous jamming behavior leading to some miss-classifications between the two corresponding classes (*Smart Attack, Continuous Attack*).

7.5.2 Evaluation under Different Interference Levels

To verify the robustness of the proposed IDS against the considered RF jamming attacks we evaluate different node density values in the area.

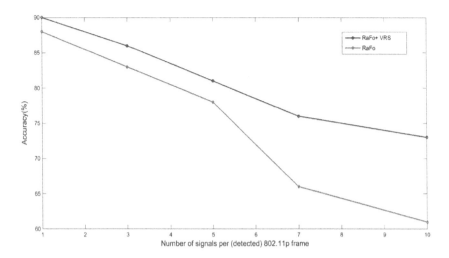

Figure 7.5 Reactive jamming detection accuracy with a "smart" jammer that differentiates its transmission rate.

The SINR feature is defined in (7.3) as the power of a certain signal of
interest (P_{Tx}) plus the power of the jamming signal sent by the jammer
to the receiver (P_{Jx}) divided by the sum of the interference power (from
all the other interfering signals) (I) and the power of some background
noise (N).

$$SINR = \frac{P_{Tx} + P_{Jx}}{I + N} \qquad (7.3)$$

Therefore, the denominator of this parameter incorporates the different
considered node density values. In Figure 7.6a the SINR values are presented for a low node density scenario with 10 interfering nodes compared
with the case in which in the same interference levels there is also a "smart"
jammer in the area. Each scenario consists of 400 time steps with red color
representing the *Interference + Smart Jammer* scenario and with blue color
representing the *Interference* only scenario. Here, we can observe that there
is a perfect separation of the SINR values between the two investigating
cases. In Figure 7.6b the SINR values are presented for a high node density
scenario with 100 interfering nodes compared with the case of the presence
also of a "smart" jammer in the area. On the contrary, using these interference levels there is no clear separation between the SINR values of the considered scenarios. This fact can lead to several misclassifications between
these cases. This is due to the fact that in the case of 100 interfering nodes
the interference power is greatly increased in the denominator relative to the
power of the jamming signal in the numerator. As a result, the effects of the
"smart" jamming attack are less obvious in these interference levels. This

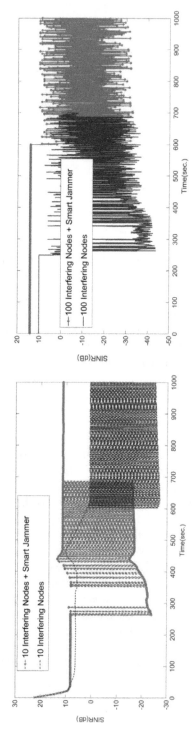

Figure 7.6 SINR values for different node density values. (a) Comparison of the SINR values between the *Interference* case and the *Smart Jamming* case in low-density values and (b) comparison of the SINR values between the *Interference* case and the *Smart Jamming* case in high-density values.

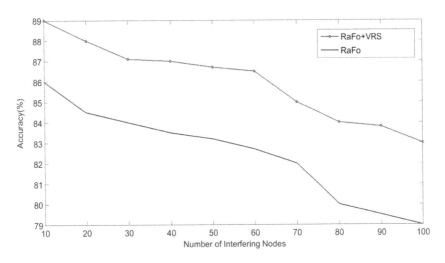

Figure 7.7 RF jamming detection accuracy with different node density values.

fact demonstrates the need for using upper layers features for the classification process that are related to the moving pattern of the jammer.

Based on the above analysis we can conclude that the higher the density
of nodes in the area, the lower the accuracy rates for detecting an RF jamming attack using the proposed IDS are (see Figure 7.7). When there are 10
interfering nodes in the area, the accuracy that is achieved using the VRS
metric is 89% and 86% without using the proposed metric. On the other
hand, when the interfering nodes increase to 100 in the area, the accuracy
decreases to 83% in the case that the VRS metric is used and at about 79%
without the proposed metric.

7.5.3 Data Fusion Results

In this subsection, we want to combine the two supervised machine learning
classifiers $(KNN, RaFo)$ to achieve better performance than a single decision from one classifier as explained in detail in Section 7.4. In Figure 7.8,
the accuracy results achieved for the RF jamming attack detection by the
data fusion technique are compared with those achieved using only KNN
or $RaFo$. The above-reported accuracy results have been plotted using a
ROC for each classifier and a different ROC for the data fusion technique.

7.6 DISCUSSION AND CONCLUSIONS

In this chapter, we presented a new approach for detecting a specific type
of DoS attack, namely RF jamming, based on a cross-layer set of features
and supervised machine learning. We introduced a novel metric from the

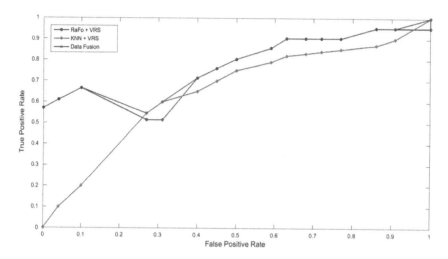

Figure 7.8 Accuracy evaluation for RF jamming attack detection comparison among Data Fusion, *KNN*, and *RaFo*.

application layer, namely the *variations of the relative speed* between the jammer and the target. The relative speed is passively estimated from the combined value of the desired and the jamming signal at the target vehicle in combination with metrics from the network, and the physical layer can be used in a cross-layer approach for detecting an RF jamming attack. To evaluate the significance of the proposed metric and its effect on detection rate, we implemented three different scenarios – two with a jammer and one with interference only.

With our work, we introduced a proactive approach against potential RF jamming attacks, which is able to differentiate interference from malicious RF jamming. Additionally, it is able to distinguish the unique characteristics of each attack, especially when the offline training is conducted with a higher speed than 15 *m/s*. We also evaluated the effect of a range of relative speed values in RF jamming detection rates. The higher the relative speed between jammer-receiver, the higher the percentages of detection probability of the RF jamming attack. This particular fact is due to the specifics attributed to the considered RF jamming attack.

Through our evaluation results, we were able to highlight the vital role of the relative speed and its variations, in addition to other metrics obtained from the physical layer, in jamming detection and unintentional jamming cases differentiation, as well as in the overall increase in the prediction accuracy. Specifically, using the proposed $V\ RS$ metric among the other features for training and testing we achieved an increase of RF jamming detection accuracy over 10% under certain conditions and "smart" jamming strategies (e.g. relative speed values, node densities in the area, or transmission rate of the jammer). Last, a data fusion method is presented that combines the outcomes of the two used supervised machine learning algorithms.

As our future work, the proposed IDS can be upgraded to a real-time RF jamming detection system, in which for the training process the past measurements named historical data will be used.

7.7 GLOSSARY

CAVs	Connected Autonomous Vehicles
ITS	Intelligent Transportation Systems
CAMs	Cooperative Awareness Messages
DSRC	Dedicated Short Range Communication
WAVE	Wireless Access in Vehicular Environments
DoS	Denial of Service
VANET	Vehicular Ad-Hoc Network
RF	Radio Frequency
KNN	k-Nearest Neighbors
RaFo	Random Forests
IDS	Intrusion Detection System
VRS	Variations of Relative Speed
HY	Physical layer
MAC	Media Access Control
RSSI	Received Signal Strength Indicator
SINR	Signal to Interference and Noise Ratio
PDR	Packet Delivery Ratio
V2V	Vehicle-to-Vehicle
MMSE	Minimum Mean Square Error
LOS	Line of Sight
ROC	Receiver Operating Characteristic Curve

REFERENCES

1. What is r? https://www.r-project.org/about.html, 2017.
2. Fran J. Aparicio-Navarro, K. G. Kyriakopoulos, and D. J. Parish. A multi-layer data fusion system for wi-fi attack detection using automatic belief assignment. In *World Congress on Internet Security (WorldCIS)*, pages 45–50, 2012.
3. Meysam Azizian, Soumaya Cherkaoui, and Abdelhakim Senhaji Hafid. Link activation with parallel interference cancellation in multi-hop VANET. In *IEEE 84th Vehicular Technology Conference (VTC-Fall)*, 2016.
4. Ikechukwu K. Azogu, Michael T. Ferreira, Jonathan A. Larcom, and Hong Liu. A new anti-jamming strategy for VANET metrics-directed security defense. In *IEEE Globecom Workshops (GC Wkshps)*, pages 1344–1349, 2013.

5. E. Bayraktaroglu, C. King, X. Liu, G. Noubir, R. Rajaraman, and B. Thapa. On the performance of ieee 802.11 under jamming. *INFOCOM, 2008 Proceedings IEEE*, April 2008.

6. A. Benslimane and H. Nguyen-Minh. Jamming attack model and detection method for beacons under multichannel operation in vehicular networks, *IEEE Transactions on Vehicular Technology*, 66(7), 6475–6488, 2017.

7. Mate Boban, João Barros, and Ozan K. Tonguz. Geometry-based vehicle-to-vehicle channel modeling for large-scale simulation, *IEEE Transactions on Vehicular Technology*, 63, 4146–4164, 2016.

8. Darren Cottingham. What is vehicle platooning? Driving Tests. https://www.drivingtests.co.nz/resources/ what-is-vehicle-platooning/, 2017.

9. S. D'Oro, E. Ekici, and S. Palazzo. Optimal power allocation and scheduling under jamming attacks, *IEEE/ACM Transactions on Networking*, 25(3), 1310–1323, 2017.

10. Z. Feng and C. Hua. Machine learning-based rf jamming detection in wireless networks. In *Third International Conference on Security of Smart Cities, Industrial Control System and Communications (SSIC)*, pages 1–6, 2018.

11. Mohamed Amine Ferrag, Leandros Maglaras, Antonios Argyriou, Dimitrios Kosmanos, and Helge Janicke. Security for 4G and 5G cellular networks: A survey of existing authentication and privacy-preserving schemes, *Journal of Network and Computer Applications*, 101, 3–15, 2018.

12. D. P. Gaikwad and Ravindra C. Thool. Intrusion detection system using bagging ensemble method of machine learning. In *IEEE International Conference on Computing Communication Control and Automation*, 2015.

13. Ali Hamieh, Jalel Ben-Othman, and Lynda Mokdad. Detection of radio interference attacks in VANET. In *Global Telecommunications Conference, 2009. GLOBECOM 2009*, pages 1–5. IEEE, 2009.

14. Alex Herm. Assume self-driving cars are a hacker's dream? Think again. https://www.theguardian.com/technology/2017/aug/30/ self-driving-cars-hackers-security, 2017. [Online; Accessed 30 August 2017].

15. S. G. Hymlin Rose and T. Jayasree. Detection of jamming attack using timestamp for WSN, *Ad Hoc Networks*, 91, 101874, 2019.

16. Dimitrios Karagiannis and Antonios Argyriou. Jamming attack detection in a pair of RF communicating vehicles using unsupervised machine learning, *Vehicular Communications on Elsevier*, 13, 56–63, 2018.

17. Dimitrios Kosmanos, Antonios Argyriou, and Leandros Maglaras. Estimating the relative speed of RF jammers in VANETs, *Security and Communication Networks*, 2019. November.

18. Dimitrios Kosmanos, Leandros Maglaras, Michalis Mavrovouniotis, Sotiris Moschoyiannis, Antonios Argyriou, Athanasios Maglaras, and Helge Janicke. Route optimization of electric vehicles based on dynamic wireless charging, *IEEE Access*, 6, 42551–42565, 2018.

19. Dimitrios Kosmanos, Apostolos Pappas, Leandros Maglaras, Francisco J. Aparicio Navarro, Helge Janicke, Eerke Boiten, and Antonios Argyriou. Intrusion detection system for platooning connected autonomous vehicles. *SEEDA-CECNSM Conference*, 2019.

20. Dimitrios Kosmanos, Nikolas Prodromou, Antonios Argyriou, Leandros A. Maglaras, and Helge Janicke. MIMO techniques for jamming threat suppression in vehicular networks. In *Mobile Information Systems*, 2016, pages 1–9. Hindawi Publishing Corporation, 2016.

21. Andy Liaw, Matthew Wiener, et al. Classification and regression by random forest, *R news*, 2, 18–22, 2002.
22. Z. Lu, W. Wang, and C. Wang. From jammer to gambler: Modeling and detection of jamming attacks against time-critical traffic. In *Proceedings IEEE INFOCOM*, pages 1871–1879, 2011.
23. N. Lyamin, D. Kleyko, Q. Delooz, and A. Vinel. Real-time jamming dos detection in safety-critical v2v c-its using data mining, *IEEE Communications Letters*, 23(3), 442–445, 2019.
24. Sharaf Malebary and Wenyuan Xu. A survey on jamming in vanet, *International Journal of Scientific Research and Innovative Technology*, 2(1), 142–56, 2015.
25. Sharaf Malebary, Wenyuan Xu, and Chin-Tser Huang. Jamming mobility in 802.11 p networks: Modeling, evaluation, and detection. In *IEEE 35th International on Performance Computing and Communications Conference (IPCCC)*, pages 1–7, 2016.
26. A. Marttinen, A. Wyglinski, and R. Jantti. Statistics-based jamming detection algorithm for jamming attacks against tactical MANETs. In *Military Communications Conference (MILCOM)*. IEEE, 2014, October.
27. N. I. Mowla, N. H. Tran, I. Doh, and K. Chae. Federated learning-based cognitive detection of jamming attack in flying ad-hoc network, *IEEE Access*, 8, 4338–4350, 2020.
28. D. Nguyen, C. Sahin, B. Shishkin, N. Kandasamy, and K. R. Dandekar. A real-time and protocol-aware reactive jamming framework built on software-defined radios. In *Proceedings of the 2014 ACM Workshop on Software Radio Implementation Forum, ser.* SRIF '14. ACM, New York, NY, 2014.
29. B. Brian Park, Katherine Asmussen, Gabriella Griener, and Inki Kim. How does a human interact with platooning automated vehicles? https://www.roa dsbridges.com/how-does-human-interact-platooning-automated-vehicles, 2019.
30. Oscar Pun˜al, Ismet Aktaş, Caj-Julian Schnelke, Gloria Abidin, Klaus Wehrle, and James Gross. Machine learning-based jamming detection for IEEE 802.11: Design and experimental evaluation. In *IEEE 15th International Symposium on a World of Wireless, Mobile and Multimedia Networks (WoWMoM)*, pages 1–10, 2014.
31. Oscar Punal, Carlos Pereira, Ana Aguiar, and James Gross. Experimental characterization and modeling of RF jamming attacks on VANETs, *IEEE Transactions on Vehicular Technology*, 64, 524–540, 2015.
32. Joseph Rocca. Ensemble methods: Bagging, boosting and stacking. https://to wardsdatascience.com/ensemble-methods-bagging-boosting-and-stacking-c9 214a10a205, 2019.
33. Christoph Sommer, Reinhard German, and Falko Dressler. Bidirectionally coupled network and road traffic simulation for improved IVC analysis, *IEEE Transactions on Mobile Computing*, 10(1), 3–15, 2015.
34. Mario Strasser, Boris Danev, and Capkun Srdjan. Detection of reactive jamming in sensor networks, *ACM Transactions on Sensor Networks (TOSN)*, 7, 1–29, 2010.
35. Oliver Sutton. Introduction to k nearest neighbour classification and condensed nearest neighbour data reduction. University lectures, University of Leicester, 2012.

36. David Tse and Pramod Viswanath. *Fundamentals of Wireless Communication.* Cambridge University Press, 2005.
37. M. Wilhelm, I. Martinovic, J. B. Schmitt, and V. Lenders. Short paper: Reactive jamming in wireless networks: How realistic is the threat? In *Proceedings of the Fourth ACM Conference on Wireless Network Security,* 2011.
38. S. Xu, W. Xu, C. Pan, and M. Elkashlan. Detection of jamming attack in non-coherent massive simo systems, *IEEE Transactions on Information Forensics and Security,* 14(9), 2387–2399, 2019.

Chapter 8

Smart Cars and Over-the-Air Updates

Panagiotis Efstathiadis, Anna Karanika,
Nestoras Chouliaras, Leandros Maglaras,
and Ioanna Kantzavelou

8.1 INTRODUCTION

Researchers have been studying ways to create the ultimate smart car. The term smart car refers to a vehicle that is provided with a specific level of driving automation. At this point, smart cars are not self-driving cars; a lot of efforts are made in that direction, but the existing technology has not reached such high levels of artificial intelligence needed for the successful automation of cars. According to the Society of Automotive Engineers, driving automation is regarded in six separate levels [10], ranging from no to some to full automation. In particular, smaller systems are being developed separately, such as systems for vision-guided automatic parking [12], context-awareness [30], [29], turn signaling [4], security using face detection and recognition [11], [21], speed control, and steering [35].

Many smart car systems are built to work in a distributed manner, therefore requiring connection and communication with other systems, over a network that is either wireless or not. Moreover, just as any other system, smart car systems have to be updated to newer versions whenever they are available. Over-the-air (OTA) updates constitute a technology that has been developed, tried, and tested in the telecommunications sector and research on it has started in the automotive industry, seeing as it has several benefits. Nevertheless, any connection with an external network is by default a security vulnerability and must be treated as such. Hence, a solution must be found to overcome such an issue and not let it cause problems to the aforementioned systems. If a threat is actually realized, systems could malfunction and be the cause of an accident that may even cost people their lives.

Even though OTA updates seem like a panacea, new vulnerabilities occur. An attacker could take control if they introduced a malicious update to a vehicle either at the back end or in transit [9]. History has shown software systems are most at risk of lapses in safety and security when undergoing change [2]. An OTA update is a substantial change; therefore, it is essential security is paramount. Having in mind to present a holistic model of a smart car that includes all different technologies that make the car "smart" European Union Agency for Cybersecurity (ENISA) issued a report last

DOI: 10.1201/9781003109952-8

year where relevant threats and cybersecurity risks pertaining to smart cars are analyzed and several security measures are proposed. The report takes into account the particularities of this highly complex, heterogenous, and volatile environment and the fact that no modern system can be analyzed in isolation. In this report, the interconnection of sensors, AI, machine learning algorithms, cloud computing, and connectivity is presented and threats that come from all these components of a smart car are analyzed. In one of the scenarios presented in the report, large-scale deployment of rogue firmware after hacking original equipment manufacturers (OEMs) back end servers affects OTA and consequently the proper behavior of the vehicle.

The rest of this section is organized as follows. Section 8.2 comprised an offer to the automotive industry. On the contrary, Section 8.3 presents a multitude of threats and vulnerabilities that arise via the use of such technology. Section 8.4 is concerned with displaying existing solutions to those problems. In Section 8.5, a discussion about our findings is exhibited. Lastly, Section 8.6 is dedicated to final conclusions on the matter of smart cars and over-the-air updates with an emphasis on security.

8.2 BENEFITS

All the way back in 2007, the authors of [25] suggested the use of the firmware update over-the-air (FOTA) technology in the automotive industry to increase client satisfaction. More specifically, they cited the following reasons as incentives for the technology's employment. First, it might not always be easy for a vehicle to be taken to the mechanic for a firmware update to be installed; this solution provides location independence. Second, the downtime for the installation can be lower when the over-the-air technology is utilized as the vehicle would not need to be taken to the mechanic. Just considering the time it takes for the trip to the dealer is motivation enough for applying FOTA. However, it is not the only reason; downtime could be delayed even further since there could be a waiting queue for the vehicle to be plugged in and its firmware updated. Moreover, as the updates' normal installation through a wire is covered in the car's warranty, technicians — and customers — are bound to lose time and money, since they could otherwise be working on a different, paying task; therefore, over-the-air updates reduce warranty cost for automotive companies and simplify the procedure for everyone involved. Further, such a conveniently easy manner of installing firmware updates could make way for an active correction cycle; in particular, new updates — including bug fixes and new features — can be installed, tested, reviewed, and extended rather fast, resulting in the achievement of vast improvements on the product's quality. Not to mention, manufacturing companies could receive diagnostics and create trustworthy statistics on the success or failure of certain features' implementation and configurations, which would allow them to have superior control with less cost. In addition, the firmware updates could be stored at a cloud server that checks for data quality and not is distributed to the multitude of dealers for them to misplace or damage the related files. This method of installation could guarantee that a vehicle is always updated to the latest software and the update's time to market (TTM) is reduced. What is more, in case the customer is not available to actively initiate the update, since an electronic control unit (ECU) sometimes must be reprogrammed without delay for security reasons, a forced update installation could be automatically scheduled for when the vehicle is inactive, just as it is already happening for personal computers and mobile devices. On top of that, FOTA could increase the safety of a vehicle; since FOTA could be responsible for a decrease in TTM, important security updates would be very likely to be installed much sooner than otherwise expected and numerous accidents that would be the result of faulty software could be avoided earlier than it would be possible with the installation of firmware updates by the dealer over a cable. Besides, the FOTA technology has already been developed and tested in the telecommunications industry and works well enough to have been established as a robust technology. Therefore, it can be adopted in the automotive industry without too many alterations; after all, the "wheel" has already been invented. Consequently, as the authors of [20] also mention, automotive software over-the-air updates will lead to higher customer satisfaction, lower maintenance expenses, quality refinement, and, last but not least, a rise in sales without too much cost.

In recent years, more and more functionalities in a vehicle have switched from mechanical to electronic implementation. Such changes have resulted in the software that is embedded into vehicles growing in size. Thus, more and larger updates are required now than ever before, and over-the-air updates can facilitate the process to the utmost extent [32].

In [5], an improvement to OTA updates for smart vehicles is proposed; instead of storing related files and offering update services from a cloud data center, the authors suggest using fog computing. Seeing as fog nodes would be much closer to the majority of associated vehicles, especially with the employment of the mobility management algorithm they propose to monitor the mobility of smart vehicles and adjust service locations, OTA update installation would become much faster.

8.3 THREATS AND VULNERABILITIES

In the continuation of our work, we will study and present some of the most important vulnerabilities of smart cars and more specifically of their feature for system updates over-the-air. As we can understand, big new automotive companies such as Tesla, alongside the old companies such as Ford or BMW, which are trying to move on from traditional cars to smart cars, are creating and testing new models and they are building new operating systems to improve critical parts of their smart cars in every sector. Therefore, if we treat all these cars as standalone computers, we will observe many common threats. In contrast to computers, mobile phones, and all the other internet of things (IoT) devices, an accident with a car can cost many human lives, so there is certainly no room for errors in these operating systems. In addition to the loss of human life, we must also consider the damage that can be brought on to a business's finances and its image to the consumer public.

8.3.1 Smart Car Components

Modern smart cars consist of about 60 to 100 electronic control units (ECUs). All these electronic control units handle all types of functions inside and outside of the smart cars as they are connected to 75 or more sensors (radar, sonar, camera, acceleration gauge, thermometer, rainfall sensor, etc.). Communication between them is achieved using a bus where any message is sent to the connected parts. The networks that are more important for our survey, and we can read more about in [28], are controller area network (CAN), local interconnect network (LIN), FlexRay (same as CAN but with significantly better speeds), and media oriented systems transport (MOST). Among these networks, the controlled area network (CAN) is the most vulnerable target. Apart from internal communication networks, automotive cars, just as any other IoT device, enable Wi-Fi, Bluetooth, and global system for mobile communications (GSM) connections, benefits that every passenger uses, but they can be dangerous, especially when they are used to update software.

8.3.2 The Attacker's Targets

The reasons why someone would attack a car, according to [28] and [27], are the following:

1. Theft
   The main problem of a traditional, vintage, human-driven car is theft. Stolen cars are divided into spare parts, and the parts that are in good condition are sold directly to illegal traders and the rest are either repaired and sold at a slightly lower price or given for scrap. Now, with respect to cars, prices are even bigger for good parts. New electronic parts are very expensive to buy, so spare parts have increased demand.
2. Planned accidents
   The hacker seeks to gain control of the vehicle in order to create a pre-planned accident. Some ways to achieve this are by (i) locking the brake system, (ii) stopping the car's engine while the car is on the road, or (iii) blocking the steering system.

3. Interception of personal data
   Information such as paired phones, call history, geolocation data, and installed applications are sensitive and could lead to other data leaks.
4. ECU source code theft
   Hackers motivated by rival motor industries could be hired to use packet-sniffing tools on automotive networks. This way someone could use a backdoor to get into a car's ECU system, get its source code, and copy patents or methodologies.
5. Tuning and other improvements
   Every car would become of higher quality if its horsepower is upgraded or its engine torque is changed. Also, cars whose mileage has been reduced are sold at higher prices. To install spare parts on smart cars, someone must have certain admin rights to bypass software restrictions. All the above processes can be avoided if the car's operating system is hacked.
6. Ethical hacking
   There are individuals who see it as a challenge to hack a smart car. They can help companies guard their cars against potential threats by finding new vulnerabilities.

Although several defense mechanisms have been developed, attackers made many successful tries. Some of the results that have been noticed are increased access to unauthorized users, corruption of data, denial of service (DoS) and distributed denial of service (DDoS) attacks on cars, and car theft.

8.3.3 Over-the-Air Updates and Security Issues

The software running on electronic devices is regularly updated these days. Vehicles are a very special and distinct category compared to other consumer devices, and as such, they are handled very carefully for safety reasons that are critical in the automotive domain. New firmware versions that will improve a vehicle's performance are deployed every day. From time to time, there have been significant vulnerabilities that have led manufacturing companies to recall massively large batches of new vehicle models, as described in [14]. As an example, Chrysler had to recall 1.4 million vehicles in 2015, while a Jeep Cherokee was remotely hacked into by two security researchers. Adversaries used the infotainment system as the entry point to dashboard functions, steering, brakes, and transmission using a laptop connected to Sprint's cellular network. Similar examples with software issues have been analyzed in [25].

Recently, several scholars have researched the area of security issues of smart cars [17] and especially those related to OTA. An OTA update system must be resilient to spoofing, tampering, repudiation, information leakage, denial-of-service, and escalation-of-privileges attacks, among others. Several security and privacy issues may arise from different parts of the ecosystem, such as cloud, service station, and car or OEM back end and several security methods must be combined in order to counter those threats. The freshness of the update information also needs to be preserved in order to prevent replay attacks. Moreover, software distribution during OTA updates must be arranged in such a way that high security, low latency, and continuous data protection are guaranteed.

8.3.3.1 Classification of OTA Update Attacks

At this point, we will analyze and classify the problems that can occur in a successful attack during OTA updates. The critical categories, according to [19], are the following:

1. Download fail
   If an attacker finds a way and achieves to stop the whole process when the vehicle is downloading the update, we can observe that this does not affect the safety of the vehicle because none of the critical services have been altered. If a scale to evaluate problems were used, this issue would have a low score on the scale.
2. Flashing fail
   Stopping and disabling a software update on a vehicle certainly causes a problem in proper functioning, and we cannot know at first glance which part was most affected, as this depends on the percentage that the update has reached. This issue has a great impact on safety as it could affect ECUs that are responsible for breaking or the steering system of the vehicle.
3. Arbitrary flashing
   In the end, the greatest success for all malicious users is to download and install their own software with which they will have unlimited rights in the management of the hardware. They will be able to change the capabilities of the engine – not only start and stop but torque and horsepower – the behavior of the braking system, the driving assistant system, etc. This would be disastrous for the safety of the passengers, whether they caused it themselves to increase the car's performance or because someone wanted to sabotage a vehicle. Here a high score would be set on the passenger safety threat scale.

   To sum up, we present Table 8.1, which describes the three categories and the safety-security scale from 2 to 8 (8 for the biggest security-safety risk).

8.3.3.2 Attacks on OTA Updates

Malicious users have very specific goals over the OTA updates. The most common issues, as per [19], are those that occur between the server and the vehicle. An attacker can "read updates", "deny updates", "deny

Table 8.1 Safety-Security Levels for ECU Categories on
Firmware Over-the-Air Attacks [19]

ECU categories	Download fall	FOTA attacks Flashing fall	Arbitrary flashing
Powertrain	5	7	8
Vehicle safety	5	7	8
Comfort	3	5	6
Infotainment	2	4	5
Telematics	2	4	5

functionality" and/or "control vehicle". Having these in mind, the appropriate candidate for the breach must have the following skills:

1. Ability to breach communications network
   Using vulnerabilities on a cellular network that is used to reach the update server or using the car's Wi-Fi, Bluetooth, and USB ports to update certain ECUs.
2. Ability to trespass security protocols of ECUs on vehicle
   The ability of an adversary to bypass security and access internal data from external sources.
3. Specialty in cryptography
   The target is to tamper with the signature of the software updates.
4. Access to repository
   Somehow, an attacker could have access to previous updates and could deal with bugs that have not been fixed or may gain access to new patches and in the long run discover new vulnerabilities.

The security attacks that someone may employ to attempt to achieve these goals are based on all the vulnerabilities we encounter between the remote database where upgrades are stored and the most useful systems of a smart car. As described in [13], they are the following:

1. Read updates
   (a) i. Eavesdrop attack
        Unencrypted packets with software updates from the repository used in the over-the-air update could lead to data leaks. To take advantage of this vulnerability, hackers stage an eavesdropping attack. The attack utilizes unsecured network communications to access data as it is being sent or received by smart cars.
2. Deny updates
   (a) Drop-request attack
        Attackers are trying to prevent a car's ECUs from getting any updates. One way to do this is by blocking all network traffic.

(b) Slow-retrieval attack

An attacker responds to clients with a very slow stream of data that essentially results in the client never completing the update process.

(c) Indefinite-freeze attack

An attacker continues to present files to a software update system that the client has already seen. As a result, the client is kept unaware of new files.

(d) Partial-bundle-installation attack

Sometimes this may happen accidentally when the vehicle is running out of power. The main idea here is to try to interrupt certain ECUs when they are in the process of installing updates.

3. Deny functionality

(a) Rollback attack

Invaders are hiding from the update system every new update and keep showing only those who have known problems and issues. Users have no evidence of new software and install only what the hacker wants.

(b) Endless data attack

An attacker accepts a download request that contains loops of streaming of data. This could cause many problems to ECUs such as creating a buffer overflow.

(c) Mixed-bundles attack

Invaders, instead of creating new software, try to install different incompatible software on different ECUs at the same time. The result is that ECUs cannot function properly and cannot interact with each other.

(d) Mix-and-match attack

On repositories, along with the official synchronous updates, there are other older ones, and as a result of this attack, the wrong packages are installed, which can confuse the operating system of the vehicle.

4. Control vehicle

(a) Arbitrary software attack

Lastly, we present the worst situation we can face, i.e., installation of illegal software is completed with or without the owner's consent. In this type of attack, attackers delete the car's official software and install what they need to achieve their goals.

8.4 EXISTING SOLUTIONS

User safety is substantially influenced by the way vehicles are upgraded. Over-the-air updates must follow certain rules in order to guarantee security and passenger safety in smart cars. As technology evolves, new innovative solutions are presented to counter the threats. In this section, we will describe the protection mechanisms that have been built and explore some of their possibilities.

8.4.1 Considerations

In order to identify the best mechanism, in terms of security of updates, [28] stated the following limitations that exist and prevent manufacturers from applying modern technologies to effectively defend a smart vehicle's system.

1. Hardware: Vehicles cannot be compared to computers and mobile phones, because their ECUs are not by any means as powerful as current CPUs. This can directly affect, for example, the application of complicated cryptographic algorithms, seeing as advanced calculations that are needed for strong encryption cannot be completed in real time. Cryptography is a key part of security, and the inability to use it in an impactful way sets smart car security back.
2. Real Time: Although vehicles' ECUs have limited capabilities, OTA updates must be completed within a certain period of time and not occupy the rest of the system for a long time.
3. Autonomy: Functions executed by the security system should be performed as autonomously as possible, without requiring interaction with the driver or owner of the vehicle.
4. Life cycle: Because vehicles have a much longer life cycle than other standard systems, we need to find a security tool that will be useful for all these years.
5. Compatibility: The system to be developed must be applicable to all car models, new cars as well as old ones. This will reduce costs. In addition, the security system should not restrict external sources that use other types of communication protocols.

8.4.2 External Protection

Having raised the above issues, we have found existing solutions that can solve them. Many of the attacks are happening on the transferred data and the communications between a car and the manufacturer's backbone. There are some projects that can secure vehicles' external communication systems.

The EVITA project [8] is a complete network solution, as it aims to protect communications from one smart vehicle to another as well as from one smart vehicle to servers on the internet. It combines hardware and software to achieve its goals. In particular, the proposed architecture entails hardware security modules (HSMs) for the secure and efficient execution of encryption operations and other security techniques.

Similarly, the SEVECOM project [22] uses a security manager as the main component in the project's architecture. It initiates and manages the components of all other HSMs and ensures the operation of the encryption module. To deal with different intrusion cases, the security manager maintains different policy sets, all of whose objective is to enable modules, disable them, or change their parameters based on the system's status so as to uphold the vehicle's security. To achieve all the above, it also makes use of HSMs to store private keys and execute cryptographic algorithms.

Furthermore, the authors of [27] suggest the utilization of a lightweight scalable blockchain that is proposed in [3] to securely interconnect vehicles, software providers, manufacturers, cloud storage, and service centers. The blockchain is implemented on a network of clusters in order to decrease the resource requirements of the original proof-of-work consensus algorithm.

The OVERSEE project [6] provides the main framework that keeps and implements all the communication protocols, like the aforementioned, on one single OVERSEE ECU.

8.4.3 Internal Protection

Attacks can also be made on the car's internal communications. Most solutions for this type of attack are based on cryptography, anomaly detection, and ECU software integrity.

To ensure confidentiality and prevent data from disclosure to unauthorized parties, they must be encrypted. Encryption is very widespread in today's environment and can be found in almost every major protocol in use. Hence, with the use of HSMs and ECUs dedicated to key management we can encrypt every packet before transferring as proposed in [34].

Another issue that can be solved by cryptography is described in [28]. Each node can start emitting if no message is currently being transmitted on the Controller Area Network, but the problem in this case is that the sender cannot be authenticated. Projects such as CANAuth [33] and LiBraCAN [7] solve this issue by implementing message authentication protocols on the CAN bus. In addition, in the field of anomaly detection, a recent project [18] proposed a way to protect ECUs and detect unauthorized transmission by monitoring all data on the bus. Each ECU detects data transmission from other ECUs that deliver Data Frames indicating their own ID. Such data transmission is regarded as an unauthorized message. If an ECU detects an unauthorized message, then it immediately transmits an Error Frame to override the message before the message transmission is completed.

Another approach that is very similar to an implementation of a traditional intrusion detection system (IDS) is described in [26]. Intrusion detection systems (IDSs) constitute one of the best ways to enhance a vehicle's security level [1]. Unlike a traditional IDS for network security, an IDS for a vehicle must be lightweight since an ECU's computing resources are quite limited. In this project, every transaction is logged, and the IDS is focused on the analysis of time intervals of messages. Every ECU connected to the bus sends messages at certain times. If the time interval between the last two sent messages is shorter than normal, then the IDS considers that message as injected. This technique can also help a lot with the detection of DDOS attacks.

Moreover, to ensure ECU software integrity, as proposed in [28], secure validation of an ECU code can be done in a way such as the secure boot mechanisms that are applied on traditional computers. With the use of OVERSEE, security can be kept at very high levels on multimedia ECUs, specifically making use of a hypervisor called XtratuM1. The hypervisor's main job is to test critical software from untrusted modules and external sources. The test is developed in virtual machines. The hypervisor using strict security policies can prevent such software from being successfully installed if it decides that it is malicious. Finally, other novel methods can be used as defense mechanisms for smart cars. Recently the authors in [16] proved that multiple input multiple output techniques could be used in vehicular ad hoc networks as active defense mechanisms in order to avoid jamming threats. Combined with novel techniques that can estimate the speed of a jammer [15] and thus calculate the area where the communication is blocked and take appropriate routing decisions can further improve OTA performance.

8.4.4 Update-Specific Protection

In [31], Uptane, a secure over-the-air update platform specifically for vehicles, was proposed. Its key idea is based on delegating specific duties to specific roles. In particular, update data that are sent from the cloud to a vehicle are signed by the repository administrator through five different roles using their corresponding private keys. When an update is received by the smart car, the pertinent ECU unpacks the files and verifies their authenticity before installing them.

The inventors of [23] created a system that stores a probability map that represents vehicle usage on a variety of segments of a time period. The system is tasked with scheduling a software update installation at the most appropriate time given the probability map and the expected downtime, and with installing the update at the scheduled time after making sure that the vehicle is indeed not in use.

8.5 DISCUSSION

In this section, we offer a brief discussion about the work that has been done on the topic of automotive software updates over-the-air. The research on this field has been spanning over a decade, since 2007. Surprisingly, ever since then, OTA software updates have not been integrated into every single new car model. And even if they do, these updates are usually not of critical importance or issued at short intervals [24].

This indicates that smart car manufacturers are still intimidated by this technology and are not ready to fully embrace it. Although its benefits are quite marvelous due to their usefulness, they do not appear to be of critical importance. Manufacturers know that their products will be sold whether or not they support OTA updates because vehicles are essential to people. With that in mind, taking the risk to implement new technology in their industry seems very dangerous to them.

And they are right since this technology can make their products much more vulnerable if not implemented correctly and as securely as possible. Over-the-air updates require wireless communication, which constitutes a new way of getting access to the car's system. Attackers can now intercept and replay messages meant for a vehicle or coming off of one and send their own messages to a car or the infrastructure it is communicating with. Such possibilities give an attacker the ability to take control of certain or all of a car system's functions. Furthermore, the car's own system could act as the attacker and try to install a new update while the car is in use. Both of these cases can result in accidents.

To solve these problems, researchers have mostly focused on securing the internal or external communication of vehicles with the use of encryption, intrusion detection, software verification, and duty-to-role delegation. Internally, smart car systems have also been developed to perform software integrity verification and update installation scheduling based on vehicle use. Such solutions cover the majority of issues that have come up on the topic of OTA updates for smart cars.

Nevertheless, gaps do exist that still need to be filled. It is our view that more research should be conducted specifically on the avoidance of update installation during the times that a vehicle is in use. A command for software installation at a specified time could bypass security mechanisms and enter the car's system. If the vehicle happens to be moving at the specified time and attempts for whatever reason to proceed with the installation, the system could shut down and render the vehicle unresponsive to digital or physical commands.

Indeed, the automotive industry should beware of this technology and do all that it can to guarantee the utmost safety to its customers. Releasing security updates should be at the top of their list as soon as even the slightest of problems are fixed and tested sufficiently. In addition, every system should have its own support team dedicated to fixing and optimizing it for as long as it is used by customers; stopping the support could prove fatal, since new threats arise on a daily basis and a solution for one system can be incompatible to others.

8.6 CONCLUSIONS

Smart cars have started taking over the world and, sooner rather than later, they might become the new normal in the automotive industry. Over-the-air software updates have been developed and established in the telecommunications industry and proven their worth. Their adaptation to the automotive industry has its challenges seeing as human lives are at stake there. A lot of work has been done to shorten the gap, so much so that this technology has already been applied to car models in the market, sometimes successfully and at other times not. Until the gap is non-existent, there is still a lot to learn and improve on. This paper has described the advantages, threats, and vulnerabilities tied to smart cars and over-the-air updates; it has gathered a list of existing solutions to them and a short examination of the situation in today's relevant research and industry.

8.7 GLOSSARY

Smart Car: An automobile with advanced electronics, artificial intelligence, and a multi-agent system that can assist a vehicle's operator.

Over-the-air (OTA): A wireless delivery of new software or data to mobile devices. Wireless carriers and original equipment manufacturers (OEMs) use OTA to send updated data to cars on the fly.

Electronic control unit (ECU): An embedded system in automotive electronics that controls one or more of the electrical systems or subsystems in a vehicle.

REFERENCES

1. Ahmed Ahmim, Leandros Maglaras, Mohamed Amine Ferrag, Makhlouf Derdour, and Helge Janicke. A novel hierarchical intrusion detection system based on decision tree and rules-based models. In *15th International Conference on Distributed Computing in Sensor Systems (DCOSS)*, pages 228–233. IEEE, 2019.
2. Thomas Chowdhury, Eric Lesiuta, Kerianne Rikley, Chung-Wei Lin, Eunsuk Kang, BaekGyu Kim, Shinichi Shiraishi, Mark Lawford, and Alan Wassyng. Safe and secure automotive over-the-air updates. In *International Conference on Computer Safety, Reliability, and Security*, pages 172–187. Springer, 2018.
3. Ali Dorri, Salil S Kanhere, and Raja Jurdak. Towards an optimized blockchain for iot. In *IEEE/ACM Second International Conference on Internet-of-Things Design and Implementation (IoTDI)*, pages 173–178. IEEE, 2017.
4. Thomas Jones Edison. Smart car with automatic signalling, U.S. Patent 13/862 263, 2014.

5. Kaneez Fizza, Nitin Auluck, Akramul Azim, Md Al Maruf, and Anil Singh. Faster ota updates in smart vehicles using fog computing. In *Proceedings of the 12th IEEE/ACM International Conference on Utility and Cloud Computing Companion*, pages 59–64, 2019.

6. Andr´e Groll, Jan Holle, Christoph Ruland, Marko Wolf, Thomas Wollinger, and Frank Zweers. Oversee a secure and open communication and runtime platform for innovative automotive applications. In *7th Embedded Security in Cars Conference (ESCAR)*, 2009.

7. Bogdan Groza, Stefan Murvay, Anthony Van Herrewege, and Ingrid Verbauwhede. Libracan: A lightweight broadcast authentication protocol for controller area networks. In *International Conference on Cryptology and Network Security*, pages 185–200. Springer, 2012.

8. Olaf Henniger, Alastair Ruddle, Hervé Seudié, Benjamin Weyl, Marko Wolf, and Thomas Wollinger. Securing vehicular on-board it systems: The evita project. In *VDI/VW Automotive Security Conference*, page 41, 2009.

9. James Howden, Leandros Maglaras, and Mohamed Amine Ferrag. The security aspects of automotive over-the-air updates, *International Journal of Cyber Warfare and Terrorism (IJCWT)*, 10(2), 64–81, 2020.

10. SAE International. Automated driving – levels of driving automation are defined in new sae international standard j3016-march 2016. Last accessed: https://www.sae.org/news/2019/01/sae-updates-j3016-automated-driving-graphic. Accessed 2 April 2020.

11. Jian Xiao and Haidong Feng. A low-cost extendable framework for embedded smart car security system. In *International Conference on Networking, Sensing and Control*, pages 829–833, 2009.

12. Jin Xu, Guang Chen, and Ming Xie. Vision-guided automatic parking for smart car. In *Proceedings of the IEEE Intelligent Vehicles Symposium (Cat. No.00TH8511)*, pages 725–730, 2000.

13. Trishank Karthik, Akan Brown, Sebastien Awwad, Damon McCoy, Russ Bielawski, Cameron Mott, Sam Lauzon, André Weimerskirch, and Justin Cappos. Uptane: Securing software updates for automobiles. In *International Conference on Embedded Security in Car*, pages 1–11, 2016.

14. Muzaffar Khurram, Hemanth Kumar, Adi Chandak, Varun Sarwade, Nitu Arora, and Tony Quach. Enhancing connected car adoption: Security and over the air update framework. In *IEEE 3rd World Forum on Internet of Things (WF-IoT)*, pages 194–198. IEEE, 2016.

15. Dimitrios Kosmanos, Antonios Argyriou, and Leandros Maglaras. Estimating the relative speed of rf jammers in vanets. *Security and Communication Networks*, 2019.

16. Dimitrios Kosmanos, Nikolas Prodromou, Antonios Argyriou, Leandros A. Maglaras, and Helge Janicke. Mimo techniques for jamming threat suppression in vehicular networks. *Mobile Information Systems*, 2016.

17. Leandros A Maglaras. A novel distributed intrusion detection system for vehicular ad hoc networks, *International Journal of Advanced Computer Science and Applications*, 6(4), 101–106, 2015.

18. Tsutomu Matsumoto, Masato Hata, Masato Tanabe, Katsunari Yoshioka, and Kazuomi Oishi. A method of preventing unauthorized data transmission in controller area network. In *75th Vehicular Technology Conference (VTC Spring)*, pages 1–5. IEEE, 2012.

19. Dennis K. Nilsson, Phu H. Phung, and Ulf E. Larson. Vehicle ecu classification based on safety-security characteristics, 2008.

20. Hesham A. Odat and Subra Ganesan. Firmware over the air for automotive, fotamotive. In *IEEE International Conference on Electro/Information Technology*, pages 130–139. IEEE, 2014.

21. S. Padmapriya and E. A. KalaJames. Real time smart car lock security system using face detection and recognition. In *International Conference on Computer Communication and Informatics*, pages 1–6, 2012.

22. Panagiotis Papadimitratos, Levente Buttyan, Tamás Holczer, Elmar Schoch, Julien Freudiger, Maxim Raya, Zhendong Ma, Frank Kargl, Antonio Kung, and Jean-Pierre Hubaux. Secure vehicular communication systems: Design and architecture, *IEEE Communications Magazine*, 46(11), 100–109, 2008.

23. J. M. Miller S. Sangameswaran, D. J. Madrid and F. Tseng. Smart over-the-air updates using learned vehicle usage, US Patent 15/902, 572, 22 August 2019.

24. A. Sergeev. Bmw now offering over-the-air updates for certain models. Last accessed: https://www.motor1.com/news/351588/bmw-over-the-air-updates/. Accessed 24 May 2020.

25. Moshe Shavit, Andy Gryc, and Radovan Miucic. Firmware update over the air (fota) for automotive industry. Technical report, SAE Technical Paper, 2007.

26. Hyun Min Song, Ha Rang Kim, and Huy Kang Kim. Intrusion detection system based on the analysis of time intervals of can messages for in-vehicle network. In *International Conference on Information Net-working (ICOIN)*, pages 63–68. IEEE, 2016.

27. Marco Steger, Ali Dorri, Salil S Kanhere, Kay Römer, Raja Jurdak, and Michael Karner. Secure wireless automotive software updates using blockchains: A proof of concept. In Zachäus C., Müller B., Meyer G. (eds), *Advanced Microsystems for Automotive Applications 2017*, Lecture Notes in Mobility, pages 137–149. Springer, Cham, 2018.

28. Ivan Studnia, Vincent Nicomette, Eric Alata, Yves Deswarte, Mohamed Kaaniche, and Youssef Laarouchi. Survey on security threats and protection mechanisms in embedded automotive networks. In *43rd Annual IEEE/IFIP Conference on Dependable Systems and Networks Workshop (DSN-W)*, pages 1–12. IEEE, 2013.

29. J. Sun, Y. Zhang, and K. He. Providing context-awareness in the smart car environment. In *10th IEEE International Conference on Computer and Information Technology*, pages 13–19, June 2010.

30. Jie Sun, Zhao-hui Wu, and Gang Pan. Context-aware smart car: From model to prototype, *Journal of Zhejiang University-SCIENCE A*, 10(7), 1049–1059, July 2009.

31. K. Trishank, A. Brown, S. Awwad, D. McCoy, R. Bielawski, C. Mott, S. Lauzon, A. Weimerskirch, and J. Cappos. Uptane: Securing software updates for automobiles. In *International Conference on Embedded Security in Car*, 2016.

32. R. V. Stokar. Updating car ecus over-the-air (fota), 16 September 2013. Last accessed: https://www.eenewsautomotive.com/content/updating-car-ecus-over-air-fota. Accessed 5 May 2020.

33. Anthony Van Herrewege, Dave Singelee, and Ingrid Verbauwhede. Canauth-a simple, backward compatible broadcast authentication protocol for can bus. In *ECRYPT Workshop on Lightweight Cryptography*, Vol. 2011, page 20, 2011.
34. Marko Wolf and Timo Gendrullis. Design, implementation, and evaluation of a vehicular hardware security module. In *International Conference on Information Security and Cryptology*, pages 302–318. Springer, 2011.
35. Shi Zhendong, Lu, Ke, Yu Qingzhou, Ouyang Lei, and Zeng Xingxing. Smart car control system based on infrared sensor, *Journal of Hubei Automotive Industries Institute*, 3, 11–14, 2007.

Chapter 9

Emerging Malware Threats
The Case of Ransomware

Aikaterini Vardalaki and Vasileios Vlachos

9.1 EVOLUTION OF RANSOMWARE

The cyberthreat landscape is constantly shifting as malicious actors find novel ways to take advantage of the security, infrastructure, and social weaknesses that arise. Ingenuity and simply trial-and-error are the driving forces, fueled by the end goal of extracting as much information or valuables as possible with the lowest risk for the attacker. Here enters the term ransomware: an infectious, self-propagating [42] malware that employs various encryption methods to deny user access to system files. Thereafter, it demands monetary value to provide a decryption key, usually in Bitcoins or in other difficult-to-trace methods of payment. By encrypting files and certain access to the system, the user is then forced to decide between the minimum of choices: either choose to pay the set ransom, [10] or risk losing all the encrypted files and consequently the system access.

The first case of ransomware infection can be traced back to 1989, where attackers started e-mailing infected diskettes that allegedly contained information about AIDS [36]. When the user inserted the diskette, the systems files were locked, and the attacker demanded a physical payment of 378$ be sent by post in a PO box in Panama City. This specific historical example was not identified as a ransomware attack at the time, although it embodies the common typology of a ransomware attack: (1) Encrypt files, consequentially holding them hostage; (2) Demand payment from infected users to unlock or decrypt the system; and (3) Provide the decryption key or choose to ignore the user, after payment is provided.

The internet organized crime threat assessment (IOCTA), with an annual report provided by Europol, aims to identify the threat landscape for cybercrimes. The IOCTA report has characterized ransomware as a top priority threat and the most dominant one in cyberspace for three consecutive years [15] (IOCTA, 2018, 2019, 2020). In other words, ransomware is becoming increasingly targeted and detailed, adapting and overcoming any security standards that may appear each year. To move forward and better understand this phenomenon, a historical overview of the most famous and damaging strains of ransomware, with a brief explanation of their typology and

DOI: 10.1201/9781003109952-9

modus operandi, is necessary. Following the historical path, the current threat landscape will be shortly presented, along with the overview of the cost of ransomware. Afterward, the most common propagation technique of ransomware and the general legal issues will be discussed. Finally, a discussion on the presented chapter will conclude this chapter.

9.2 EMERGING THREATS

To gain a better understanding of the ransomware phenomenon, it is necessary to discuss the pre-ransomware era. At the beginning of the millennium, novel types of cyberfrauds emerged. *Scareware* campaigns, as they were cleverly named from their coercion tactics, targeted inexperienced users with clever social engineering ploys. The goal was to either convince them to purchase the useless software in order to rid themselves of imaginary viruses [20] or to pay the ransom to avoid prosecution for cybercrimes they had never committed. The two most common scareware campaigns were *Fake AntiVirus Software* and *Lockers*.

A considerable number of fake antiviruses (FakeAV) software and other ineffectual cybersecurity products were sold by cybercriminals to naive users [46]. Initially, the perpetrators exploited various known bugs and vulnerabilities of inadequately protected personal computers (PC), running the Microsoft Windows Operating system or the Internet Explorer web browser. Thereafter, they repeatedly displayed numerous fake warning messages to the owners of said systems. The messages falsely claimed that the PC was infected with a plethora of viruses. The proposed solution was to purchase a suggested antivirus product to clean and repair the system. In reality, the suggested program was useless. The fake AntiVirus did not encompass any useful functionality besides a Graphical User Interface that supposedly showed the disinfection progress. As a result, the users were manipulated to buy a non-functional application to clean a non-infected system from non-existent computer viruses and other fictional cyberthreats. These campaigns were also present in various fake advertisements on websites. One company named innovative marketing (IM) even employed a team to handle scareware campaigns and appeared to gain a revenue of 163 million dollars between 2004 and 2008 [20] while operating in Ukraine. Usually, the average price paid by the victims ranged from $60 to $80, while the total profit for the cybercriminals was close to $130 million [47]. In one case alone, the Federal Bureau of Investigation (FBI) dismantled a criminal network that used scareware to infect 960.000 users [1] and collect ransom close to $72 million.

Another prevalent scareware campaign was the "Police Locker", "Police Trojan" or "Police Ransomware". Users that have supposedly committed cybercrimes, related to illegal sexual activities (child pornography) or other socially unacceptable sexual behavior [13], could buy their freedom by paying a ransom. Cybercriminals used known vulnerabilities that existed in popular software such as Java, Flash, and PDF viewers to gain access to their systems. Thereafter, they were able to lock it and display a message on the main screen, allegedly communicated from the FBI or other national police forces, depending on the geographical location of the user. The message was an offer for the user to pay a ransom to avoid prosecution.

In both cases, the targets of these attacks were mostly inexperienced users, incapable of distinguishing the signs of fraud. It would be wholly unreasonable to expect the FBI, or any other national police force, to allow a suspect of a serious crime run free just because he or she agreed to pay a small fee. Nevertheless, it is highly uncommon for a technically advanced user to believe their personal computer is infected with multiple strains of viruses simultaneously, all the while the fix is easy and just a convenient click away. The common denominator of most scareware threats is that their success [43] can be attributed more to effective social engineering tactics and less on the technical novelty of the implementation of the attack. In most cases, the infected system could be restored and repaired without loss of its contents. The operation was quite simple, and it did not require any specific knowledge, programming skills, or custom equipment.

Despite the financial success of the FakeAV and the Police Locker campaigns, cybercriminals decided to employ more aggressive tactics. The CryptoLocker, CryptoWall, and other imitating strains of ransomware were prolific and groundbreaking between 2013 and 2015. To begin with, the CryptoLocker in 2013, using the P2P Gameover ZeuS malware, a botnet based on a former Trojan, sent bulk spam emails with malicious links [28]. This is the first time in history that ransomware was distributed using dedicated networks of already infected computers and infected websites. It also utilized phishing emails to target Microsoft Windows users. A successful attack was followed by the encryption of various files with strong asymmetric encryption using a 2048 bit RSA key-pair. This means that decrypting the affected files is only made possible by a private key, provided by the attackers, and only if 300$ is paid within the first three days of infection [36]. CryptoLocker is started by affecting enterprises and businesses and then advanced to personal home computers. CryptoLocker came down in 2014 after Operation Tovar, a joint law enforcement operation between the FBI, Interpol, academics, and other security experts. At the time, imitators already had copied its modus operandi. Considering how rapidly the cyberlandscape is affected, the rise of CryptoLocker's successor, CryptoWall, came as no surprise. By 2015, almost $18million was suspected to have been stolen from victims, which caused the FBI to release a statement of caution.

The Petya and NotPetya ransomware used the same method which allowed them to adapt and mutate to avoid detection. Unlike the

CryptoLocker and CryptoWall variations, Petya targeted the entire system, overwriting the master boot record (MSB). In 2017 a new version of
Petya, later named NotPetya, exploited a vulnerability in Windows called
EternalBlue. Eternal- Blue was part of NSA's cyberarsenal and was developed to successfully spread throughout an internal network, extract login
information from other systems and finally use them to propagate laterally
to other networks [17]. EternalBlue was leaked online by a hacker group
known as *Shadow Brokers*. The group also revealed that the NSA pos-
sessed their own version of Mimikatz, a powerful password-stealing tool.
NotPetya would end encrypting and overwriting more than 100 different
file extensions and demand 300$ in Bitcoins for the decryption. The infec-
tion methods used by Petya and NotPetya included phishing campaigns to
gain access to selected targets. In fact, NotPetya turned out to be one of
the most dangerous and damaging ransomware worldwide. Later analysis
deemed the encryption routine used by NotPetya as impossible to decrypt.
Even the attackers themselves could not provide a decryption key, making up the infected data and systems completely irreversible and lost [17].
According to the US Department of Justice, NotPetya was developed by the
Russian military intelligence agency, GRU, as part of a global cyberwar-
fare operation that started the attacks against the Ukrainian Government
and other Ukrainian Critical Infrastructure [16]. Recent evidence suggests
that Russian hackers used NotPetya to disrupt a multitude of activities. For
example, it allegedly disrupted the PyeongChang 2018 Winter Olympics,
obstructed the Novichok poisoning investigation of Sergei Skripal and his
daughter held by the Organization for the Prohibition of Chemical Weapons
(OPCW), attacked the United Kingdom's Defence Science and Technology
Laboratory (DSTL), and finally interfered with French elections [1]. In 2017,
a Danish shipping company with a global presence named Moller-Maersk
got infected with Not- Petya and reported financial losses of between
250 and 300 million dollars [4]. Similarly to Petya and NotPetya, the
WannaCry ransomware was so catastrophic that paralyzed corporations in
150 countries. It exploited the same EternalBlue vulnerability that helped
the spread of Petya and NotPetya ransomware [38]. In terms of codifica-
tion, WannaCry is considered a hybrid between a worm and ransomware.
Furthermore, it was using Windows vulnerabilities in the Server Message
Block (SMB) protocol to gain access and a propagation strategy of random
and localized scanning [11] to select new targets. Therefore, it can spread
with zero human interaction throughout the network. Consequently, the
healthcare sector and the National Healthcare System (NHS) in the UK
suffered significant ramifications. In addition, the WannaCry 2.0 ransomware has strong similarities with the MACKTRUCK malware, which has
been used against Sony Pictures Entertainment (SPE). Allegedly, the North
Korean government used ransomware as retaliation against Sony Pictures
because of the circulation of the known satirical movie "The Interview".

US officials claimed that evidence points to North Korea being centrally involved in the cyberattack.

While the first variants of the WannaCry failed to achieve increased propagation rates, its latest version substantially improved the infection rates. After the massive impact and significant losses that were experienced by hundreds of thousands of users, a decryptor was launched through the *No More Ransom* initiative, fronted by Europol, the Dutch Politie, McAfee, and Kaspersky [12]. What's more disturbing is the now well-documented evidence presented by the US Department of Justice that implicates the government of North Korea with the development and deployment of the WannaCry strain. A Department of Justice (DoJ) Criminal Complaint was revealed, charging Park Jin Hyok for three legal charges, criminal conspiracy, conspiracy to commit wire fraud and bank fraud based on the analysis of the malware and the correlation with similar attacks to banks.

As a result, one can make three main observations, perspective wise, from the aforementioned cases: (a) the persistence of ransomware throughout the years, (b) the adaptability from the attackers' side to remain successful and relevant, and (c) the involvement of state-sponsored actors in many prominent cases, either directly using serving officers or indirectly by providing protection to known cybercriminals. Ransomware is a global phenomenon that appears enduring and prevalent [24]. Although one could hypothesize that hackers and malicious actors are growing more innovative and knowledgeable, this is not always the case. Reality lies in a multitude of reasons, one being that the weakest link of the interaction is always the human factor. The second one lies with the driving force behind the motive of the common attacker, which is none other than the investment of time and risk for monetary gain. The third one is the most catastrophic of the now documented cases, the political pressure. It is worth noting that some of the higher impact ransomware campaigns were supported by rogue states that are deploying dangerous malware to gain minor tactical advantages. However, important the bigger picture for the deeper reasons behind the attackers' psyche and choices, the financial effectiveness of ransomware infections speaks for itself. This next section will provide an overview of the current landscape and the driving force behind a large number of documented ransomware attacks: the financial gain.

9.3 FINANCIAL IMPACT

Due to the fact that cybercrime is entirely human-centric [33], social engineering poses cybercriminals as a viable and effective tactic that offers high return rates with minimum risk [19]. The end cost for the user or corporation will be further discussed to assess the overall impact of ransomware infections. To begin with, the use of Bitcoins, being the most prominent cryptocurrency in ransomware crimes [41], is creating an environment of security toward the malicious actor. Bitcoin transactions are challenging to trace, although not impossible, nevertheless cultivating the persistence of cybercriminals and the hardship for justice to act on ransomware attacks. Today, Bitcoin payments remain the necessary medium to transfer the ransom in all recorded cases. This eventually leads to the inability to propose mitigation strategies with a fail-safe result. Furthermore, Ransomware-as-a-Service, firstly emerging in 2015 [44], meant that an attacker could buy a ransomware strain for a fee and even have the necessary help from its creators to use it effectively. In other words, anyone could exploit the human vulnerabilities with a pre-made code that did not necessarily demand any significant skills to use and gain monetary value from. In some cases, that value amounted to millions of dollars, depending on the victims. The heterogeneity of different possible targets, corporations, and individual users with distinct characteristics creates a unique extortion value for each with minimum upkeep for the offender.

Ransomware, as any criminal activity, adapts for different targets and the expectations are shaped for each end goal. In the case of a private and personal home system infection, the data in danger include personal information, pictures or home movies, and sometimes work files. For the infected individual, personal files might be important enough to justify paying the ransom. This would add up to 400$ paid in Bitcoins. The individual maintains the option of not paying the ransom and thus risking losing their files. If compared with corporations, the same infection could add up to millions every year, without even considering the undocumented cases. The average cost of infection of a company reaches 2.6 million dollars, as recorded in the annual cyberthreat report of Accenture in 2019. Still, the true difference with the infected organization is that they cannot simply format the system and start over. This option is not viable. The financial cost might be worth paying for if the organization can bury the incident to avoid a hefty GDPR fine for placing client information at risk. Not to mention the much-expected loss of consumer trust when the public finds out about the infection.

Larger organizations may be considered as the gold at the end of the rainbow by criminals, as reported by McAfee Labs threat report of August 2019, although small and medium (SME) enterprises are in greater danger. SMEs are targeted more frequently by malicious actors than individuals and thus carry greater risk. This can be attributed to a plethora of reasons. For one, smaller companies avoid reporting previous attacks made against them, either to avoid a fine for a breach imposed by legislative acts or to avoid being targeted again by other actors [44]. This creates a shadow number of infections due to a vast majority of ransomware attacks that remain unreported. Additionally, SMEs are perceived as easy targets, because most of them do not maintain a dedicated cybersecurity team [24], hoping they will not become targets. They also store valuable data, similarly to larger corporations, and may not have insurance in place, as larger organizations usually invest in. This might further be explained as false confidence, since smaller businesses feel they are not visible enough, leading to delaying updates or patching their systems [48], thus retaining security holes unkempt for longer. Being an easy target fuels criminals, giving them the confidence and leeway to continue the unlawful activity, while benefiting greatly from the cover-up of the incident.

It is worth noting that the cost of dealing with ransomware is not completely covered by the ransom itself. Hidden costs include remediation, legal expenses, and as mentioned before, possible fines. Usually, the size of the organization correlates with the recovery cost, as the Sophos report on the state of ransomware in 2020 acknowledges. Basic considerations of loss include downtime, employee time, device costs, network costs, and lost opportunities of capital gain. In their annual report of 2019 concerning the state of ransomware in the United States, Emsisoft assesses that on average, ransomware incidents cost 16 days of downtime. Nevertheless, one must consider the lost trust from customers as their data is obviously not sufficiently protected, while the publication of such an event deters future prospective customers from using that corporation or organization. For government infections or local municipalities, the mandate states that they have to register the attack with the authorities [29]. However mandated it might be for the private sector as well, it is now evident by current research that organizations and corporations may seek to avoid the interference with law enforcement, thus creating the shadow number of undocumented cases. Consequently, it is not possible to estimate the true cost of ransomware attacks, but the hypothesis lies with the certainty that it is absolutely higher than the one we are aware of and is documented.

It is important to highlight the existence and role of a parallel economy to cybercrime, the cybersecurity insurance services. Insurance companies offer agreements to pay the ransom if their customers are compromised to avoid loss of data and to minimize the downtime, which could last from weeks to months. Sophos noted that only one in five organizations are not covered by insurance in case of ransomware. In most cases, the firms that maintain a ransomware cyberinsurance policy have the ransom paid for them by said insurance. Surprisingly enough, the public sector is not usually covered by insurance, probably deterred by the high cost and upkeep. Evidently, the existence of ransomware insurance benefits and perpetuates the criminal narrative: "eventually someone will pay." In most corporate cases, that someone is the insurance. It guarantees payment to the perpetrator and is sustained by the fear of the downtime result and public defamation.

The undocumented cases, the multitude of companies that choose to pay the ransom to avoid implications, and the insurance companies that are guaranteeing payment to criminals are inadvertently fueling ransomware activity. The SamSam strain, for example, has raised the amount of ransom requested in 2019, leading the value from 10.000 to 50.000 dollars, as stated in the annual threat report of 2019 of Sophos Labs. Criminals seem to know that eventually they will get paid, regardless of the amount of ransom demanded. Sophos reports that the SamSam strain used to infect systems at least once per day. This adds up to a minimum of damages of $70.000 per week, and if each infected system pays the ransom, it will sustain and fuel the criminal activities like never before. Another strain, Gandcrab, was already reported overpriced, compared to previous years and similar strains, by demanding a sum of 1.000 dollars from infected users. In their annual threat report of 2019, ENISA (the European Union Agency for Cybersecurity) claims that 45% of victim organizations paid the ransom in 2019. Symantec in their threat reports emphasizes that SamSam mainly targeted organizations within the US. Nevertheless, the fact remains that ransomware cases are growing and so are their ransom demands. However important financial value is to ransomware perpetrators, the end user is equally involved, as a victim, to the criminal activity. To further understand the globalized phenomenon, the end user needs to be discussed along with the most common propagation method: phishing.

9.4 RANSOMWARE AND SOCIAL ENGINEERING

While it is an uncontested fact that the methodology behind the propagation of malware is in its functional basis, a technical phenomenon, the receiving end of an attack, the user, needs to be considered. There are various important studies discussing the models and the attack cycle used [12, 30], the methods of propagation mechanisms [3], and even mitigation practices [8] while still considering only one end of the activity spectrum. This involves the security measures in place, the unpatched holes, network segmentation, and the overall safety of the targeted system. However, the human aspect of security can be easily manipulated and without as much effort as a physical attack would need. Humans are governed by characteristic traits, emotions, ideologies, curiosity, empathy, fear [2], and plain mood changes. Therefore, their everyday behavior can lead to exploitation [7].

Social engineering is described as the art of prompting users to compromise information systems [27], a form of attack that has been gaining popularity with ransomware infections [18]. For ransomware and malware, no other means of propagation besides exploiting system vulnerability or using social engineering [14] exists. Social engineering is considered as the path of least resistance, by virtue of employing the user himself to assist in the propagation. Kevin Mitnik has identified a model of social engineering attack cycle that includes four attack phases: information gathering, developing rapport and trust, exploiting said trust, and finally using the results from the previous phases [37]. This follows a logical and practical narrative. First, attackers gather the necessary information to scam the user, learning about their habits and most viewed websites or even their email client. Second, they approach them and provide information naturally and effortlessly. Third, exploiting the trust they have created, they prompt the user to download and run an executable or click on a link or provide sensitive information themselves. Lastly, using the information they gathered, the attacker proceeds with the final steps of the criminal activity.

Similar to the aforementioned model, Gallegos-Segovia et al. in their research on social engineering as a deployment method for ransomware, identify three different types of social attacks, namely the ego attack, the sympathy attack, and the bullying attack [18]. The ego and sympathy attack models are similar, by means of employing trust and direct communication with the victim to effortlessly persuade them to act. The bullying model uses intimidation and coercion while maintaining a sense of urgency. It is worth mentioning that the sense of urgency is common in social engineering attacks to stop the victim from realizing the logical gaps in the attacker's narrative. The less the victim contemplates the actions they are fulfilling, the timelier and more efficient the attack is. The aforementioned techniques are especially dangerous in cases of mass infections, such as in businesses where employees are exploited by malicious actors to gain entry [31]. Therefore, it is crucial to address the number one social scheme attack of ransomware: phishing.

Phishing is highly efficient as a method because cybercrime is solely based on the characteristics of the human psyche. Human interaction with a system can be the cause of its exploitation [7]. In cases, sympathy attacks can be more efficient than intimidation attacks [18] due to the high chance of a positive reaction from the victims, meaning that feelings of reward or winnings will lead to the download of the malware. For example, phishing looks like clicking on a seemingly harmless advertisement online about free coupons or air miles from your commonly used airline. This consequently means that the motivation behind the user to achieve their goals [34], a driving force in the human psyche, is exploited by using a positive affirmation. Goals, as mundane as they can be, booking a flight or looking for recipes, can be exploited by malicious actors to bait victims with high success rates. What if a user were employed in a large-scale organization and a similar email address from a coworker requested a typical money transfer to finalize a contract? Maybe the user's bank requested them to change their past e-banking passwords after 6 months of use. These examples are used as common phishing scams, prompting the user to click on seemingly innocent links or provide sensitive personal information. By noticing the uniform resource locator (URL) a user could potentially avoid victimization. Criminals try to imitate a convincing URL, similar to the purpose of the prompt used to lure clicks. Avoiding suspicion is a priority for a successful phishing attack. An intimidation attack, on the other hand, leads to users seeking to consult from third parties, lowering the possibility of a download. Evidently, one human error could lead an entire network or organization to collapse, especially if no segmentation measures are in place to stop the spread of the infection to certain systems.

Although it is challenging to comprehend the full extent of the reasons and the motivation behind human interaction with security threats, awareness training is one of the few effective routes organizations can take to mitigate the human factor. While the security of the system may be up to date, monitored, and supervised, there is always the chance of a naive user introducing malware into their computer [26], or in the worst-case scenario, in an organization. Technology alone cannot combat all the possibilities of the forms the human vulnerability takes. Implementing solid human-oriented practices to increase awareness of decision-making [9, 22], establishing a clear communication line between users and security departments in case of a mistake, implementing standard policy regulations in such cases, and repeating security trainings can minimize the effect and reach of a ransomware attack.

Even though security trainings have been used in the past to lower infection chances, they may not be enough to mitigate the risk. Especially for non-technical people who resist trainings or do not retain the training, [26] learning new skills with zero experience in the security department can be challenging. Furthermore, the training may not be monitored by the organization well enough [19] to prove effective or not repeated and thus constituting the acquired knowledge lost. Another interesting theory to be considered is the reactance theory. Restricting employees, threatening them with punishment when they do not comply, or simply removing some of their freedoms can potentially lead to non-compliance with directives and trainings. In Lowry and Moody's research, reactance is defined as a negative emotion, a coping mechanism that causes the directive to be rejected [31]. This is the result of threatened freedom that the user is fighting to re-establish. Reactance can be avoided with explanatory awareness trainings to employees, instead of simply establishing new guidelines and directives with no previous warning. The sense of lost freedom should be replaced with a deeper knowledge and the preservation of an educated choice. Furthermore, it is considered highly effective to inspire and encourage end users to implement security policies and follow security directives. However, a tailored threat-oriented message, providing information on susceptibilities in security, will enhance the effect of awareness in end users [25]. In short, using real-life security incidents alongside positive awareness trainings and avoiding harsh punishment to the end user, newly implemented security measures will be more efficient and the risk of phishing will be effectively lowered.

9.5 LEGISLATION CHALLENGES

The discussion on new yet persistent threats, such as ransomware, against societies would bear no constructive addition to a unilateral solution if it did not involve a legislative viewpoint. Each new technology and the endless uses it can offer are creating areas of interest that are not yet bound by any legal constraint and are challenging to legal concepts [40]. The law is an adaptable tool [39] and serves the purpose of responding to societal issues, providing guidance and clarification along with resolution. The issue with new-age threats, especially in the cyberdomain, is the globalization aspect and the fact that effective prosecution is often impossible. Defining the unlawful act is a tedious task when technology and means of forensic research at a state level are not compatible with the criminal's abilities. However criminal extortion may be, some countries like the United States are constantly evolving and taking steps to adapt legislation to cover ransomware attacks. For example, in Maryland, a discussion has begun since January to establish whether the possession of ransomware constitutes an unlawful act, even without the intent to use it. Although the legal aspects of ransomware cannot be exhausted in this subchapter, the most relevant points include two main themes: (a) The globalization of the phenomenon and the need for legislation to modernize and create an overarching cybercriminal law and (b) Whether law in its nature is enough to act as a deterrent to mitigate future ransomware attacks.

Ransomware, in its nature, cannot be contained within state borders. As discussed previously, it has been used, on multiple occasions, in order to apply political pressure in rival countries. Prosecution issues arise when countries with no collaboration treaties or agreements clash. For example, ransomware that was created and deployed in Pakistan has little to no chance to reach the courts of Ukraine. If it does, it is almost certain that the developers and offenders will not be sanctioned in a Ukrainian court of law. The legislative issues may be remediated if the offending country belongs in and attacks within the borders of the European Union [32]. This is attributed to the Budapest Convention, a treaty proposed in 2001, which provided a framework for cybercrime, an attempt to harmonize cybercriminal law and create cooperation between the signing countries. Issues arise when one considers which countries have signed the treaty. Even though it counts 65 countries, in comparison with the 27 within the European Union, some key countries leading in cybercrime are missing, namely Iran, China, Russia, and India. India, for example, is considered the country most hit by ransomware in 2020. Lastly, there is a plethora of criticism against the Budapest Convention, especially concerning the treaty's broad terminology and abstractness. However, legislated ransomware is, within the EU and US, the payment method used in ransomware attacks, Bitcoin, is very difficult to trace and may be directed in uncooperative jurisdiction. This is evident by the fact that no case law is available with convictions against ransomware attackers [32]. On the other hand, the US has prosecuted two individuals, Anthony R. Murgio and Yuri Lebedev, for operating a Bitcoin exchange financial system, commonly used by the victims of ransomware attacks [45]. The two have essentially violated federal US anti-money laundering laws. Notably, the two already resided in the US and operated under US federal law. Even though the US has been the most responsive in ransomware laws since the 2019 massive state ransomware infections, the fact remains that there is no overarching cyber federal law covering ransomware in the US. The US federal law possesses only one act that can cover ransomware cases, namely the Computer Fraud and Abuse Act (CFAA) [5], which is codified in Title 18 USC 1030. It was enacted in 1986 and amended multiple times [35]. Evidently, the CFAA does not specifically mention ransomware but covers federal computers, bank computers, and computers that have access to the internet and have been accessed without authorization [6, 21, 5]. Individual states have legislated provisions to include ransomware, so far them being California, Connecticut, Michigan, Texas, and Wyoming and more recently Maryland with its Senate Bill 30, of January 14, 2019. No equal or similar framework or overarching legislation exists at a European level. This is hypothesized to be difficult to implement in multiple countries due to different socio-economic backgrounds and ideologies. Establishing a common path toward safer cyberspace requires time and vast amounts of research. In the example of GDPR and its mandatory implementation, one could notice the hardship and confusion it brought on in the first months and can still wreak havoc in small organizations. Moreover, it is not applicable to countries that have not signed it, like China or Russia. Only businesses and corporations that operate on EU grounds will have to comply with its regulations. It is clear that the law will not be effective if there is no way to enforce it. The law acts, among other ethical and societal structures, as a deterrent [23]. However, if forensics and jurisdictional issues are there, then political issues will be always present, which means the law is rendered ineffective. In 2019, the Emsisoft report on the state of ransomware claimed that the only way to stop the infections is to make it unprofitable, acknowledging the issue at heart: no current mitigation strategy is working. It is obvious that criminals are constantly adapting and becoming more and more refined in each attack, with or without a legislative framework. A step toward a mitigating legal framework would be to implement a similar approach to the Budapest Convention on an international level. By establishing international cooperation in jurisdictional matters, with the option of extradition when needed, the law may become more effective as a deterrent with the first convictions. This step would require unimaginable negotiation hours, drafting attempts, and amendments; however, it would be the first step in producing legislative results. Finally, until a point of legal effectiveness is established, the responsibility of staying ransomware-free falls in the realm of the end user.

9.6 CONCLUDING REMARKS

In this chapter, the dangers of ransomware and the implications it causes toward society and law were discussed. The phenomenon has now been extensively reported since 1989, while constantly changing and adapting to avoid being detected and rendered ineffective. This tactic strengthens the attack result ratio and causes monetary damages that amount to millions of losses from individuals and enterprises alike. From the early days of scareware and fake antiviruses to refined and targeted political-oriented attacks against neighboring countries, ransomware is still considered the most dangerous active malware for the last three consecutive years (IOCTA, 2018, 2019, 2020). This chapter considered ransomware as a current and active threat against personal home computers and professional systems and equipment alike. Thus, concise research was conducted, contemplating a brief history of the infection, the financial impacts caused by the payments of ransom, the downtime of businesses and the restoration cost of damages, the spreading and propagation methods, and finally the legal challenges that ransomware causes require judicial intervention.

Some prolific strains of ransomware include the famous CryptoLocker, CryptoWall, Petya, NotPetya, and WannaCry. Each one exploited different vulnerabilities in MS Windows operating systems, used complicated encryption methods, and finally infected multiple government facilities, personal computers, corporations, and healthcare institutions. All different malware strains had various stages of deployment and improvements with constant adaptations from their developers, or mirrors that copied some parts of the infection process and then created their own details. Some of them were developed by whole criminal teams and deployed against countries to force them toward decisions or to enforce political pressure. The fact remains that damages are still considered unmeasurable and the true financial cost remains hidden due to underreporting from enterprises and individuals alike. Moreover, a parallel economy has risen from the infection rates. The notion of ransomware cybersecurity insurance is common within corporations and large organizations, which secures the payment to the criminals if an infection happens to the aforementioned firms. Still, the monetary gains for the perpetrator alongside the anonymity Bitcoins offer remain to be the two most fueling causes for attackers to continue adapting malicious code and propagating ransomware. Further reasoning behind the success of propagation is pointing toward (a) lack of judicial enforcement and (b) the social factor.

Social engineering has been examined as the path of least resistance since the end user is the one who opens the door to the infection. No need for refined hacking techniques or sophisticated code; the infection can happen with ordinary activities such as downloading a recipe or booking airplane tickets. The social engineering model, firstly identified by Kevin Mitnik, comments on four attack phases: information gathering, developing rapport and trust, exploiting said trust, and finally using the results from the previous phases [37]. More sociological models have been examined after the aforementioned one, but the important factor is the manipulation of human qualities to gain unauthorized entry into a system. Taking advantage of notions such as trust or the sense of urgency leads to infections. Phishing is the most common and notorious method of ransomware propagation for individuals and mass infections alike. Even though awareness trainings have been employed for the past years to counteract the human factor, they are not enough to mitigate the true ransomware risks. Adaptations and repetition are deemed necessary for the new information to be retained in employees. Seminars should be presented in a way that common freedoms of the user are not threatened to avoid the reactance theory phenomenon, where the user flushes new directions because of fear of restriction. The proposed solutions to lower phishing statistics would be to use real-life security incidents, positive awareness training, and avoid punishment to the user.

Lastly, this research explained the jurisdictional and judicial issues ransomware legislation faces. Common problems such as the globalization of the phenomenon and the hardship of defining the cyberworld create issues with the effective prosecution of ransomware crimes. Regulatory statutes and laws are present in countries such as the US and economic or political unions such as the EU. On the other hand, bringing criminals in a court is deemed almost impossible, since there is no case law available for ransomware prosecution. Furthermore, the disagreements between rival countries create extradition issues, which then pose a threat to the legislative procedure. Similar to the US, the EU does not pose an overarching cybercrime law covering ransomware, only the Budapest Convention, which is now in great need of a timely amendment. The law is a tool, and in its nature is adaptable. Establishing a common global path toward safer cyberspace is the only solution to successfully mitigate the ransomware risks.

This chapter attempted to explain and discuss the fundamental problem trajectories of ransomware with each societal and legal aspect it represents a risk to. We acknowledge that in no way, shape, or form is this research completed. Many more research papers with an interdisciplinary viewpoint are needed to explain the phenomenon in full and establish applicable solutions prior to the long-term approach of a globalized entity responsible to bringing cyberextortionists to justice. This research is the first stepping point for a long-needed discussion to truly attempt to mitigate and lower ransomware infection rates, thus breaking the three-year cycle of ransomware being the top cybersecurity threat globally.

REFERENCES

1. Department of Justice Disrupts International Cyber Crime Rings Distributing Scareware, Current On-Line (December 2020): https://archives.fbi.gov/archives/news/pressrel/press-releases/department-of-justice-disrupts-intern ational-cybercrime-rings-distributing-scareware, 2011, June.
2. Sherly Abraham and InduShobha Chengalur-Smith. An overview of social engineering Malware: Trends, tactics, and implications, *Technology in Society*, 32(3), 183–196, 2010, August.
3. Maxat Akbanov, Vassilios Vassilakis, and Michael Logothetis. WannaCry ransomware: Analysis of infection, persistence, recovery prevention and propagation mechanisms, *Journal of Telecommunications and Information Technology*, 1, 113–124, 2019.
4. Craig H. Allen. Developing and implementing a Maritime cybersecurity risk assessment model. Available at SSRN 3302772, 2018.
5. Alden Anderson. The computer fraud and abuse act: Hacking into the authorization debate, *Jurimetrics*, 447–466, 2013.
6. Patricia Bellia. A code-based approach to unauthorized access under the computer fraud and abuse act, *The George Washington Law Review*, 84, 1442, 2016.
7. Bowen Brian, Salvatore Stolfo, and Ramaswamy Devarajan. Measuring the human factor of cyber security. In *Conference on Technology for Homeland Security (HST)*, pages 230–235. IEEE, 2011, May.
8. Krzysztof Cabaj and Wojciech Mazurczyk. Using Software-defined networking for Ransomware mitigation: The case of CryptoWall, *IEEE Network*, 30(6), 14–20, 2016.
9. Nobles Calvin Botching human factors in Cybersecurity in business organizations. *HOLISTICA - Journal of Business and Public Administration*, 9(3), 71–88, 2018, December.
10. Anna Cartwright and Edward Cartwright. Ransomware and reputation, *Games*, 10(2), 1–14, 2019, June.
11. Zesheng Chen, Chao Chen, and Chuanyi Ji. Understanding localized-scanning worms. In *IEEE International Performance, Computing, and Communications Conference*, pages 186–193, 2007.
12. Aniello Cimitile, Francesco Mercaldo, Vittoria Nardone, Antonella Santone, and Corrado Aaron Visaggio. Talos: No more Ransomware victims with formal methods, *International Journal of Information Security*, 17(6), 719–738, 2018.
13. Sancho David and Hacquebord Feike. The *"Police Trojan"*. Technical Report, Trend Micro, 2012.
14. Aaron Emigh. The crimeware landscape: Malware, phishing, identity theft and beyond, *Journal of Digital Forensic Practice*, 1(3), 245–260, 2006, September.
15. Europol. Internet Organized Crime Threat Assessment (IOCTA). 2018, CurrentOn-Line (December2020): https://www.europol.europa.eu/activities-services/main-reports/internet-organised-crime-threat-assessment-iocta-201 8, 2018.

16. Sharifah Fayi. What Petya/NotPetya Ransomware is and what its remidiations are. In *15th International Conference on Information Technology – New Generations, Las Vegas*, pages 93–100. Springer International Publishing, 2018, January.

17. Steven Furnell and David Emm. The ABC of Ransomware protection, *Computer Fraud & Security*, 2017(10), 5–11, 2017.

18. Pablo L. Gallegos-Segovia, Jack F. Bravo-Torres, Victor M. Larios-Rosillo, Paul E. Vintimilla-Tapia, Ivan F. Yuquilima-Albarado, and Juan D. Jara-Saltos. Social engineering as an attack vector for Ransomware. In *Chilean Conference on Electrical, Electronics Engineering, Information and Communication Technologies (CHILECON)*, pages 1–6, 2017.

19. Ibrahim Ghafir, Saleem Jibran, Mohammad Hammoudeh, Hanan Faour, Vaclav Prenosil, Sardar Jaf, Sohail Jabbar, and Thar Baker. Security threats to critical infrastructure: The human factor, *The Journal of Supercomputing*, 74(10), 4986–5002, 2018.

20. Jim Giles. Scareware: The inside story, *New Scientist*, 205, 38–41, 2010.

21. Lee Goldman. Interpreting the computer fraud and abuse act, *Pittsburgh Journal of Technology Law & Policy*, 13(1), 1–38, 2012.

22. Lee Hadlington. Human factors in Cybersecurity; Examining the link between internet addiction, impulsivity, attitudes towards Cybersecurity, and risky cybersecurity behaviours, *Heliyon*, 3(7), e00346, 2017.

23. Kai-Lung Hui, Seung Hyun Kim, and Qiu-Hong Wang Cybercrime. *Deterrence and International Legislation: Evidence From Distributed Denial of Service Attacks*. Technical Report 2, Research Collection School Of Information Systems, 20

24. Gavin Hull, Henna John, and Budi Arief. Ransomware deployment methods and analysis: Views from a predictive model and human responses, *Crime Science*, 8, 1–22, 2019, December.

25. Allen Johnston and Merrill Warkentin. Fear appeals and information security behaviors: An empirical study, *MIS Quarterly*, 34(3), 549–566, 2010.

26. Mahmoud Khonji, Youssef Iraqi, and Andrew Jones. Phishing detection: A literature survey, *IEEE Communications Surveys & Tutorials*, 15(4), 2091–2121, 2013.

27. Katharina Krombholz, Heidelinde Hobel, Markus Huber, and Edgar Weippl. Advanced social engineering attacks, *Journal of Information Security and Applications*, 22, 113–122, 2015. Special Issue on Security of Information and Networks.

28. Kevin Liao, Ziming Zhao, Adam Doupe, and Gail-Joon Ahn. Behind closed doors: Measurement and analysis of Cryptolocker Ransoms in Bitcoin. In *APWG Symposium on Electronic Crime Research (eCrime)*, pages 1–13, 2016.

29. Allan Liska. Early findings: Review of state and local government Ransomware attacks. *Recorded Future* 10, Current On-Line (December 2020): https://go.recordedfuture.com/hubfs/reports/cta-2019-0510.pdf, 2019.

30. Wanping Liu and Shouming Zhong. Modeling and analyzing the dynamic spreading of epidemic malware by a network Eigenvalue method, *Applied Mathematical Modelling*, 63, 491–507, 2018.

31. Paul Benjamin Lowry and Gregory D. Moody. Proposing the control- reactance compliance model CRCM to explain opposing motivations to comply with organisational information security policies, *Informations Systems Journal*, 25(5), 433–463, 2015, September.

32. John MacRae and Virginia Franqueira. On Locky Ransomware, Al Capone and Brexit. In *International Conference on Digital Forensics and Cyber Crime*, pages 33–45, Springer, 2017.

33. Barbara J. Mann. *Encyclopedia of Crisis Management*, Vol. 27. Thousand Oaks, CA and London: Sage Publications, 2013.

34. Julie L. Marble, William F. Lawless, Ranjeev Mittu, Joseph T. Coyne, Myriam Abramson, and Ciara Sibley. The human factor in Cybersecurity: Robust & intelligent defense. In Sushil Jajodia, Paulo Shakarian, V. S. Subrahmanian, Vipin Swarup, and Cliff Wang, eds., *Cyber Warfare - Building the Scientific Foundation*, Vol. 56 of Advances in Information Security, pages 173–206. Springer, 2015.

35. Jarrett Marshall, Michael Bailie, Ed Hagen, and Scott Etringham. *Prosecuting Computer Crimes*. Technical report, Office of Legal Education Executive Office for United States Attorneys Accessible from US Justice Department, 2010.

36. A. K. Maurya, Neeraj Kumar, Alka Agrawal, and Raees Khan. Ransomware evolution, target and safety measures, *International Journal of Computer Sciences and Engineering*, 6, 80–85, 2018, January.

37. Kevin Mitnick and William Simon. *The Art of Deception: Controlling the Human Element of Security*. John Wiley & Sons, 2003.

38. Savita Mohurle and Manisha Patil. A brief study of Wannacry threat: Ransomware attack 2017, *International Journal of Advanced Research in Computer Science*, 8(5), 1938–1940, 2017, May.

39. Marianne Mollmann. Change is possible: The law as a barrier and a tool, *City University of New York Law* Review, 15(2), 277–281, 2011.

40. Annamart Nieman. Cyberforensics: Bridging the law/technology divide, *Journal of Information, Law and Technology*, 1, 1–30, 2009.

41. Masarah Paquet-Clouston, Bernhard Haslhofer, and Benoît Dupont. Ransomware payments in the Bitcoin ecosystem, *Journal of Cybersecurity*, 5(1), tyz003, 05 2019.

42. Chen Qian and Robert Bridges. Automated behavioral analysis of Malware: A case study of Wannacry Ransomware. In *16th IEEE International Conference on Machine Learning and Applications (ICMLA 2017)*, pages 454–460. IEEE, 2017.

43. Moheeb Abu Rajab, Lucas Ballard, Panayiotis Marvrommatis, Niels Provos, and Xin Zhao. The Nocebo effect on the web: An analysis of fake anti-virus distribution. In *Large-Scale Exploits and Emergent Threats*, 2010.

44. Ronny Richardson and Max North. Ransomware: Evolution, mitigation and prevention, *International Management* Review, 13(1), 10–21, 2017.

45. James Sherer, Melinda McLellan, Emily Fedeles, and Nichole Sterling. Ransomware - Practical and legal considerations for confronting the new economic engine of the dark web, *Richmond Journal of Law & Technology Annual Survey*, 23, 1–49, 2017.

46. Brett Stone-Gross, Ryan Abman, Richard Kemmerer, Christopher Kruegel, Douglas Steigerwald, and Giovanni Vigna. *The Underground Economy of Fake Antivirus Software*. New York, NY: Springer, 2013.
47. Kurt Thomas, Danny Yuxing Huang, David Y. Wang, Elie Bursztein, Chris Grier, Tom Holt, Christopher Kruegel, Damon McCoy, Stefan Savage, and Giovanni Vigna. Framing dependencies introduced by underground commoditization. In *14th Annual Workshop on the Economics of Information Security, WEIS 2015*, Delft, The Netherlands, 22–23 June 2015.
48. Adam L. Young and Moti Yung. Cryptovirology: The birth, neglect, and explosion of Ransomware, *Communications of the ACM*, 60(7), 24–26, 2017, June.

Chapter 10

Holistic Immunization

A Comprehensive Model to Tackle Hybrid Threats in the Cyber Domain

Athanasios Kosmopoulos

10.1 INTRODUCTION: BACKGROUND AND DRIVING FORCES

Over the past years, hybrid threats and operations have evolved from a theoretical framework to an actual fact, applied in contemporary battle domains [1]. This chapter presents and discusses a model to tackle hybrid threats not in a defensive manner but rather developing immunity to them in a broader sense [2]. Immunization refers to the set of processes developed in a state in order to predict, detect, respond, and neutralize hybrid threats and their structural components at their initial stage prior to becoming attacks. The chapter also focuses on the elements needed in order to present an effective and efficient response to the issue at hand. Holistic immunization increases the ability of an organization or state to respond successfully to a hybrid threat before the need for actual defense is presented. The main methodology to create immunity is to establish consecutive levels of detection and responses starting with fake news/disinformation [3] tracking, cyber defense, critical infrastructure protection, and homeland security/army defense. The holistic immunization model offers the ability to react proactively before the impact of a hybrid operations initiative has been fully deployed and still is at the initial phase [4]. Our main focus stands with cybersecurity and cyber-defense measures.

10.2 PROBLEM DEFINITION – THE CYBER CRISIS MANAGEMENT

The advent of "cyber conflict" and "cyber war" serves as examples for the use of new technologies within the scope of hybrid threats [5]. Cyber war refers to a sustained computer-based cyberattack by a state (or non-state actor) against the information technology infrastructure of a target state [6]. An example of such hostile action occurring in the fifth dimension of warfare is the 2007 Russian attempt to virtually block out Estonia's Internet infrastructure as a unilateral countermeasure and retribution for

DOI: 10.1201/9781003109952-10

Estonia's removal of World War II Soviet memorial from the center of the city of Tallinn [7]. This incident was followed by the employment of sophisticated cyber operations against Georgia in 2008.

These present "cyber" hybrid threats; one can state that it is new and readily available technology that makes these threats so potent [8]. Command and control capabilities may be established in relatively short notice and with little effort [9]. The media can be used for influencing public opinion as a means of psychological operations (PSYOPS), both at home and abroad. Cyber threats strike at the core of modern warfare by affecting command and control abilities, which have become increasingly vulnerable to cyberattack. Such cyber threat capabilities also strike at the core of our post-industrial, modern society [10]. The use of "cyber" as a threat category on its own or as an aiding tool for carrying out other multi-modal attacks is highly likely to increase, and consequently, its overall role within the context of hybrid threats will rise [11].

While in the cyberspace many different actors may play a role.

The need for a joint operational model in cyber defense is not new [12]. The findings and lessons identified by public inquiries and inquests have highlighted cases where the technical-level services could have worked better together and shown a much greater degree of communication, cooperation, and coordination with the strategic-level decision-makers [13]. That is why improved operational level management is needed to act in the middle.

Along with improving joint working between the technical- and strategic-level stakeholders, it is clear that the need for all responding entities to operate in a joint and coordinated approach.

Policies and procedures that promote joint working form the basis of the doctrine for responding services. Applying simple principles for joint working is particularly important in the early stages of an incident when clear, robust decisions and actions need to be taken with minimum delay, in an often rapidly changing environment.

Those principles are demonstrated below. They will often, but not always, be followed in the order in which they are presented.

- **Colocate** all operations staff as soon as practicably possible at a single, safe, and easily identified location.
- **Communicate** clearly using a common understandable language. Meaningful and effective communication between technical- and strategic-level entities strengthens effective joint working and guarantees that efficient communication will be delivered to the public. Sharing and understanding information benefits the development of shared situational awareness, which underpins the best possible outcomes of an incident.
- **Coordinate** by agreeing on the leading issue. Identify priorities, resources, and capabilities for an effective response, including all incoming technical data.

- **Jointly understand risk** by sharing information about the likelihood and potential impact of threats and hazards to agree on potential control measures.
- **Shared situational awareness** established using common standard operation procedures (SOPs) to implement a Joint Decision Model and deliver a decision proposal for the strategic level.

The main points that raise challenges for an operational management model have to do mainly with [14]:

- **Coordination,** that is to say, synchronize competences so as to improve decision-making and risk management,
- **A common understanding of risks** among stakeholders,
- **Improvement of intelligence and situational awareness** as to recognize threats from weak signals in early stages in order to quickly promote analysis,
- **Advance coalitions** across sectors spanning public and private, foreign and domestic divide,
- **Informing** policy recommendations and decision-making within existing structures,
- Reassuring that **information will be designated as a critical domain,** especially for public communication purposes,
- **Exercises and training.**

An operational management scheme shall provide planning, implement and control the SOPs needed to meet requirements, and implement the actions determined by:

- Establishing criteria for the Standard Operating Procedures,
- Implementing control of the Standard Operating Procedures in accordance with the criteria, and
- Keeping documented information to the extent necessary to have confidence that the Standard Operating Procedures have been carried out as planned.

One of the biggest problems regarding efficient cyber crisis management is the inability to have a comprehensive picture of what is exactly happening, what is precisely the impact to society, and what mitigation measures should be activated in order to handle the aforementioned impact.

It is very significant to alleviate fusion and to underpin the flow of intelligence with regard to operational level actors. This will facilitate the strategic-level entities to bring together the available info, reconcile potentially differing priorities, and then make effective decisions. Different kinds of intelligence, originating from diverse actors, have to be combined and assessed at the operational level.

In this context, establishing a common operating picture is of outstanding importance and it is obtained via the leverage of a comprehensive situational awareness.

We define a common operating picture as "A common overview of an incident that is created by assessing and fusing information from multiple sources, and is shared between appropriate command, control and coordinating groups to support joint decision-making".

In the language of practice, building a "common operating picture" is essential for clear communication and coordination of actions among emergency response organizations. This means achieving a sufficient level of shared information among the different organizations and jurisdictions participating in crisis management operations at different locations, so all actors readily understand the constraints on each and the possible combinations of collaboration and support among them under a given set of conditions. A common operating picture is a single point of reference for those involved and supports joint decision-making.

Generally, data provided by the technical-level actors are not observed or understood to their full extent by the decision-makers. Interpretation is a need. Answering the questions below helps develop a common operating picture and helps establish shared situational awareness:

- **What?** – What has happened, what is happening now, and what is being done about it?
- **So what?** – What might the implications and wider impact/harm be?
- What might **happen in the future?**

The form of the common operating picture first depends on technical requirements and practices. It has to be updated as events and inputs change and also as the results of further work become available, such as analysis that answers the "so what?" or "what might?" questions.

The common operating picture should have a clear relationship with the established command, control, and coordination groups (including computer security incident response teams (CSIRTs)) and should be accessed through a suitably resilient and secure common information-sharing platform.

In other contexts, the common operating picture at the operational level may be a dynamic dashboard that provides an overview of the incident, using maps and graphics as well as text.

A major cyber crisis could be the main element of a combined set of hybrid operations targeting an entity.

Countering hybrid threats is at the top of the list of joint actions endorsed by the EU and NATO in December 2016. The concept of "hybrid threat" is both ambiguous and widely criticized: no one seems to know exactly what the term means. However, it has had a prominent place in European security debates in recent years and has made its way into the core documents of the EU and NATO [15].

The EU has broadly defined hybrid threats as a "mixture of coercive and subversive activity, conventional and nonconventional methods (i.e. diplomatic, military, economic, technological), which can be used in a coordinated manner by state or non-state actors to achieve specific objectives while remaining below the threshold of formally declared warfare" [16].

The key concept in responding to hybrid threats – resilience – is also elusive. It generally refers to a "capacity to withstand stress and recover", with critical infrastructure and civil preparedness playing a key role [17]. While the resilience of each society primarily depends on national measures, contemporary societies are closely tied to transnational networks and flows (of people, goods, energy, information, money, etc.).

These networks are a source of both major opportunities and vulnerabilities. Security of networks requires cooperation between states, and between organizations such as the EU and NATO.

Major cyber crisis management involves an entity's lead role that is not always self-evident. Examining modes of network governance between EU and other internal/external actors, specifically regarding the decision-making process, we may identify three basic models:

- Participant-governed networks,
- Lead-organization-governed networks, and
- A network administrative organization.

The first model concerns what is called "shared governance" by the network members themselves and is characterized by the equality of members and high levels of trust within the network.

The second model (a lead-organization model) uses a more centralized and hierarchical approach, with the lead agency responsible for the coordination of activities and decisions within the network.

The third model (a network administrative organization) involves a separate and external entity to specifically govern the network's activities. These models are theoretical ideal types: in practice, institutional constructs and procedures often display a combination of characteristics and elude a clear categorization. What constitutes a determining trait of a specific model can also be debated. A network administrative organization, for example, is defined by the external position of its coordinating organ while the lead organization is regarded as a full member of the network.

In this chapter, we argue that the second model is the best to be followed in managing major cyber crises.

Whatever model is applied, the critical factor is making fast decisions while adapting accordingly to the changing environmental parameters.

A rapid decision-making system uses implicit guidance and control methods to move from environment observation to decision and then to action.

One of the best and widely adopted decision-making analytical frameworks elevated to an ideal cyber-defense model is the OODA loop (Observe/Orient/Decide/Act loop). In literature, it is combined with the National Security Agency (NSA) Methodology for Adversary Obstruction to create a new cyber-defense model.

The OODA loop assumes that continuous improvement is a cohesive part of the decision-making process, permitting to learn from previous experiences, feeding lessons learned into the loop activities to achieve better performance every time the four steps are completed.

The OODA loop, in the military context, describes the ability to acquire, process, and act upon information in comparison to one's adversary's ability to do so. The common phrase, "getting inside their decision cycle", is a reference to being able to cycle through this loop faster than your adversary. Figure 10.1 outlines the comparison of Boyd's OODA Loop and other common cycle approaches.

As Boyd hinted in his Aerial Attack Study (1964), the focus of the OODA (See Figure 10.2) loop is not about making faster decisions but rather to manipulate the environment in such a way as to "inhibit an adversaries capacity to adapt to such an environment (suppress or distort observations)". Instead of the environment being a valuable information source for the adversary to analyze and use to improve its attitude against us, Boyd saw the environment as a means of disorientation to disrupt the adversary's decision-making process. Disorientation is the intentional result of exploiting ambiguity, deception, superior mobility and surprise to subvert, disrupt or seize the connections, centers, and activities that allow the adversary to function. The goal of manipulating the environment is to "bring adversaries system into an area of confusion and disorder by causing them to over and under react because of activity that appears uncertain, ambiguous or chaotic".

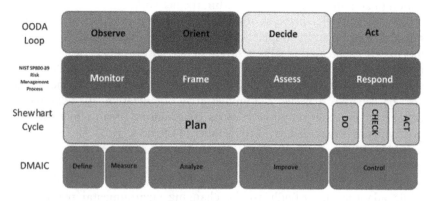

Figure 10.1 Comparison of OODA loop to other cycle processes.

Boyd describes the adversarial correlation in terms of competing mental models that evolve while circumstances change against a backdrop of time constraints. This is a conflict that unfolds in the minds of the adversaries. The minds of the adversaries compromise the cognitive dimension of the information environment. It is for this reason that the addition of the cognitive dimension as a fourth layer in the model of cyberspace was advocated.

The first three of these layers, as described in Joint Publication 3-12(R), Cyberspace Operations, are:

1. **The physical network** layer comprises the physical elements of cyberspace. These physical elements are the hardware, systems software, and infrastructure that supports the network.
2. **The logical network** layer contains those elements of the network that are related to other, abstracted from the physical layer. JP 3-12(R) gives the example of a website that can be hosted in multiple locations but is accessed with a single URL.
3. **The cyber-persona** layer is a higher level of abstraction that uses rules that apply in the logical layer to develop digital [18] representations of the user.

Adding **the cognitive dimension** to cyberspace changes the analysis of cyberspace operations from a search for vulnerabilities in hardware and software into an engagement that includes information operations. The proposed revised layers of cyberspace are shown in Figure 10.3.

The genius of OODA loop analysis was Boyd's recognition that an adversary's perspective predictive analysis could be weaponized, leading to a future loss of situational awareness. That is to say, taking actions

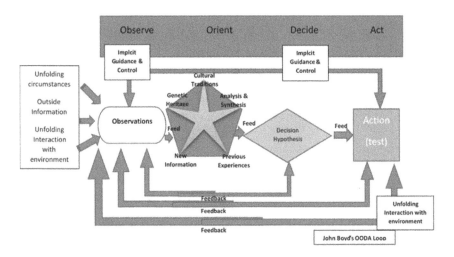

Figure 10.2 The OODA loop.

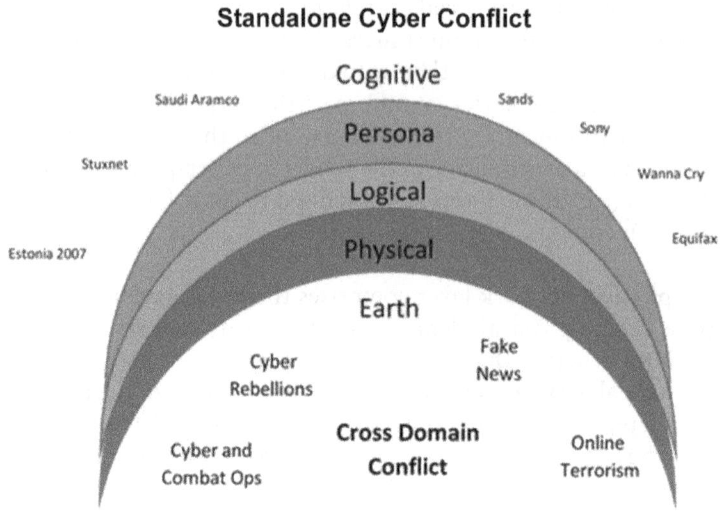

Standalone Cyber Conflict

Figure 10.3 The four layers of cyberspace.

inconsistent with the adversary's expectations, thereby depriving the adversary of situational awareness.

For the reason that "present loops shape the character of future orientation" Boyd set forth five techniques that place information into the environment with the intent to disrupt future orientation. These five OODA loop manipulation techniques are:

- **Ambiguity:** Alternative or competing impressions of events as they may or may not be.
- **Deception:** An impression of events as they are not.
- **Novelty:** Impressions associated with events/ideas that are unfamiliar or have not been experienced before.
- **Fast transient maneuvers:** Irregular and rapid/abrupt shift from one maneuver event/state to another.
- **Effort:** An expenditure of energy or an eruption of violence focused on, or through, features that permit an organic whole to exist.

Collecting and analyzing historical events is a retrospective explanatory analysis. Applying past knowledge to current events is concurrent situational awareness. Anticipating that future attacks will mimic prior attacks is prospective predictive analysis. While there is no doubt that more rapidly identifying, analyzing, and understanding new attacks allow defenses to be more quickly adapted to changing events, this is not a predictive activity, and this is a reactive activity. The importance of AI and machine learning systems are of exceptional importance since they are in a position to process historical information more quickly than humans can perform this task.

Nowadays examining the "hybrid threats" landscape we can clearly distinguish four main pillars:

1. **Mis/Disinformation and Fake news** [19]
2. **Destabilization** – Awakening and support of domestic groups on an ethnic or ideological basis
3. **Cyberattacks** – Cyberterrorism, attacks on critical infrastructure
4. **Conventional means** such as political, military, diplomatic, financial, and religious.

The aforementioned pillars may be encountered either in conjunction or just one of them depending on the specific deployment and nature of the hybrid operations in hand [20].

In this chapter, we are focusing mainly on the third pillar.

In order to respond successfully to this challenge, the key stakeholders should work in a comprehensive way for the development of:

1. **Situational awareness**
2. **Incident response**
3. **Public communication**

I argue that the three aforementioned domains should be serviced in a predictive manner rather than a responsive one.

Currently, the different threats are interconnected in such a way that hybrid defense as a response is not sufficient. It is too late to deploy defense measures as soon as a hybrid operation is detected. The damage is already ongoing and not easily stoppable.

10.3 PROPOSED MODEL

I propose a hybrid, holistic multilayer immunization model that is going to effectively protect state assets beforehand and cover vulnerabilities in advance, prior to a hybrid operation is deployed.

This model consists of different layers of SOP and stakeholders involvement, from different domains and states, forming a focused working group that evaluates and assesses constantly all available data.

Figure 10.4 illustrates the model.

The first layer is about a mechanism to detect fake news [21] that usually follows a major cyber event.

The second layer has to do with anti-misinformation operations in order to respond in a proper manner regarding public communication needs during cyber crisis management.

The third layer involves the homeland security forces and intelligence related to possible threats [22].

Hybrid Immunization

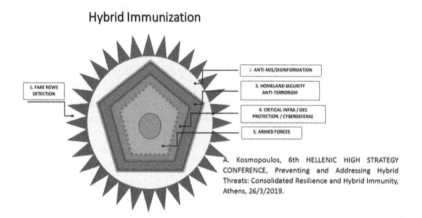

A. Kosmopoulos, 6th HELLENIC HIGH STRATEGY CONFERENCE, Preventing and Addressing Hybrid Threats: Consolidated Resilience and Hybrid Immunity, Athens, 26/3/2019.

Figure 10.4 Hybrid immunization model.

The fourth layer consists of the traditional cybersecurity entities (CSIRTs, SOCs, etc.) mainly the operators of essential services and critical infrastructure in general.

The fifth and last layer entails the Armed Forces and involves their cyber-defense capabilities.

The Holistic Hybrid Immunization Model offers the ability to achieve a level of readiness and preparedness in such a way that no defense model can present.

All these layers of proactive nature guarantee an effective level of readiness and resilience, so as to respond sufficiently to a future hybrid operation, deployed by a state or non-state actor.

Sharing relevant information is an important aspect of an effective approach to hybrid resilience, as it serves the interest of both public and private stakeholders [23]. This is because it increases collective awareness and, thereby, enables every stakeholder to adapt their security posture to the evolution of the threat landscape. Collective response on the other hand is the best way to prepare successfully for difficult times albeit the best response has to be a prediction.

10.4 CONCLUDING REMARKS

Threats and attacks have traditionally been at the center of organizational security and cyber-risk discussions, as noted by the US National Institute of Standards and Technology (NIST); looking at these is an intuitive response, since to prevent cyber-harm we must know how we might be attacked in cyberspace. One approach to assess the resulting harm is to be able to anticipate such threats and their likely intent. An alternative to such a threat-driven approach is to focus security risk analysis on assets and impacts first [24].

The general Cybersecurity Crisis Response Framework is at a crossroads with respect to integrating objectives and modalities of cooperation. The relevant actors, institutions, and authorities have to be identified concerning their operational contribution to responding to a major cyber crisis. Standard Operation Procedures have to be developed regulating situational awareness, incident response, and communication requirements in order to identify evolving hybrid threats.

At the technical level, a major concern is observed on "risks and threats impact". At the operational level "harm" is more relevant when it comes to responding to hybrid operations.

Situational awareness is a multidimensional and well-studied phenomenon, which can be looked upon from several different perspectives. For the operational command and control case, it is argued here that the technical and cognitive sides of situational awareness are closely related and somewhat intertwined. Cybersecurity is not to be focused solely on hardware, software, and network issues but is to expand as to embrace cognitive issues included in a hybrid operation in the cyber domain [25].

The most challenging part of the incident response process is precisely detecting and assessing possible cybersecurity incidents – determining and identifying whether an individual incident has occurred, then defining what the objectives are for the response activities – and finally investigating the situation in an appropriate manner to examine if the incident is contained within a combined hybrid operation context. The next step is to contain the damage and finally recover and restore everything to normal operation.

An important component at the operational level management is the crisis communications plan. Strategic-level decision-makers have to be able to respond promptly, accurately, and confidently during an emergency in the hours and days that follow. Many different audiences must be reached with information specific to their interests and needs. The handling of a major cyber incident is not only a technical issue to be addressed but it has communication and reputation additions that have to be addressed.

The image of the response mechanisms can be positively or negatively impacted by public perceptions of the handling of an incident. The operational level should be able to provide a suggestion on proper communication.

Operational management and decision-making process, through a deliberate OODA loop-based process of collecting data, making sense of that data, and creating constructive, informed decisions and controlled actions will permit to utilize its advantages, especially when a cyberattack is deployed in the context of a generic hybrid operation [26].

Most importantly, a single autonomous competent entity within a state or corporate environment has to take over (command, control, and coordination) all operational level activities and conduct the fusion of all available data, intelligence, and information from the technical level.

The focus and direction for governing cybersecurity must come from the highest levels within an entity, whether a state or a corporation. The method for achieving an acceptable level of security must be adequately promoted (fostering a security-aware culture), resourced, monitored, and managed in the same fashion as any other mission-critical program or service. Active and visible leadership, sponsorship, and oversight are necessary to ensure that goals are achieved as expected. Operational management of cybersecurity must be aligned with and support the achievement of the central strategic objectives. Focusing on these objectives provides the rationale for investing in cybersecurity activities – because they enable every entity to achieve its mission. Without each of these actions, an entity will not achieve its desired security posture and will likely fall short in its ability to adapt to, respond to, and recover from disruption and stress and thus to continue to provide mission-critical services during normal and disrupted operations.

10.5 GLOSSARY

Hybrid threats: a mixture of coercive and subversive activity, conventional and nonconventional methods (i.e. diplomatic, military, economic, technological), which can be used in a coordinated manner by state or non-state actors to achieve specific objectives while remaining below the threshold of formally declared warfare.

Comprehensive approach: A holistic model that implies a whole-of-government and a whole-of-society involvement in countering hybrid influence.

OODA loop: (Observe/Orient/Decide/Act loop), by John Boyd, that proposes to manipulate the environment in such a way as to "inhibit an adversaries capacity to adapt to such an environment (suppress or distort observations)".

REFERENCES

1. H. G. Sascha-Dominik Bachmann. Hybrid wars: The 21st-century's new threats to global peace and security, *Scientia Militaria, South African Journal of Military Studies*, 43(1), 77–98, 2015.
2. R. Johnson. Hybrid war and its countermeasures: A critique of the literature, *Small Wars & Insurgencies*, 29(1), 141–163, 22 December 2017.
3. M. Wigell. Hybrid interference as a wedge strategy: A theory of external interference in liberal democracy, *International Affairs*, 95(2), March 2019.
4. Gregory F. Treverton et al. *Addressing Hybrid Threats*, Swedish Defence University, Center for Asymmetric Threat Studies, The European Centre of Excellence for Countering Hybrid Threats, Stockholm, pp. 73–75, 2018.
5. A. Lupovici. Cyber warfare and deterrence: Trends and challenges in research, *Military and Strategic Affairs*, 3, 49, December 2011 .

6. F. Hoffman. Hybrid threats: Neither omnipotent nor unbeatable, *Orbis*, 54(3), 441–455, 2010.

7. T. Ian *The Guardian*. 17 May 2007. [Online]. Available: http://www.guardian.co.uk/world/2007/may/17/topstories3.russia

8. European Union Agency for Cybersecurity. *Threat Landscape for 5g Networks, ENISA*, November 2019, p. 75.

9. Patrick Cullen and Erik Reichborn-Kjennerud. *Understanding Hybrid Warfare*, Brussels: Multinational Capability Development Campaign, 2016.

10. E. Berg-Knutsen. From tactical champions to grand strategy enablers: The future of small-nation SOF in counter–hybrid warfare, *Combating Terrorism Exchange*, 6, 61, 2016.

11. S.-D. Bachmann and H. Gunneriusson. Terrorism and cyber attacks as hybrid threats: Defining a comprehensive 21st century approach to global security, *The Journal on Terrorism and Security Analysis*, 9, 2–11, Spring 2014.

12. R. D. Thiele. Crisis in Ukraine – The emergence of hybrid warfare, ISPSW Strategy Series: Focus on Defense and International Security, Issue No. 347, May 2015.

13. CREST. *Joint Doctrine: The Interoperability Framework Edition 2*, JESIP, July 2016.

14. *Cyber Security Incident Response Guide, Version 1*, CREST, 2013.

15. M. V. M. Ćurčić. The evolution of European perception of the term "hybrid warfare", *Vojno delo*, 70(1), 5–21, January 2018 .

16. D. H. C. Ştefănescu. Nato strategy to defeat enemy forces in the hybrid war. In *International Conference of Scientific Paper*, Brasov, 2015.

17. Duane Verner, Agnia Grigas, and Frederic Petit. *Assessing Energy Dependency in the Age of Hybrid Threats*, Helsinki: The European Centre of Excellence for Countering Hybrid Threats Publ, January 2019, p. 18.

18. D. Omand. Understanding digital intelligence and the norms that might govern it. Chatham House Paper Series: no. 8, March 2015.

19. Azhar Unwala and Shaheen Ghori. Brandishing the Cybered Bear: Information war and the Russia-Ukraine conflict, *Military Cyber Affairs*, 1(1), 7, 2015.

20. L. DR. OFER FRIDMAN King's College. The danger of Russian hybrid warfare, Cicero Foundation Great Debate Paper no. 17/05, 2017.

21. A. T. A. Jason. Wiseman Secretary General, Terrorist and Cyber-Attacks, unstable energy supply, social media & information warfare, sabotage, corruption as part of the hybrid warfare equation. In *Nato Advanced Research Workshop Proceedings, Critical Infrastructure Protection Against Hybrid Warfare Security Related Challenges*, Stockholm, 2016.

22. A. Ion. Cyber defense and citizens rights in the virtual environment. In *"Carol I" National Defence University, Centre for Defence and Security Strategic Studies, International Scientific Conference Strategies Xxi The Complex and Dynamic Nature of the Security Environment*, Bucharest – Romania, 2015.

23. H. Gunneriusson. Hybrid warfare and deniability as understood by the Military, *Polish Political Science Yearbook*, 48(2), 267–288, 2019.

24. I. Agrafiotis, J. R. Nurse, M. Goldsmith, S. Creese, and D. Upton. A taxonomy of cyber-harms: Defining the impacts of cyber-attacks and understanding how they propagate, *Journal of Cybersecurity*, 4(1), tyy006, 2018.

25. Reinhard Meyers. White Knights versus Dark Vader? On the problems and pitfalls of debating hybrid warfare, *On-line Journal Modelling the New Europe*, 21, 3–28, 2016.
26. Bachmann Sascha-Dominik and Gerhard Kemp. Aggression as "organized hypocrisy" – How the war on terrorism and hybrid threats challenge the Nuremberg legacy, *Windsor Year Book of Access to Justice*, 30, 233, 2012.

Chapter 11

The Cyber Skills Gap

Ismini Vasileiou

11.1 INTRODUCTION

The cybersecurity field is growing fast and directly affected by Industry 4.0. Across all sectors, government, education, and industry, partnerships are developing to address the skills gap. It has recently been calculated that 48% of the businesses have a skills gap (Pedley et al., 2020), and actually, two-thirds of those stakeholders face issues with cyber skills, whether that is low-level or advanced skills. Over the years, there has been a plethora of qualifications and certifications developed and introduced in the discipline of Computer Science but also in an interdisciplinary approach in order to bridge those gaps. The growing demand across countries and governments on how to close the skills gap and the Digital Revolution of the continuous economic restructure in Europe, the US, and all over the world develop new areas and skills needed and at the same time create skills shortage. The Skills Mismatch Index that was put together to indicate and forecast the skills gap by 2020 noted that in the Eurozone alone we experience 900,000 shortage of professionals in STEM (Francis and Ginsberg, 2016). The recent research published in 2019 evidenced that these figures are set to get worse and revealed that there could be 7 million under-skilled or their job requirements (Industrial Strategy Council, 2019).

Some claim that the cybersecurity discipline is a relatively new profession and often organizations are not able to recruit the specialized skills they need. Although a Computer Science graduate can be seen as suitable for all IT specializations, still within the cyber field it is needed to carefully select those professionals who will bring the expertise and knowledge to reduce the skills gap and create a more secure online environment, whether that is in businesses, in organizations, or even at home.

Understanding cybersecurity is important and vital to all users in the IT field. Despite years of experience and a steep increase in the use of technologies, it is often found that organizations of any type are exposed to cyber-attacks. The lack of security awareness and compliance among staff can often be the root of recent incidents and breaches. Developing and maintaining cyber skills can be done in many settings, starting from early on at

DOI: 10.1201/9781003109952-11

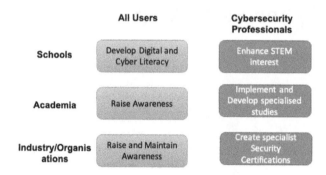

Figure 11.1 The SETA pathways for general users and cybersecurity professionals.

the school level, higher education, and within organizations (Vasileiou & Furnell, 2018). By addressing the gap and skills from early on, society can build and integrate cybersecurity knowledge and skills in various ways and at different levels. Figure 11.1 demonstrates the different pathways on how to become a cyber professional and maintain those skills in the field.

This chapter takes a multidimensional approach in demonstrating not only the need for developing those cyber skills we need during the Fourth Industrial Revolution (Industry 4.0) but also the ways we can use in order to close the gap and make the sector as a whole but also the home users, awared, educated and more secure.

11.2 THE SKILLS GAP IN THE LANDSCAPE OF INDUSTRY 4.0

Industry 4.0 has affected the business sector on the whole. Technology has pushed most, if not all, business interactions to take place online in a remote approach. Technology has become inseparable from all business functions and as such cybercrime has grown fast. In 2020, the World Economic Forum ranked the cyberattack as a top-ten risk in every category of their "Long Term Global Risk" report. It was also a notable fact that they forecasted 74% of organizations could be hacked in the upcoming year.

11.2.1 The Skills Gap

The skills gap is an ongoing discussion among employers, academia, and any sector developing the standards to address digital skills. As this is not a new problem, governments have been focusing on identifying ways to fund those opportunities that arise in big data, AI, and Cyber. The schemes being put forward by various governments across the globe require technical skills, such as understanding and managing databases and manipulating data, programming, and also those soft skills that employees can use to support their lifelong learning, such as project management. The continuous change created themes such as "learning to learning to learn" and a variety of meta-skills to support the ongoing development of the individual. This has led to having three tiers of responsible areas to develop those digital skills that will also address the cyber skills gap.

11.2.2 Tier 1: Employers

Organizations are looking to meet compliance requirements and develop a security-conscious workforce. Employers have a responsibility to continue upskilling their staff and provide them with the education to understand the different tools and techniques needed. Employers and organizations have a responsibility to not only create those skills needed but also take into account the diverse learning strategies individuals might have.

Cybersecurity includes a wide range of specialized skills and roles and it is felt that not a single educational program, whether that is a degree, an apprenticeship, or a certification, can cover all aspects of those skills the sector needs. Recently, National Initiative for Cybersecurity Education (NICE) emphasized that the current landscape of education does not provide a concrete set of skills needed to address the skills gap. It is worth noting that many programs emphasize policy making and planning, or compliance audits and not those substantial skills required to support organizations with cybersecure systems. It was observed that many educational programs were focusing on the theory and not on the hands-on experience. As such, from the employers' perspective, to address the gap, it is vital that we address those issues in an applied learning approach.

Organizations face severe challenges in identifying and recruiting cyber specialists. While they need to protect their systems, they also need support to identify the pool of talents that can be not only educated but also prepared with practical experience and build a more robust pipeline of professionals.

11.2.3 Tier 2: Academia

The UK government has been continuously exploring the skills gap and how to support higher education institutions to create new sets of cyber skills. The nursing and midwifery (NMC) (2016) report offered a five-year horizon for higher education institutions and identified the main areas the research identified that the use of technology could improve teaching and learning and offer more opportunities within the higher education sector. In particular, their research focused extensively on developing competing educational models in an attempt to assist institutions to move away from traditional courses, and although such approaches could have implications on policy, leadership, and practice, it was still seen as a breakthrough approach.

For years, there has been a strong incentive to address and develop further the relationship between higher education and employers. Higher education is called to become more responsive within Industry 4.0 advancements and to enhance the knowledge and skills while empowering the critical reflective learner. The government has produced various reports discussing the future of higher education, such as the 2003 UK government report, the 2008 HEFCE report, the 2011 Government White Paper (Vasileiou, 2018), and the 2015 Advance HE Framework on enabling employability.

Higher education institutions have made employability one of the key aspects of organizational commitment and vision. In traditional degrees, short, work-based learning modules are offered where students are experiencing doing an academic piece of work alongside an employer (GOV.UK, 2017). In addition, students can go for a year-long optional placement at the end of Year 2 before they enter the final year of their degree.

The UK Advance HE framework is often being adopted on embedding employability and can be tailored depending on the type of the degree and desirable outcomes. It is important that any higher education establishment becomes a key driver in developing a curriculum with embedded employability addressing the skills gap. The UK universities tend to get their degrees accredited against professional bodies. Within the Computer Science discipline and its related fields such as cyber, it is highly important that curriculum updates rather regularly in order to develop employable graduates and reduce the skills gap. Professional bodies such as BCS (The Chartered Institute for IT) play a leading role in developing and accrediting courses by meeting the higher education quality assurance standards. In addition, they support and empower a relationship between (Higher Education) HE and employers, and a greater understanding of the skills-based approach. Having said that, this could also create new problems, where professional bodies do not understand the quality assurance standards of higher education and awards and accreditations becomes a competitive behavior rather than an informative on developing teaching excellence (Vasileiou, 2020).

In many European countries, the development of the Degree Apprenticeships programs was initiated around 2016. It relies mainly on the skills set needed by graduates as it is defined by each government's analysis on the skills gap and the standards published (Vasileiou, 2020). The Degree Apprenticeship bachelor's degrees combine learning with employment and the final certificate is not only a degree on understanding the discipline but also a verification of the skills an individual has acquired. The apprenticeship standard that was developed and introduced is a combination of a job with the skills needed and the learning that needs to be undertaken. In other words, one cannot exist without the other. The learning skills in the UK are mapped to the professional standards with a great emphasis on the SFIA framework (2018) and the CIISec Skills Framework (CIISec, 2019). These professional bodies work rather closely with the government and inform the relevant trailblazers of the apprenticeship standards to ensure that not only we bridge the gap academically but it is also well received by the cyber society. While developing any academic element can enrich the field of cybersecurity, a mapping exercise is constantly needed to provide regular updates of the skills acquired and needed now and in the future.

11.2.4 Tier 3: Government

The government has been responsible for supporting both the education sector and the stakeholders to engage in discussions around aligning those efforts into a joined approach. The governments, through trailblazer groups, continuously identify the new skill set needed to bring together academia and employers. In the US, NICE works heavily on standardizing performance measurements and aligning them with the NICE Cybersecurity Workforce Framework. Similarly, in the UK, the UK Cyber Training Academy is developing short course intensive programs to upskill the workforce. Finally, as mentioned above, a lot of effort and design has been put into creating new types of degrees, the Degree Apprenticeships that combine the hands-on experience with the theory.

11.3 DEFINING AN AGENDA FOR CYBERSECURITY SKILLS

The cybersecurity workforce skills gap is one of the major concerns for both economic development and security. In this rapid digitization of the global economy, it is vital we build an ecosystem that will encompass cybersecurity education, problem-based training, and continuous workforce development. In order to reduce the skills shortage, the aim should be to develop a common approach in cybersecurity skills context.

The UK report on identifying the cyber skills gap (Furnell, 2020) noted that there was no change since the 2018 report. The report reiterates the fact that organizations spend more time on developing policies and training their workforce on how to identify the cyber risks and neither enough upskilling takes place nor adequate entry routes into cyber.

Areas such as cloud computing, AI, and machine learning often accompany the skills gap in the cyber sector. There are various discussions around the future skills needed and on how to improve the talent pool. It is interesting that there are numerous reports discussing the skills gap in the cybersecurity sector. What is clear across all those reports is that the focus of the outcomes is around the importance of education. It is highlighted that cyber skills education needs to start as early as primary school years.

11.3.1 Evolution of the Cyber Discipline

When originally the Chartered Institute of Information Security developed the Skills Framework, it was divided into two sections: the technical skills and the soft skills. Initially, it was designed in such a way that it would define the requirements of specific jobs and activities. It is important at this stage to show how the Skills Framework looks like. Figure 11.2 shows how the skills were grouped and what they covered.

This initiative was adopted by various cyber professionals, such as e-Skills UK, and later by National Cyber Security Centre (NCSC).

Security Discipline	Skills Groups
A - *Information Security Governance and Management* Capable of determining, establishing and maintaining appropriate governance of (including processes, roles, awareness strategies, legal environment and responsibilities), delivery of (including polices, standards and guidelines), and cost-effective solutions (including impact of third parties) for information security within a given organization).	A1 – Governance A2 – Policy and Standards A3 – Information Security Strategy A4 – Innovation and Business Improvement A5 – Behavioural Change A6 – Legal & Regulatory Environment and Compliance A7 – Third Party Management
B - *Threat Assessment and Information Risk Management* Capable of articulating the different forms of threat to, and vulnerabilities of, information systems and assets. Comprehending and managing the risks relating to information systems and assets.	B1 – Threat Intelligence, Assessment and Threat Modelling B2 – Risk Assessment B3 – Information Risk Management
C - *Implementing Secure Systems* Comprehends the common technical security controls available to prevent, detect and recover from security incidents and to mitigate risk. Capable of articulating security architectures relating to business needs and commercial product development that can be realized using available tools, products, standards and protocols, delivering systems assured to have met their security profile using accepted methods	C1 – Enterprise Security Architecture C2 – Technical Security Architecture C3 – Secure Development
D - *Assurance: Audit, Compliance and Testing* Develops and applies standards and strategies for verifying that measures taken mitigate identified risks. Capable of defining and implementing the processes and techniques used in verifying compliance against security policies, standards, legal and regulatory requirements.	D1 – Internal and Statutory Audit D2 – Compliance Monitoring and Controls Testing D3 – Security Evaluation and Functionality Testing D4 – Penetration Testing
E - *Operational Security Management* Capable of managing all aspects of a security program, including reacting to new threats and vulnerabilities, secure operational and service delivery consistent with security policies, standards and procedures, and handling security incidents of all types according to common principles and practices, consistent with legal constraints and obligations.	E1 – Secure Operations Management E2 – Secure Operations and Service Delivery
F - *Incident Management, Investigation and Digital Forensics* Capable of managing or investigating an information security incident at all levels, including the use of digital forensic techniques.	F1 – Intrusion Detection and Analysis F2 – Incident Management, Incident Investigation and Response F3 – Forensics
H - *Business Resilience* Capable of defining the need for, and of implementing processes for establishing business continuity.	H1 – Business Continuity and Disaster Recovery Planning H2 – Business Continuity and Disaster Recovery Management H3 – Cyber Resilience
I - *Information Security Research* Original investigation in order to gain knowledge and understanding relating to information security, including the invention and generation of ideas, performances and artefacts where these lead to new or substantially improved insights; and the use of existing knowledge in experimental development to produce new or substantially improved devices, products and processes.	I1 – Research I2 – Applied Research
J - *Management, Leadership, Business and Communications* Recognizes the importance of wider communication and interpersonal skills in order to enable the effective communication and integration of cybersecurity within an organizational context.	J1 – Management, Leadership and Influence J2 – Business Skills J3 – Communication and Knowledge Sharing
K - *Contributions to the Information Security Profession and Professional Development* Recognizes the need for ongoing development of cybersecurity practitioners, and their potential to contribute to the wider community and profession.	K1 – Contributions to the Community K2 – Contributions to the IS Profession K3 – Professional Development

Figure 11.2 Skills against security disciplines.

11.4 A FRAMEWORK TO ADDRESS THE SKILLS GAP IN CYBER

The skills gap in cyber applies in all disciplines and fields. As the pool of data grows, the manipulation and evaluation of data become dominant; whether we are looking at healthcare, IT, education, etc., it is becoming important to propose a way to upskill and identify new talent. This is where the work-based learning approaches have proved to be positive and have an impact on closing the gap (Advance HE, 2015). In areas such as healthcare or education, the route of apprenticeships is the norm. Nurses, doctors, and teachers learn by doing. When we look at the cyber profession, many questions arise as to how it can be implemented in a similar successful way.

As Degree Apprenticeships grew, it was evident that a new framework was needed. The "knowledge" and "competence" frameworks are beginning to foster practice-based academic qualifications (Lester, S., Bravenboer, D. and Webb, N.,2016). In Degree Apprenticeships, learning is also employer-led. While stakeholders start thinking about how to develop such routes into cyber, they will face some difficult decisions. How do you balance academic learning with professional learning (Anderson, A; Bravenboer, D; Hemsworth, D., 2012)? This new integrated approach in higher education can really address the skills gap. The professional bodies such as BCS and CIISEC may now map their standards against skills such as critical thinking, evaluation, and reflection. Those professional values of HE transform the Degree Apprenticeships route, and the barriers are removed. Transdisciplinary skills reflect the generic competence a graduate needs in academic work and the integration of both academic and professional standards becomes the core.

While patterns and processes are transforming higher education, they equally change the industry. The rise in tuition fees in the UK has changed the landscape. There have always been discussions and comparisons between apprenticeships, degrees, and certifications. Students have been making those hard decisions since their early adult lives (Vasileiou, 2020). We often see competent students often not able to attend university. To date, the Higher Apprenticeships have not been offering this holistic approach to learning the Degree Apprenticeships do (Beech and Bekhradnia, 2018). Despite the opportunities that arise, still either the young population is struggling to find employment that will lead them to an apprenticeship, or their employers are not investing in their holistic and lifelong education. Therefore, it is of high need that when developing the Degree Apprenticeships they are not being sold as a financial investment for the employer but in collaboration with the government and the professional bodies to inspire and develop the new generation (NCSC, 2019).

Training and teaching learners at the same time becomes a theme of significance but it can equally create a new set of problems. Integrating a variety of pedagogical approaches, moving away from the traditional didactic approach, can enhance and empower the learner and the process of achieving a degree. Understanding just the regulatory framework is often not enough. The Degree Apprenticeships are not delivering just a set of standards. They explore collaborations and opportunities to promote the flexible learning needed to support equal opportunities and cater to diverse backgrounds. Some examples are neurodiversity, more females into cyber, and any other areas that are unrepresented. Such approaches are well received by employers and students.

The cyber programs need to be developed with careful consideration of looking into the future and how the discipline expands. Looking present only is not enough, and upon the creation of new skills by the professional bodies it would not be achievable to reach positive results or it would lead to delays revamping the curriculum. Such holistic approaches and new routes into the cyber field benefit the employers a great deal as they became more compliant with the skills frameworks and developed a deeper understanding of the field.

11.5 RECOMMENDATIONS

The implementation of Degree Apprenticeships can be seen as a fantastic route and approach to closing the skills gap in Cyber. As there are many stakeholders involved in such developments, Table 11.1 summarizes the steps and recommendations on how academia, employers, and the government can come together to build the pipeline.

Looking ahead, the above recommendations can be used by each stakeholder interested in developing Degree Apprenticeships to address the skills gap. In addition, it can also be used by those organizations that face skills shortages and are looking for ways to upskill their staff.

Employers can introduce organization-wide strategies on how to identify the skills gap and either make existing employers to upskill or recruit new talent. Table 11.1 can facilitate those discussions between all parties and assist them in designing strategies to increase participation in Degree Apprenticeship schemes.

11.6 CONCLUSION

This chapter reflected not only on the widely known issue of the skills gap in cybersecurity but also on the development of cyber Degree Apprenticeships within higher education. The aim of this chapter is to demonstrate a new route for developing cyber professionals and highlight that such routes can be valuable for employers and actually address and improve the skills gap. As more and more employers identify their organizations' skills gap in the cyber field, professional bodies such as CIISec and NCSC (2019) are accepting, promoting, and recognizing the Degree Apprenticeship routes. This has

Table 11.1 Steps in Creating the Pipeline in Closing the Skills Gap in Cyber

Issue(s)	Academia/Higher education	Organizations	Apprentices
Strategic	To create an Institutional approach to implementing Degree Apprenticeships.	Degree Apprenticeships should be part of the CP0 activity of an organization.	Implement such approaches to support the management of work and education.
Collaborative approach	Engage employers from early on.	Collaboration between the industry and higher education. Develop degrees that meet the organization's needs.	Create and implement a triage with mentors, academics, and line managers.
Triangulation	Empower and embrace the three different types of experience: employer and academic.	What is your skills gap? Identify that particular skills shortage and build on it with apprenticeships. Continuing Professional Development (CPD) support for staff and identify the possible route of Degree Apprenticeship.	Continuous development on CPD.
Continuing Professional Development (CPD)	Redefine and redesign the delivery of approaches to Teaching and Learning.	CPD support for staff and identify the possible route of Degree Apprenticeship.	N/A
Outreach	Promotion of Degree Apprenticeships to schools and colleges.	Neurodiversity: Identify new talent.	N/A
Professional skills	Embed professional bodies' skills and frameworks.	Embed professional bodies' skills and frameworks within the apprentices' work and training.	N/A

led to rapid growth across many organizations and higher education institutions to either upskill or employ new cyber professionals. For example, even big companies such as HP and IBM are either upskilling existing staff in this area or investing in new talent via the Degree Apprenticeships route.

Although it is felt that any strategic approach might not be 100% perfect at this stage, still the implementation of Degree Apprenticeships has proven to result in steady talent recruitment in the cyber discipline. Similarly, academia entering the world of apprenticeships and transforming the teaching and learning approaches can be seen as a breakthrough for organizations. The development of such routes is found to be a promising strategic approach for apprentices, academia, and employers. What is found to be the most important factor affecting a quick growth in cyber professionals was aligning the development of apprenticeships with the higher education strategy and the employer's vision and mission. Employers who have an understanding of the field can drive change and see ahead. Alongside it, developing the curriculum around cybersecurity is becoming highly important. Although there is a high need from all sides to deliver those cyber skills that are currently missing and rapidly growing, the same degree but in different formats, to meet the employers' needs, equally it has been a great challenge to identify not only suitable staff but also staff with capacity.

Other areas that still need to be explored are widening participation and inclusivity. HE provides a provision for all types of learners, giving everyone an opportunity to develop as a person, as a graduate, and contribute to society. Although such educational models can inspire and remove barriers for students who are unable to get a student loan, still HE can influence less and less student population and intakes. Employers will be providing their workforce and by embedding professional standards into the curriculum, the widening participation aspect is outsourced to all those stakeholders.

Irrespective of the fact there are new challenges and the landscape of higher education is changing, it is worth noting at this stage that professional bodies collaborate with employers and the government in an attempt to redefine what degree education means. While universities are still developing and establishing a variety of Degree Apprenticeships, reflection is required on the role of employers and professional bodies (Husband, S., 2018). The latter two should be supporting the higher education establishments in developing and adapting their material to close the skills gap (Lester et al., 2016). Currently, the implementation of such degrees does not hold the employer or the professional body responsible, but with a triangulated approach it is recommended that there needs to be an accountability system where all parties and stakeholders work collaboratively in addressing the cyber skills shortage. It is important that any government, any employers, and all the professional bodies adapt and understand that reducing the skills gap can only be derived by a common approach and by allowing space for growth. If this is achieved, then the policy contexts can change, become more inclusive, and align any university qualifications with the needs of businesses and organizations.

The cyber skills gap is not reducing as fast as one would have hoped based on all those incentives (Gov.uk, 2020). On the contrary, the rapid online developments, the impact of Covid, and the impact of digital transformation mean that any degree or qualification in the Computer Science discipline will need elements of embedding skills and knowledge around security and privacy. The cyber field can be fully and successfully supported by the Degree Apprenticeships routes while the trainees and/or students will have ongoing exposure to the real problems and challenges of their daily job and not just focusing on the theoretical aspects. Employers are offering most of the time cutting-edge technologies, and as such, this is offering academia the opportunity to stay current and offer the latest theoretical frameworks. It is as such more important than ever to get the professional bodies involved too. They are the ones collecting, collating, and framing the profession, offering that ongoing support and guidance. Evidently, embedding those frameworks within the rapidly changing and growing cyber field can be not just a challenge for academia but also an opportunity to reshape their offerings and produce such graduates that will come with professional and academic experience (Vasileiou, 2020). An embedded approach into cyber, alongside the embedded skills frameworks, will develop such cyber professionals supported by lifelong learning characteristics that, in return, will be an asset for any organization and the cyber profession.

The topic of the skills gap in cybersecurity is the one that comes before anything else. It should be given priority and for all stakeholders to appreciate the need to educate the new generation in this field. Governments are still working on understanding how Degree Apprenticeships should look like and are exploring the next steps. Similarly, employers have been evaluating the effectiveness of those routes into cyber and, of course, given the sudden impact of Covid-19, it has become an interesting point of discussion. The financial difficulties that many businesses face due to the impact of Covid often cause concerns about the future of Degree Apprenticeships. Nevertheless, the skills gap in cyber is growing, and the pandemic has exposed systems even more. While there are numerous certifications out there on specific skills, a holistic approach such as that of the Degree Apprenticeships in cyber can be an innovative strategic approach to bridge the gap.

REFERENCES

Advance HE. Embedding employability in higher education, 2015. https://www.advance-he.ac.uk/guidance/teaching-and-learning/embedding-employability

Anderson, A., Bravenboer, D., and Hemsworth, D. The role of universities in higher apprenticeship development, *Higher Education, Skills and Work - Based Learning*, 2(3), 240–255, 2012.

Beech, D. and Bekhradnia, B. *Demand for Higher Education to 2030*. HEPI report 105, 2018. www.hepi.ac.uk/wp-content/uploads/2018/03/HEPI-Demand-for-Higher-Education-to-2030-Report-105-FINAL.pdf

CIISec. CIISec skills framework, Version 2.4, Chartered Institute of Information Security, 2019, November. https://www.ciisec.org/CIISEC/Resources/Capab ility_Methodology/Skills_Framework/CII SEC/Resources/Skills_Framework .aspx

Evans, K. and Reeder, F. A human capital crisis in Cybersecurity, 2010. https:// www.csis.org/analysis/human-capital-crisis-cybersecurity

Francis, K. and Ginsberg, W. The Federal Cybersecurity Workforce: Background and Congressional oversight issues for the Departments of Defense and Homeland Security, 2016. https://digitalcommons.ilr.cornell.edu/key_wor kplace/1491/

Furnell, Steven, and Bishop, Matt. Addressing cyber security skills: The spectrum, not the silo, *Computer Fraud & Security*, 2020(2), 6–11, 2020.

GOV.UK. How to develop an apprenticeship standard: Guide for trailblazers, 2017. www.gov.uk/government/publications/how-to-develop-an-apprenticeship-st andard-guide-for-trailblazers

GOV.UK. Cyber Security skills in the UK labour market 2020, 2020. https://www .gov.uk/government/publications/cyber-security-skills-in-the-uk-labour-mar ket-2020/cyber-security-skills-in-the-uk-labour-market-2020

HEFCE. When the levy breaks–facts and the future of degree apprenticeships, Knowledge Exchange and Skills, Higher Education Funding Council for England, Bristol, 2016. http://blog.hefce.ac.uk/2016/03/16/when-the-levy-b reaks-facts-and-the-future-of-degree-apprenticeships.

Husband, S. Can apprenticeships help increase diversity and address an ageing workforce? 2018. www.peoplemanagement.co.uk/voices/comment/apprenti ceships-increase-diversity-ageing-workforce

Industrial Strategy Council. UK skills mismatch in 2030, 2019. https://industrialst rategycouncil.org/sites/default/files/UK%20Skills%20Mismatch%202030 %20-%20Research%20Paper.pdf

Lester, S., Bravenboer, D., and Webb, N. Work-integrated degrees: Context, engage-ment, practice and quality, Quality Assurance Agency, Gloucester, 2016.

NCSC. NCSC degree classification, 2019. https://www.ncsc.gov.uk/information/ ncsc-degree-certification-call-new-applicants-0

NMC Horizon Report. Higher Education Institutions. 2016. https://www. sconul.ac.uk/sites/default/files/documents/2016-nmc-horizon-report-he-EN-1.pdf

Pedley, D., Borges, T., Bollen, A., Shah, J., Donaldson, S., Furnell, S., and Crozier, D. *Cyber Security Skills in the UK Labour Market 2020 – Findings Report*. Department for Digital, Culture, Media and Sport, 2020, March. https://www. gov.uk/government/publications/cyber-security-skills-in-the-uk-labour-market-2020/cyber-security-skills-in-the-uk-labour-market-2020

Skills Framework for the Information Age (SFIA), 2018. https://www.sfia-online .org/en

Vasileiou, I. An evaluation of accelerated learning degrees. In *HEA STEM Conference Newcastle*, UK, 31 January–1 February 2018, 2018.

Vasileiou, I. Cybersecurity education and training: Delivering industry relevant education and skills via degree apprenticeships, HAISA, July 2020, 2020.

Vasileiou, I., and Furnell, S. *Enhancing Security Education-Recognising Threshold Concepts and Other Influencing Factors.* SciTePress, 2018.

Index